# Haunted
# Liverpool 32

## Tom Slemen

The Tom Slemen Press

ISBN-10: 1701946246
ISBN-13: 9781701946248

For
The Count of St Germain

# CONTENTS

"I do not fear death. I had been dead for billions and billions of years before I was born, and had not suffered the slightest inconvenience from it."

– Mark Twain

# IT HAPPENED IN A TAXI

This chapter is concerned with three supernatural incidents that either occurred inside a taxi or in the vicinity of a cab. Like police officers, taxi drivers are often out after dark and they not only encounter every type of person from all walks of life, they also have skirmishes with the paranormal from time to time if the many phonecalls, letters and emails I have received from cabbies over the years are anything to go by. Let us put the meter on and start with the first fare. It all began on a blustery rainy evening in November 1978. Taxi driver Barry Jones, who had recently turned thirty, had a terrible row with his wife Thelma over something rather silly; she'd clean forgotten to make him a treacle pudding because she'd been so caught up in the latest episode of the TV soap *Crossroads* and he'd gone out of his way earlier in the day to stop off at the supermarket to get a packet of Atora suet mix and a tin of Golden Syrup so she could make the pud. 'Barry, I'm sorry, I didn't do it on purpose,' Thelma had told him during the row, and Barry had reacted childishly by storming out of his Edge Hill home on Botanic Road, slamming the front door hard behind him and getting into his hackney cab. He just wanted to get lost in the night. He headed for a chippie on Myrtle Parade, picked up two bags of chips and two battered cods, then drove to the tiny cramped flat of his friend Mike on Catharine Street. He was lucky to find him in, as Mike practically lived in his local pub, the Blackburne Arms. Mike was thankful of the fish and chips and scoffed away as Barry unburdened himself of his imagined marital troubles - all over the treacle pudding he never had.

Mike crunched into the batter-covered cod and issued a warning to his friend. 'You wanna start living mate; you're thirty now. These young dolly birds will start looking at you as a dirty old man soon if you don't get a move on. Get out there while you can. Once you hit forty you're just a streak of nowt to these young birds.'

'I'm a married man, Mike,' said Barry, despondently noticing the floppy, soggy chip he was holding. 'I'm not going to start seeing women behind Thelma's back because she forgot to make a treacle pudding.'

'Nah, it runs deeper than that mate,' said Mike, peeling a chip off the greasy tracing-paper thin wrapper. 'You don't seem happy with married life. You seem crotchety nowadays.'

'I'm not,' objected Barry, 'I'm fairly happy – it's just one of those nights.'

'Well, this week I'm going to that club Cindy's on a date with a bird, and a few days later I'm meeting a girl at Baileys, and I've also got my eyes on this classy bird who teaches at the polytechnic. You wanna see her mate, she looks like that actress who plays Wonder Woman.'

'You're just a bedpost-notcher, Mike – don't you want to stay with one person and settle down?' Barry asked, and looked at his watch.

'The only time I'll settle down is when they plant me six-feet under, mate,' Mike replied, gazing at Barry with amused contempt. He tossed a chip into his mouth, looked up at the ceiling, then said, 'Lynda Carter. That's the name of the one who plays Wonder Woman. Spit of that teacher she is.' Barry left the flat and walked through a thin rain to the hackney cab. He thought of the lecherous Mike's warnings and gently shook his head. He drove off and curved left onto Myrtle Street. Town seemed deserted tonight. Around 1am Barry picked up his first fares – a couple standing outside the Hofbrauhaus club on Mount Pleasant. The stocky man looked shrewd, and the woman was blonde, thin and clingy; she nestled her face against her partner as soon as they got into the back of the vehicle.

'Where to?' asked Barry with a stock smile, looking at the man via the rear-view mirror.

'Chelwood Avenue – the Childwall Valley Road end,' said the man.

'Okay boss,' said Barry, moving off with the windscreen wipers swaying. 'Had a good night?'

With a dull expression the man nodded. 'Not bad,' he said, begrudgingly, 'they had five strippers on in the erm, Hofbrauhaus.'

'Didn't your girlfriend object, like?' asked Barry with a smile, and he winked into his mirror at the blonde. The man seemed puzzled by the question and said, 'I haven't got a girlfriend.'

'Well your wife then, is it?' Barry queried with a faux

smile, and he halted the vehicle at the lights of the Rodney Street junction. 'I've got no wife,' said the man, and there came an awkward pause which prompted the taxi driver to suggest places to go for a night out. 'The New Montrose is alright; I go there now and then with me missus, and that wine bar on Bold Street – what's it called now? Whispers – nice decent place it is.'

At this point, the blonde holding onto the man's arm started singing the old Rita Coolidge song, *We're All Alone*. She had quite a voice which Barry found mesmerising, and yet his male passenger started to disrespectfully doze off. She stroked his head and smiled at Barry as she sung. When she stopped singing, Barry said, 'You should go on *New Faces*; you've got a cracker voice.'

'Thank you,' said the woman, and she looked at her snoring partner and said, 'Rob's had a hard day. I'll always love this man. Married to him for seventeen years.'

Straight away, Barry thought about his stupid tiff with Thelma, and under his breath he muttered, 'Congratulations.'

When the cab reached Chelwood Avenue, Barry turned and saw that the woman had gone. He thought she had collapsed but Rob said he had been alone during the journey. 'Don't talk daft mate,' said Barry, 'she *must* be there.'

But she wasn't there. Barry gazed at the floor of the cab and saw that the woman had gone. He was more baffled and confused than scared. Rob told the driver he had buried his wife yesterday morning at Allerton Cemetery and was in no mood to have his leg pulled.

'Look, I swear I am not joking with you,' said Barry, as his annoyed passenger stuck out his hand and offered him the fare. 'Look, she called you Rob – is that your name?'

'Do I *know* you from somewhere?' asked Rob with a suspicious look in his eyes.

'I'd never set eyes on you before tonight,' Barry told him, 'and she told me she'd been married to you for seventeen years. Look, why would I even make stuff like this up?'

Rob suddenly looked sober. What Barry had just told Rob had evidently struck some chord in him.

'She started singing but you fell asleep;' Barry recalled, 'it was that song, *We're All Alone* - honest Rob. She had a good voice.'

'And you say she sat with me through the journey?' Rob asked, his eyes glittering as tears formed in them.

Barry nodded. 'Yes, her exact words were: "I'll always love this man," – I'm sorry if this is upsetting you, mate.'

'That song you mentioned;' Rob said in a choked-up voice,' that had been her favourite song.'

'She looked so real,' said Barry, realising he had conversed with an actual ghost.

'Come in with me a minute please,' said Rob, and he burst into tears as he walked to the gate of his house. Barry went with him into the house and Rob showed him the photo album featuring many treasured photographs of his wife Elaine. Barry went cold when he saw these snaps, for he could see beyond a shadow of a doubt that they were of the woman who had talked to him in his cab earlier. Barry refused to take the money from Rob and he sat with him for a while and the two men supped coffee and chatted till almost 2am.

Barry drove home in a daze and let himself in. His wife came down the stairs in her nightie and with a wonky smile she said, 'I made you that treacle pudding.'

'Come here love,' said Barry with a tear in his eye, and he hugged Thelma as she reached the bottom step. He told her what had happened, and she knew he was telling the truth because she'd never seen him cry in the seven years she'd been married to him. 'Let's never take one another for granted eh?' he said, and hugged his wife tightly. Barry does not consider himself as psychic in any way and he has not seen anything remotely paranormal since that rainy morning in 1978, so he wonders why he was able to see the ghost of Elaine.

We move forward now – 21 years – to the October of 1999, to a foggy day outside of a Liverpool hospital. Paul, a 22-year-old taxi driver, walked with his head bowed, along a grey pavement stippled with fallen leaves of olive green, jonquil, and burnt orange. His separated wife Bethel came out of the hospital and hurried towards him as her boyfriend Stuart loitered near his car, making a roll-up cigarette. 'Paul,' Bethel almost groaned the name, 'are you coming in to see her later?'

Bethel was referring to their practically lifeless eighteen-month-old daughter Ella, now lying in her cot in the hospital on a ventilator. The infant had been diagnosed with mitochondrial disease, which meant the baby's body was incapable of making enough energy in its cells to live. Ella could only breath with the assistance of the ventilator and she had been unconscious now for over a week. Her mum, Bethel, had taken impressions of the tot's palms and feet, and the parents were preparing for the worst. The doctors had warned them that the end was drawing near now for the poor baby.

Paul had flown into a rage when the baby was first diagnosed with the disease and went on a drunken rampage. He had frightened his wife with his violent behaviour and she had turned to Stuart, an old friend for consolation – but in recent weeks it had turned into a relationship and now Bethel and Paul had separated.

Paul stood there, gazing at his hackney cab in the hospital car park. He seemed to be in a dream.

'Paul, are you coming in to see Ella tonight?' Bethel asked once more.

'What for?' he replied at last, and turned to face his estranged wife with red, tearful eyes. 'It'll just tear me up even more.'

Bethel looked at him, and she could see a desert in the eyes of her unloved husband. It was like looking into the eyes of a stranger. 'Well, we're coming in anyway,' said Bethel, 'and Stuart said he'll give you a lift anytime if you want.'

'I'm going,' said Paul, heading for his cab, 'see ya!'

He drove off in his hackney cab, biting his lip, wanting to cry but fighting the volcano of sorrow rumbling inside. He turned on the radio and heard that song by Boyz II Men - *End of the Road*. That did it. When he heard the part of the song that said 'We'd be forever' – he burst into tears. He drove past a man waving frantically at him, unable to stop to pick up the fare. He pulled over on Mill Lane, not far from the Jolly Miller club, switched off the radio and he hid his sobbing face in his palms. He was startled by a tapping on the window.

'Piss off!' he cried, without looking, then looked to his right and saw the face of a policeman who was stooping to look in on him. He wound down the window and tried to apologise.

'It's alright kid,' said the policeman, 'you alright, eh?'

'It's a lot – lot of things – ' Paul tried to talk but he was too strangled by grief.

'It's okay pal,' said the constable, 'just that I saw you with your head in your hands and wondered if you were okay.'

'Thanks officer,' came the muffled reply from Paul as he pressed his face against his palms.

'Ah, is he alright?' asked a passing girl of about thirty who was walking towards the pub. She was a very pretty brunette and she came over to the cab.

'Yeah, it's alright love,' said the policeman, 'he's just a bit upset.'

'Ah, why?' asked the girl; she was quite tall in her platforms and so she had to stoop to look in at Paul.

'What's happened?' asked an old man behind the policeman. He was walking his dog and came from one of the houses on Mill Lane.

'He's upset,' the girl told the old man.

'Did someone run off without paying?' asked the elderly man in all seriousness.

'I'm okay, honest,' said Paul, regaining his breath for a moment. He looked up at the three concerned faces; they were all blurry because of the tears in his eyes.

A middle-aged black man approached from the

other side of the cab and when he saw Paul's tear-streaked face he asked the policeman, 'Everything okay?'

'Someone ran off without paying, I think,' said the old man, 'and he's awfully upset.'

The policeman rolled his eyes. 'Where do all of you people come from?' asked the policeman.

Paul looked at him and smiled as he wiped his tears away with the backs of his hands.

'I just live over there,' the old dog-walker told the policeman, pointing to his home.

'Here's why I'm upset,' said Paul, his voice still broken. He produced his wallet and took out a Polaroid of his baby daughter lying in her cot at the hospital. She was hooked up to a ventilator. After two false starts at trying to reply because he was choked up, Paul managed to say: 'That's my eighteen-month-old daughter, Ella. She's got mitochondrial disease and they say she won't survive.'

'Oh no!' said the pretty young lady and the policeman sighed and closed his eyes for a moment as he surveyed the photograph. The black man took hold of the photograph, shook his head as his eyes filled with sorrow, and the old man took hold of the picture and scrutinised it closely as if he was far-sighted. 'Oh, I am so sorry, young man,' remarked the old man.

'No use being sorry,' said the black man, 'you have to do something about this.'

'What can I do?' asked Paul. He looked helpless.

'Prayer,' said the black man, 'let's all say a prayer. I believe you see, and if anyone else here does, let him join me in prayer.'

'I do as well,' said the young lady, 'I believe. I'm a

believer.'

'It's worth a try,' said the policeman, and he took off his tall helmet, put it under his arm and pressed his palms together. 'All fails when faith fails,' the officer of the law added.

The black man started to recite the Lord's Prayer, and the other three joined in. Paul was so moved by these people praying for his daughter, he could hardly say the words to the prayer. The black man asked God to give Paul a sign of hope, and after a few minutes, he walked away after shaking hands with Paul. The girl leaned into the cab and kissed Paul, and the old man and the policeman shook hands with the cabbie as well. Paul somehow felt a little less sad now. He drove home and for the first time he actually ate a meal. He was back out on the road in the evening, even though he felt a bit weary; he just wouldn't be able to sleep for obvious reasons. The fog had worsened and just after midnight he was driving up Speke Road in Woolton, not far from St Julie's High School, when he saw a vague silhouette with a raised arm, standing at the kerb. Paul slowed and the headlights showed the customer to be a nun. He unlocked the rear kerbside door and the nun got in. She looked as if she was in her fifties, and in a well-spoken voice she said, 'Thank you driver. Could you take me to Hope Street, please?'

'Yes, of course, Sister,' Paul found himself addressing the holy woman. This harked back to his days as an altar boy when he was twelve.

'You haven't put your meter on,' said the nun.

'Oh – oh yes, thanks for telling me,' said Paul. 'Terrible night isn't it?'

The nun said nothing in reply.

Paul turned left onto Allerton Road and asked, 'If you don't mind me asking Sister, what are you doing out on such an inclement night?'

The nun told him. 'I had to pay a visit to a sick man. His name's James Rake.'

'Not James Rake who lives on Manor Road?' asked Paul.

'Yes,' came the flat monosyllabic reply.

'Small world,' said Paul, 'I went to school with him. What's wrong with him?'

'It's confidential, but I knew he was a friend of yours,' came the intriguing reply.

'How did you know I knew him?' Paul wanted to know.

'Paul, never mind that,' said the nun, 'you need help for your baby, don't you?'

Paul felt his heart palpitate as the nun mentioned his sick daughter. He slowed down and asked, 'Who *are* you?'

The passenger did not reply. Paul switched the light on in the rear of the vehicle and saw she was sitting there calmly, and he noticed how blue the nun's eyes were.

'Paul,' she said, 'you must return to your faith. You believed in the Lord unquestioningly when you were small, and your faith was unshakeable – but somewhere along the line you not only lost your faith, you started to blame God for every misfortune.'

'I know, and I'm sorry,' said Paul, and he had to pull over. 'I don't know what happened, but everything started revolving around me. I started putting myself first and I stopped helping the less fortunate Sister.

How do I get back to the person I was when I was

younger?'

'By believing Paul. And you must stop blaming God and everyone for your faults and predicaments,' replied the nun, and then she added, 'I will save Ella.'

'Oh please do,' said Paul, and tears started to fall from his eyes. 'Have you been sent because of those people who prayed for me?'

The nun nodded. 'Paul, you must return to your faith. You must promise that when Ella make's her First Communion, she must dress in blue.'

'Yes, I promise I'll do that, Sister, I give you my word,' said Paul, and he started crying.

'Don't cry Paul; cry for those who have lost their way,' said the Nun.

Paul nodded and started the cab. He then seemed to go into some sort of trance state. He travelled six miles in around twenty minutes and the next thing he knew, he was pulling up in Hope Street opposite the Everyman Theatre, outside the John Foster Building. The nun got out and walked off into the fog. The words 'don't forget the promise' echoed in his mind.

He was just about to drive home when a blonde girl of about seventeen appeared at the nearside window and said, 'Excuse me, I need to get home but I only have a fiver.'

'It's alright love, get in,' said Paul, squeezing his eyes shut for a moment. He felt as if he'd just awakened from some lucid dream.

'I live up in Litherland,' said the girl, 'I'm sorry about not having enough money only I lost a twenty-pound note.'

'It's alright love,' said Paul, 'now where about in Litherland?'

'Moss Lane, near Stanley Park,' said the girl.

'Oh I know the place,' said Paul, and he set out on the six mile journey, and when he reached the girl's home just over 25 minutes later, he saw her mother waiting for her on the doorstep. He refused to take the fiver off the girl and drove home. The next morning, Paul received a call from the hospital. They wanted to tell him something but they weren't allowed to divulge the news over the phone; Paul would have to call into the hospital in person. He wondered if his beloved daughter had died – or had the nun kept her word and had she brought divine help? When he reached the hospital he bumped into his wife Bethel and her boyfriend Stuart in the reception area. A doctor came out to talk to them and before he opened his mouth the couple saw he was smiling. The doctor told them that Ella's oxygen levels had gone back to normal overnight, the child had opened her eyes and was breathing unaided without the ventilator. Ella had also told a nurse she was hungry. The doctor also said that a specialist seemed to be at a loss to explain the 'miraculous' recovery. The doctor did warn the parents that Ella was by no means out of the woods yet – they were still keeping her under observation for the time being. Paul and Bethel started to cry and held one another. Stuart looked awkward, and meekly hugged Bethel. Eventually, Ella made a full recovery, and Paul told his wife about the strange encounter with the nun in the cab. He told her he had to keep his promise – he wanted Ella to wear a blue dress for her First Communion. Bethel thought the nun Paul had picked up had just been a real flesh and blood nun and not some messenger from God. Paul said he had discovered that a convent had existed near St Julie's – where he had picked the nun up that night in the fog, and he had also been told that the name of the building the nun had walked towards on Hope Street that night was the John Foster Building, now used by the Liverpool John Moores University – but years ago it had been a Catholic teacher training college run by the Sisters of Notre Dame. A few days later, Paul heard some sad but intriguing news from a friend; his old schoolmate Jimmy Rake had passed away from cancer. He'd only been 22 – the same age as Paul. Paul, of course, immediately recalled the nun telling him she had been looking after his old friend.

Bethel and Stuart split just under a year later, and Paul and his wife got back together. When Ella turned eight, in 2007, she was due to make her First Communion, and Paul had a dream about the nun who had entered his cab, and in the dream she was dressed in a blue habit. She had said to him in the dream, 'Remember the promise you made to me, Paul.'

When Paul awoke he told his wife about the dream, and Bethel asked him what shade of blue the nun had worn. Paul looked about, but could not see the type of blue he'd seen in that dream – and then he smiled and looked straight into Bethel's eyes. 'What?' she asked, puzzled and a bit annoyed.

'Your eyes – that's the exact shade of blue the nun wore,' he told his wife.

The couple went to a priest and they expected him to be a bit sceptical about the dream of the nun but he told Paul and Bethel that the colour they were describing is what is known as "Marian Blue" – a colour always associated with the Virgin Mary. She had always been depicted wearing garments of that colour in religious paintings down the centuries. Bethel went to a fabric store on Stafford Street near TJ Hughes where her mother had often bought dressmaking materials, and she obtained a sheet of cloth that closely matched the blueness of her eyes and a pattern for a dress that would become the communion dress. Bethel's best friend, a lady named Rita, was a gifted seamstress, and she made the dress, but she told Bethel that Ella would get some strange looks from the parents attending the First Communion service, but Bethel said she didn't care; she believed she was keeping a promise to the nun from beyond who had saved her daughter's life all those years back. The ceremony took place, and Ella was the last in line that day when the girls came into the church in a procession. As Ella knelt at the altar rail to receive the host, the sun emerged from a cloud outside and a beam of blue light filtering through a stained-glass window fell upon her. At that very moment, the statue of the Blessed Virgin was seen to change from white to a shade of blue. Seconds later, the statue returned to its pallid colour.

To this day, Bethel and Paul believe that the nun who Paul met on that foggy night near St Julie's High School was some envoy from God who not only saved Ella, but also helped Paul to regain his faith.

Another supernatural incident concerning a taxi took place just after 7.45am on the Tuesday morning of 19 May 1970. Steven Bryant, a 30-year-old hackney cab driver from Kensington had been on the job since midnight and was about to clock off for some breakfast and some shut eye as he drove homewards along Ullet Road when a woman ran out from Aigburth Drive and straight into the path of Steven's car. He braked and beeped his horn. The woman had rushed out of Sefton Park, completely oblivious to Steven's cab, and only for his reflexes he would have hit her. This woman fled down Windermere Terrace and Steven was about to continue on his way when another figure came running out of the park, and this was a very bizarre-looking man who was wearing what looked like a pointed dunce's hat – and he was brandishing a sword. He looked demented, and he slowed down for a moment, then bolted after the woman who had just run across the road. Steven swung the cab around and sped after the oddly-dressed swordsman beeping his horn. The weird man was closing in on the woman. Steven pulled up, grabbed the crowbar he kept concealed under his seat in case someone tried to mug him, and jumped out of the vehicle. One half of the cabbie's mind was screaming for him to stop and telling him it was a stupid and dangerous thing to do, but another part of Steven was urging him to intervene and save this woman from being cut down by the crazed man.

'Oi!' Steven shouted, and the man in the pointy hat turned, startled, and lifted his sword-wielding hand as if he was about to take a swipe at the taxi driver with the fearsome-looking blade. 'This whore shouldn't be on the streets dressed like that! She's asking to be slaughtered!'

The woman he was referring to looked as if she was in her late twenties and she was cowering from the deranged man in the driveway of a rather grand looking house. 'Put that sword down before you do some harm!' shouted Steven, but the man turned to look at the woman and walked towards her, and he still held the sword aloft in his right hand, ready to strike.

Steven rushed at the man and swung the crowbar hard at his right shoulder. The force knocked the stalker to the ground, and the woman screamed and rushed past Steven.

'Get in my taxi!' Steven shouted at her, and she ran to the vehicle. Steven left the stunned man on his knees and he rushed back to the cab, opened the passenger door and almost pushed the lady in, and then he got in and drove off. As the hackney cab past the man there was a terrific bang and the woman screamed. The weirdo had struck the cab with the sword, taking the right wing mirror clean off with the blade. Steven was so infuriated at this damage to a vehicle which provided him with a living, he reversed into the crazed attacker – and the man fell under the vehicle and the taxi went over him. Steven looked through the windscreen in horror. The man's body lay in the road face up, and he could see the cab had left a tyre track that went up the man's right leg, across his hip and shoulder. He was not moving and the sword was still in his right hand.

'You – you ran over him,' muttered the traumatised lady behind him as she eyed the inert body in the roadway, but then as she and Steven looked on, the man sat up turned around, and charged at the cab as he screamed something unintelligible. The passenger yelped and Steven reversed into Ullet Road, then halted for a moment to see if there were any vehicles coming his way. He drove off and sped around Princes Park and asked the woman who the nut was.

'I haven't a clue,' she answered with a tremor in her voice, 'I was taking a short cut through the park to get to my work on Leece Street, and he just came out of nowhere. He kept shouting "Repent!" and then I looked back about a minute later and he was still following me, and then I ran.'

The woman's name was Verity Slade, and she worked at a newsagents shop on Leece Street. Steven drove her to her workplace and when she asked him how much she owed him he shook his head and said, 'No, its okay love, you just get into work and if I was you I'd call the police and tell them what happened. Mention me if you want; I'm a witness - my name's Steven Bryant.' Steven gave his address to the woman and advised her to avoid Sefton Park when she made her way home.

Driving home to his flat on Kensington's Boaler Street, Steven recalled how the madman had recovered very quickly from being run over by a taxi weighing two thousand kilograms and he had not even suffered any visible injury despite a crowbar smashing into his shoulder. The suspicion that there was something supernatural about the swordsman started to creep up on him, and he wondered what the meaning of that dunce's hat the man had worn could possibly be. After reaching his home, Steven had a look at the spot where his right side-view mirror had been, and he asked his friend in the nearby garage if he could fit a new mirror. The new mirror was put on in minutes.

A very weary Steven returned home, had a small shot of whisky, and then he climbed into bed at 10am and had five hours of restless sleep. He had felt uneasy when he had awakened in his bed almost every twenty minutes. He wondered how Verity was, and acting on impulse he showered, shaved, then rode his cab to the newsagents where the woman worked, arriving there a little after 5pm. She was surprised to see him. She said she hadn't reported the matter to the police because she thought they'd find her story a bit dubious; a man in a dunce's cap with a sword, and a man who had survived being run over by a taxi.

'I'll run you home if you want,' said Steven, buying a copy of the *Liverpool Echo*.

'No, its okay,' said Verity, 'I don't knock off till six; it's only a quarter past five.'

'I don't mind killing time in town till then,' said Steven.

'No, don't be daft, I'll be okay,' said Verity, smiling, but Steven could see uneasiness in her eyes. 'I'll take the long way home and go right round the park.'

'Well, be careful then; bye now,' Steven said, and he left the shop and drove up Leece Street, through Hardman Street and onto Myrtle Street, where two young ladies flagged him down outside the Philharmonic Hall. One of the girls asked Steven to take them to an address on Elmswood Road, Aigburth. Steven had to go round Sefton Park, and he kept an eye out for the weird man with the sword, but couldn't see him. He told the girls – both art students from the polytechnic – to be careful when they were walking through the park because 'a strange-looking fellah with a sword' was about, and one of the girls surprised Steven because she nodded with a grave expression and asked, 'You mean the nutter with the big pointed dunce's cap?'

'Yeah, have you see him?' asked an intrigued Steven.

'Yes, I've seen him twice,' said the student, 'I was walking my old neighbour's dog in the park by the Palm House and he came out of nowhere saying, "Repent," and then he said my skirt was too short and that I shouldn't be wearing boots. I picked the dog up and ran back to the flat. Then I saw him standing outside our flat a few nights later about ten, and he waved to me with the sword and shouted "whore!" '

'Yes I heard him shout that,' said the second student.

'Didn't you call the police?' Steven asked the first student and she shook her head and told him, 'No. He ran off towards Aigburth Vale and I locked the door. He must have escaped from a mental hospital or something.'

After Steven had dropped the students off at their flat, he drove slowly to the place where he had encountered the sinister figure, and then he drove down Windermere Terrace, and there was his smashed wing mirror lying in the gutter. Steven had the unsettling feeling he was being watched. He'd heard birdsong up until a few moments ago, but now there was a peculiar hush hanging in the air. He drove down Aigburth Road and upon reaching the junction at Ullet Road he saw Verity and a female walking towards him. He beeped his horn at them and turned the cab around. He leaned over to the nearside window, wound it down and with a smile on his face he said, 'Verity – I'm not following you love – I've just dropped off two students by the park. Get in!'

'No, we'll be okay Steven,' Verity assured him, and the blonde lady she was with stooped to have a look at Steven in the cab.

'Alright, get straight home now, bye!' Steven

shouted, and he drove up Aigburth Road. The cabbie had only travelled about a hundred yards when he happened to glance to his right, and there, coming from Colebrooke Road was the creepy man with the sword, and again he had that pointed hat on. He was looking towards Verity and her friend. Steven turned the cab around and there was a chorus of disharmonious car horns from drivers behind him as he performed the manoeuvre. He drove back to Verity and pulled up by them on the wrong side of the road with a screech of tyres. He wound down the window and shouted, 'Get in! He's up there!'

Verity shot a puzzled look at Steven, and then she turned her head left and her eyes widened as she saw the figure of fear running down Aigburth Road towards her. She and her friend, a workmate named Karen, quickly got into the cab and the hackney shot off into Ullet Road.

'We've got to report this,' said Steven and he drove to the nearest police station – on Lark Lane. The police seemed a bit bemused by the description of the attacker's tall pointed cap with the block letter "D" emblazoned upon it but promised to investigate.

Steven started to date Verity and they later moved to a flat in Aigburth. Neither of them saw no more of the frightening weird man with the sword, but years later, when the couple had married, they moved to a house in Mossley Hill, and held a housewarming party. This was in the autumn of 1981, and at the time, a rapist was at large in the Sefton Park area. A 23-year-old student had been subjected to a dreadful sexual assault and it had generated waves of fear that went rippling through the trendy flat-land district. Girls had reported being followed by an assortment of strange men, and everyone was dreading the news of the next rape. At the housewarming party was a couple who lived near Sefton Park, and they told everyone how they were scared to go out after dark because of the rapist at large. A representative of the Student's Union was requesting extra protection from the police for the student population, especially around the Halls of Residence. Verity's Auntie Margaret was a guest at the housewarming party and she said something which really caught the attention of Verity and Steven. The old woman said, 'There's a strange atmosphere in that park near the old folk's home on Aigburth Drive. I was coming back from that home one night – it must have been around 1969 – I'd been to see my old Auntie Flora. Anyway, it was dark and the moon was out, and I heard this man shouting. It was coming from the park. I turned and looked and it was really quite odd because the person who was shouting had this tall pointed hat on, like a witch's hat only without the brim – or a magician's hat come to think of it – and he was waving this huge sword.'

Steven and Verity looked at one another and Verity clutched Steven's hand.

Aunt Margaret continued, 'I could see the moonlight reflecting off the blade of this sword, and I started to run – and *he* started to run, and he shouted, "repent you so and so" – it was a very rude word. Well by the time I reached my home I was in tears. When I told my mother about the unbalanced man she told me he'd been seen way back in the 1930s and was supposed to be a ghost.'

Verity and Steven then told Margaret about their two

encounters with the apparently paranormal character, and the rest of the night was filled with drink and the telling of ghost stories. The back-story behind the violent dunce-hatted ranting psychopath is still unknown, but perhaps someone out there – someone with a dark family secret – knows a lot more.

The next taxi tale of terror takes place in the January of 1979. It was a freezing Saturday night creeping into a Sunday morning and the snow was falling heavily across the North West. A 62-year-old cabdriver named Dennis Humphreys was driving through Speke, wondering whether he should call it a day on account of the worsening weather conditions, but it was a weekend and there was so much money to be made from clubbers stuck in the city centre in this big freeze. He'd just left the filling station, and after topping up the cab he had heard from the station attendant that the weather was so bad, matches and race meetings were being cancelled. It was three minutes after midnight when Dennis saw a woman in a dark blue anorak waving to him at the side of the road. He slowly pulled up because the macadam was deep with snow and beneath it was the layer of ice from the night before. The gritters hadn't been out and there was a shortage of salt because of a lorry driver's dispute. The woman got into the cab and she had a tartan scarf wrapped around her head inside the anorak hood, and her eyes were glistening with the glacial razor blade cold. She spoke with a muffled and nasally congested voice. 'Could you please take me to Llangollen?' she asked. There was a slight Welsh accent, Dennis thought.

'*Where*, sorry?' Dennis hoped he'd misheard the girl.

He leaned back to listen as her voice was so muffled.

The woman, who struck Dennis as being in her early twenties, said: 'Llangollen – it's in Wales. I need to get there tonight; a family member is seriously ill you see.'

'I thought you said that. Are you serious?' Dennis asked with a painful smile. 'That's about fifty miles away, and there's a heavy snow forecast – '

'I know but my mother's dying, and I've got the money – as much money as you want,' said the girl, and the desperation in her filtered through the muffled voice as she talked through that tartan scarf.

'I – I don't know, I could get stranded out there,' said Dennis, unsure what to do. Money was his god and he quoted an inflated figure off the top of his head. 'You're talking about a ton at least,' he said, and recalled he'd just topped up the taxi's gas, but he was worried about the snow; he watched the huge flakes kissing the windscreen and turned on the wipers. One hundred quid was still a lot of money in the mind of Dennis, but did she have the money on her or at least some form of security? The girl seemed to read his mind, because she took off two gold rings and thrust them at the square hole in the security grille. 'They're worth over a hundred alone,' she said, 'take them as security if you want.'

'No, love I trust you, but if this taxi breaks down or gets stuck in a snowdrift you'll have to pay me to get it picked up,' Dennis warned the girl, and she nodded and reclined back into the padded grey seat.

'You cold there?' Dennis asked, and the woman didn't reply, but he turned on the heater anyway and drove off up Speke Boulevard. A few minutes into the journey Dennis asked, 'What's wrong with your mum, anyway?'

'She has cancer,' came the reply, 'lung cancer. She used to smoke a lot.'

'Yeah, ciggies are killers,' said Dennis, and the cab joined the Speke-Widnes Link Road. 'Just packed them in myself; I've started eating more though.'

The girl seemed so still with her head bowed, as if she was dozing off, perhaps because of the heat being blown into the cab. Dennis switched on the radio and found some easy-listening music on BBC Radio 2. Presenter Ray Moore introduced some schmaltzy song by a crooner and Dennis surveyed the white snowscape beyond the swaying windscreen wipers. They passed over the Runcorn Bridge, a white arched skeleton against a dark grey sky, and minutes later on the M56, the snow was so heavy, the visibility had dropped to about fifty yards. In all of his years on the road, Dennis had never seen snow like this; the wipers seemed like a waste of time – they swept away the sticky goose-feather flakes but more stuck in the wake of the wiper, and Dennis had to slow down somewhat. He felt a right idiot – there wasn't another car on the motorway – at least as far as he could see, which was less than fifty yards. The thought of the hundred quid kept him going. A severe weather bulletin from the Met Office interrupted Ray Moore's *Late Show*; the weathermen were warning people not to venture out onto the roads unless the journey was absolutely essential, and then there was a mention of a shortage of grit. The music resumed, and the taxi wound its way towards Wales. They passed the outskirts of Chester and the peripheries of Wrexham, and the taxi had to crawl along because the snow was so deep. Dennis swore and said the roads should have been gritted, and then he shouted to his passenger, 'I wouldn't be surprised if this engine seizes up! Are you asleep there, love? You'll have to guide me; the signs are covered in snow. I knew it was a mistake coming out here!'

The girl looked at the window and said, 'I can't see anything – the window's iced up.'

'Look through this window, love!' shouted Dennis, nodding to the windscreen, 'Anything look familiar?'

'I can't see a thing, it's just all snow,' the girl replied.

'Does that say – Llangollen?' Dennis muttered, looking through the side window. He slowed the cab, wound down the window and the blast of icy wind stung his eyes. 'Bastard! I think it said Llangollen 10 miles,' he said, winding the window back up. He turned the steering wheel and the cab curved into a road that was covered in a foot of snow. The handling of the taxi changed immediately and Dennis started cussing and squinting through the windscreen. The lighting in this area was terrible. The road seemed to have no end, and then Dennis got the scare of his life – he realised he had somehow gone up a mountain. He could see the frightening snow-covered gradient to his left, descending into a grey limbo of a million snowflakes. He turned and growled, 'Don't you know where we are? You *are* from around here aren't you love?'

'This looks like Bower's Road – you've gone the wrong way,' said the girl.

'Well I don't know this part of Wales, but I thought you might at least have been able to guide me!' roared Dennis. He went down a lane that was the same width as the cab – just under seven feet, and the girl started to giggle – possibly with nerves.

'Not funny at all love,' Dennis chided her, 'and I might have to charge an extra fifty quid now!'

'Listen to that wind,' said the girl, drawing the cab driver's attention to the moaning winds blowing across the mountain.

'Jesus, look at that,' Dennis saw the windscreen turn white, and the wipers were now a waste of time. 'I'll have to radio for help,' Dennis said, his hand fumbling for the microphone of the radio transceiver. 'What is it now? The Victor waveband,' he whispered, then swore. 'It's dead. Isn't that bloody typical, eh? Just a hissing noise. Let's try this; no – nothing.'

The taxi stuttered to a halt. Dennis tried to restart it – but the abnormal cold had thickened the engine oil, and the battery seemed to be flat now. 'I should never have come out here!' moaned Dennis, trying again to restart the cab but it just wasn't having it.

He tried to open the door – and discovered that the snow had already piled up against the taxi, so he could only open the door by about six inches. 'We're going to freeze to death in here because of you, you dozy cow!' Dennis informed his passenger. 'We'll be buried in this blizzard!'

'Dennis,' said the passenger.

How does she know my name? Dennis wondered in the midst of his rant. He looked at her as she took off her hood. It was a face he had not seen since 1949. It was Cathy. She unwound the tartan scarf, and there was the crimson isosceles triangle where a nose had been. Back in 1949 on that terrible January night, he and his beautiful girlfriend Cathy had been in a car.

Dennis had been at the wheel, but had been

drinking, and the car had slid on black ice and there had been a horrific crash. The rear view mirror had sliced off Cathy's nose. Plastic surgery was unheard of in post war Liverpool, so they made no attempt to rebuild the nose, and Dennis had left the disfigured girl. He had been engaged to another girl anyway, and the abandoned Cathy had hanged herself from the banisters in her auntie's house. Now it all made sense – Cathy had been Welsh; she had family in Llangollen. This was her ghost sitting in the cab. She was smiling at him and her face was as white as the fields of snow outside.

'Don't be afraid, Dennis,' said the solid-looking apparition, 'you'll go to sleep with the cold and then you'll be with me.'

Dennis turned without a word of reply and he tried desperately to open the door next to him, but the packed snow was stopping that door from fully opening. He swore and pushed as hard as he could and then he somehow managed to squeeze through the gap, scraping off skin on his leg as he did. He ran in a panic into the white void and those giant whirling snowflakes stung his eyelids and burnt his face. He looked back and saw Cathy slip out of the car and walk towards him in the howling wind. Dennis tried to run but the snow was up to his knees, and it impeded him to such an extent he fell face first into it. He shouted for help but his cries were lost in the howling wind. He felt Cathy touch his left arm and he turned and saw her white bony hand on his shoulder. He tried to run away but felt as if his lungs were on fire as he gasped for air – icy subzero air – and then he fell, clutching his chest. He had no energy and he lay there, face down, unable to get up. It all seemed unreal, like a dream, and he felt drowsy with the numbing cold. He saw a jumble of images and scenes in his mind: his cat, Arthur, sitting in his fireside chair, his divorced wife Agnes, standing by him in a pub, and then everything faded away and he blacked out. A police Land Rover came upon the scene at first light and they found Dennis barely alive with a faint pulse. He was rushed to hospital and treated for severe hypothermia and frostbite. When Dennis woke up, a specialist told him he had come close to losing his nose through frostbite. The nose of the cabbie had turned dark and would have become gangrenous if it had not been treated in time. At the mention of the frostbitten nose, Dennis recalled the ghost of Cathy, and of her ghastly accident all those years ago when she lost her nose. He told the doctor about his ghostly passenger but the police had found no one else in the taxi and only one trail leading from the vehicle, made by Dennis. He assured them he really had encountered a ghost but the doctor told him he'd hallucinated Cathy because of the arctic temperatures. 'Why do you think I was out in the middle of Wales in a blizzard?' Dennis asked the doctor, 'Because I was taking that woman to her home in Llangollen.'

No one ever believed the story Dennis told – that his first girlfriend had returned from beyond the grave on the anniversary of her suicide in an effort to bring Dennis into the afterlife. He visited Cathy's grave in Allerton Cemetery and left flowers there after saying a little prayer.

# THE FETCH

I've had to change a few names in the following uncanny story for legal reasons but beyond that, the account is exactly as it was related to me. In 1970, a 50-year-old Huyton bachelor named Noel Peake was getting rather fed up with his humdrum life. For the past twenty years he'd been the company director of a cardboard factory and did nothing all day but sit in his office on Greenland Street, filling the long hours signing a wad of cheques, poring over reams of invoices or gazing out the window at the bleak brick wall of the warehouse facing his own grim-looking premises. Sometimes there were meetings with major shareholders in the firm, but every one of them was a septuagenarian and each meeting was mind-numbingly boring. Noel had taken over the position as company director from his uncle a few years before the latter died, and although the money was more than okay, Noel felt as if he was stuck in a clockwork routine from which there was no escape. He talked to his 78-year-old mother about selling the business on a few occasions and she would always become teary and say her brother – Noel's late uncle – would turn in his grave if the business changed hands. Noel had a few holidays each year, but coming back from Spain or Florida to the grey world of the factory always sent him down into the depths of depression. Mr Peters, the 75-year-old who filled in for Noel when he went abroad was currently in hospital with pneumonia, so even going on a short holiday would present an insurmountable difficulty for now. One lunchtime, Noel got into his burgundy Triumph Herald and drove to Bessie's Café on Islington's Soho Street - a place where he had once met a beautiful girl named Gina each weekend in his younger days – until she met someone. She had wanted him to move into a flat in London with her but Noel's domineering mother had told him his future lay with the cardboard factory. Noel walked into Bessie's Café where, as chance would have it, he met an old friend from his college days – Maurice Pickering – a strange individual who studied – and dabbled in – the Occult. Noel had always regarded him as an oddball, but being utterly depressed and in need of friendship he was so glad to see him. Over coffee and cakes, Noel told Maurice about his boring, soul-destroying existence and how he would give anything to have a new, exciting life. Maurice smiled for a while, seeming to be in contemplation, and as Noel became a little annoyed at the pause in the conversation, Maurice said, 'I think I may have the answer, Noel.'

'I'd love to hear it but I bet it involves the supernatural knowing you,' said Noel.

Maurice nodded and replied, 'Yes it does; you know me so well. I've made a *lot* of progress in the study of the Occult since you last saw me, and I had a nervous breakdown because of it five years back. I went a little too far – and I almost lost my mind. There are things – powers – we humans should keep well away from – but I suppose it's like telling Adam and Eve not to go near that Forbidden Fruit.'

'I think I'll just have to break my mother's heart and

tell her I want out,' said Noel, feeling guilty of desertion just talking about it. He knew deep down he was stuck with that factory until his mother – or he – went to Heaven via Anfield Cemetery. 'It's not fair the way some parents control their offspring,' he added.

'Anyway,' Maurice sighed the word, 'you probably won't be able to take this in Noel – no offence but it does require high intelligence – but there is a sort of dimension running alongside our one and I call it the Altern Void.'

'A dimension next to ours – yes – I can take that in, go on,' said an annoyed Noel, hurt by the condescending way his friend had dismissed him as a blockhead.

'The Altern Void is where most *doppelgangers* come from – exact doubles of people that have been documented over the years – they're close copies of us but they're a little dim because they have a different type of consciousness than us.'

'You're not pulling my leg with all this?' Noel asked, and twitched a nervous smile. He offered Maurice a cigarette from his pack of Rothman's King Size.

Maurice accepted the cigarette and said: 'Straight up, Noel, and I now know how to bring a person's double from the Altern Void to our reality – so do you see what I'm getting at?'

'Er, no, not really, Maurice' admitted Noel, clicking his lighter - lighting his own cigarette then Maurice's.

'I could bring your double into this world, and he'd look exactly like you and because he's rather dense, I could tell him what to do and how to behave; he'd be like a human robot – only he'd be subhuman really because they're like an inferior version of us. Anyway, he could run your cardboard factory and you'd be free to do whatever you wanted. You've described the boring routines Noel, and they'd be right up the carbon-copy-Noel's street.'

If anyone else had heard Maurice's plan, they'd have dismissed him as a fantasy-prone crackpot or someone with a mental illness, but Noel Peake *knew* his friend could somehow produce some strange phenomena with his in-depth knowledge of the Occult; he'd witnessed a lot of extraordinary and inexplicable things Maurice had pulled off – and those powers his friend possessed frightened him.

'No, don't start messing about with all that Black Magic stuff, Maurice,' said Noel, looking a little disconcerted, 'I'll just have to retire and find a more exciting line of work.'

'You're scared,' said Maurice, gritting his teeth, 'but just look at yourself Noel; life will pass you by soon and you'll be too old to break free. The bedpan years are looming my friend.'

'I suppose I am a bit scared,' admitted Noel, 'but it's just because there are certain things we shouldn't dabble with, and the Occult is one of them. Once you start meddling with those forces they start to affect your life and bad things start to happen.'

'Rubbish,' laughed Maurice, 'hundreds of thousands of years ago – probably millions of years back – someone produced fire for the first time, and that person would have been feared at first, for they'd be seen to be in control of a living, destructive, supernatural flame, but thank the stars they were brave enough to give the rest of the human race fire, because it could warm us in winter, cook food and scare away man-eating predators. If you had been back in that age we'd be living in a cold and dark cave eating raw meat!'

People seated at other tables turned their faces to the ranting Maurice.

'Now that's a daft analogy, Maurice,' laughed Noel, 'and er – let's not argue – I'm just glad I have someone to unload my gripes to. Can I get you another coffee?'

'No thanks, I haven't finished this one,' Maurice nodded to the mug. 'This isn't an argument, Noel, it's a discussion; I'm trying to *help* you.'

'I know old chap,' Noel nodded slowly and smiled and patted Maurice's tightly-clenched fist on the table. 'It's just that I don't want some spooky double of me swanning about, running the factory.'

'You could be living the life of Riley as your *fetch* puts in those long grinding hours Noel,' Maurice continued in a whispering voice as people all around turned their attention back to their own personal universes. 'They call these doppelgangers fetches in Ireland and it's a good name really because they can fetch and carry and do all the menial tasks – '

'No, Maurice,' Noel interrupted, then rolled his eyes to the ceiling, 'knowing me, with my blasted luck, something would go wrong.'

'Look, there's nothing that can go wrong,' Maurice insisted, and he grabbed a pepper shaker that was standing in the centre of the table and placed it down on another part of the red and white gingham table cloth. 'That's you, Noel Peake, and this – ' he picked up the salt shaker – 'this is your fetch, Leon – your name spelt backwards – and he is being brought over from the Altern Void. I give an intense hypnotic instruction to Leon and tell him where he lives, who he is and what he's supposed to do, and he will do nothing but go to work and come home at the exact same time every day – just as you do – and you can go to the Bahamas or live in an Amsterdam brothel for a month. No one will know the difference.'

'Friends would know!' Noel said in a combination of coughing and laughter.

Maurice posed a cutting question: '*What* friends?'

'Friends I play poker with each month, and people I sometimes talk to down the pub,' said Noel, and he knew very well he hadn't played poker for nearly six months and rarely went down to his local because the conversations there bored him to tears. 'And if this – er, Leon lives in my house, won't he wonder who I am? You haven't thought this through really, have you Maurice?'

'You're loaded, Noel!' roared Maurice, 'You could get another place to live. You'd have to keep away from your Altern Void self because it confuses the doppelganger – so I *have* thought this through!'

'Hey, will you simmer down there, foghorn voice?' a huge man seated at a nearby table said to Maurice.

'Stay in your cave, Noel!' Maurice said, and he got up and stormed off to the toilet.

'Your mate's a bleeding fanatic!' an elderly man shouted to Noel from another table.

'I'm sorry,' Noel replied, 'he's had a few health issues recently. He's not normally like this.'

When Maurice returned to the table, Noel looked at his wristwatch and said, 'No rest for the wicked. I better be getting back.' He shook hands with Maurice and the hand that did the shaking contained a piece of paper with Noel's home number on and two ten-pound notes wrapped up in it.

When Maurice saw the money he smiled and nodded at his old mate. 'Thanks,' he said.

'And remember now, Maurice, don't be conjuring anything up. Keep in touch,' said Noel with a wink, and he went and paid for the coffee and cakes, then left Bessie's Café in an optimistic mood.

On the following morning at his Huyton home, Noel had lathered his face with shaving foam and was about to use the old trusty cut-throat razor that had belonged to his late father – when he noticed something which unsettled him; his reflection looked odd. It was hard to put his finger on just *what* was different about his mirror image at first, but as Noel shaved his face and occasionally stared at his reflected image – looking at it straight in the eye – it became clear that the man in the mirrored door of the medicine cabinet was *not him* - the resemblance was 'off' and the mirror image seemed to lag; when he shaved, the razor seemed unsynchronized. It was the same when Noel looked in the full length wardrobe mirror. He stood there in his Y-fronts, and again the face looked a little different; it reminded him of people who were so-called lookalikes of celebrities who were in fact bad facsimiles of a pop or movie star. When he drove to work, Noel saw what seemed like a stranger gazing back at him in the rear view mirror. He became so distracted by the bizarre mirror mystery he pulled over, had a cigarette, then decided to go and see his physician Dr Robert Spinnery. He talked to the receptionist at the surgery and she told him a patient had just telephoned to cancel an appointment so he could take her place. At 9:10am Noel was called to see

Spinnery.

He walked into the surgery and without looking up from some notes he was reading, the white-haired doctor said, 'Morning Noel, what's troubling you?'

Noel sat at the desk and felt silly, and with a false chuckle he replied: 'Well, you'll probably refer me to a psychiatrist doctor, but, well – here goes; I was having a shave this morning and I noticed – and I know this will sound bizarre but, well – '

Dr Spinnery looked up from his notes with an expression of curiosity as he eyed Noel over the top of his reading glasses. 'You noticed what?'

'I feel as if I'm wasting your time really but – when I look at myself in the mirror, it doesn't look like me,' said Noel, sheepishly, adding, 'the image staring back doesn't seem to correspond - it - it looks unfamiliar.'

'Smile,' said the doctor, gazing intently at Noel as he leaned forward on his desk.

'Sorry?' Noel was baffled at the request.

'Smile – just checking you haven't had a stroke,' said Spinnery.

Noel gave an awkward smile.

'Smile seems symmetrical – no drooping on one side of your face,' the doctor noted, and then he asked: 'Any weakness in either arms or any difficulty when you walk – like as if you're dragging your leg?'

'No, no, I feel fine doctor,' Noel replied.

'Sometimes, when people have strokes, they find they can't recognise close family or friends because the part of the brain that deals with visual recognition is damaged. There was a case ten years ago where a devoted couple in Old Swan was in a bad car crash.

The wife had whiplash injuries and the husband was

suffering from concussion, but at the hospital, the husband claimed that his "real wife" had died in the crash and that the woman claiming to be his wife was an impostor. It's known as Capgras Syndrome, and it's very distressing. The Old Swan crash victim refused to sleep with his wife and tried to divorce her, thinking she was some stranger who merely resembled her. She stuck with him until she sadly died from cancer a few years ago. The husband wouldn't even attend her funeral.'

'I haven't been involved in any car crashes and I'm sure I haven't had a stroke doctor,' a worried Noel told the physician, fidgeting with the button on the sleeve of his coat.

Dr Spinnery pinched his bottom lip and said, 'When you say your reflection doesn't look like you, does he actually look different or is it a case of you noticing how you've aged when you look in the mirror? A lot of people say they feel younger than the person gazing back at them in the mirror - I know I do.'

'No, he – well *I* – my mirror image – doesn't look authentic, and sometimes if I move my hand or turn my head, the image in the mirror doesn't do the same; there's like a delay of a split second. Is it my brain, doctor?'

'Would you say you've been under a bit of stress recently?' Spinnery asked.

Noel nodded with a soft grin on his face. 'Well, I'm always under stress doctor; I'm not happy at all at work; I feel as if I'm trapped in the most boring job in the world.'

'And you're not happy with yourself or the way things are going in your life?' Spinnery queried with a knowing look.

'I'd be content if I could just get out of my god-awful job, doctor;' admitted Noel, and then he paused and narrowed his eyes and asked, 'and you think my self-hate, or self-loathing or whatever it is – is somehow manifesting itself with this mirror thing?'

'You've put it pretty well Noel – but you're not a psychiatrist and neither am I. Look, if this isn't down to stress, and if it persists, you'll have to come and see me again and I'll refer you to a clinical psychiatrist. None of this means you're going "nuts" or anything, it probably *is* down to stress, but we've got to find out what it's all about. In the meantime, I'd suggest getting as much sleep as you can, and indulging in a bit of relaxation; read a book, and perhaps potter about in the garden.'

'You don't think it's serious though, doctor?' Noel asked Spinnery.

'I personally think it's a minor thing but see how it goes,' the doctor told him.

It was only when Noel was sitting at his office desk later that day when the thought struck him out of the blue: was Maurice Pickering somehow responsible for the way he was perceiving his mirror image? Wasn't a doppelganger a type of *mirror* image – only one that could somehow leave its looking glass world and step into this one? Noel had the growing feeling that his hunch had hit the nail on the head.

Sure enough to confirm his suspicions, Noel Peake received a rambling letter three days later at his home. It was from Maurice Pickering. He picked the envelope up off the doormat and took it to work. He sat reading the handwritten note at his office desk as he waited for the morning coffee, and it was obvious from its incoherent wording that his old friend was mentally unstable. He said he'd conjured up "Leon" and that the double would soon take over Noel's job, thus freeing him. Leon would also be moving into Noel's home on Roby Road shortly and Maurice would telephone to give Noel a day's notice. If anything went wrong with Leon, Maurice promised he'd intervene and send him back to the Altern Void. The handwriting style in the letter then became erratic and illegible towards the end. Noel crumpled the letter and threw it in the wastepaper bin. 'I told him not to mess around with that rubbish!' he hissed. His secretary, 47-year-old Mrs Donders came in with the tray of coffee, biscuits and the morning mail.

'Thank you Mrs Donders – I really need that,' Noel said, slicking his quiff back with his hand as he eyed the cup. Mrs Donders poured him a coffee and added just the right amount of milk, cream and the usual Tate & Lyle sugar cube.

That morning, Noel left the office to go to the toilet and he dreaded looking at his reflection in the small square mirror above the wash basin, but he was a little relieved to see that his mirror image now looked *authentic* again. When he returned from the toilet he happened to glance through the window in the top half of his office door – and saw his double, seated at the desk. He was dressed exactly the same, but had his hair parted on the left. This really frightened Noel and in a confused state he backed away from the door, then turned and rushed to the stairwell. 'Pickering you bloody idiot,' he gasped. Pickering had somehow summoned that doppelganger just as he said he could.

Noel left the factory and drove about aimlessly, wondering what to do. His left eyelid started to twitch and flicker and he felt his heart palpitate. He called upon his ex-girlfriend Lucy at her home on Huskisson Street. In times of trouble or when he was feeling down, Noel often paid her a visit because she had a knack or reassuring him that things would turn out okay – but she answered the door with a black eye.

'How dare you come back here!' she bawled, and tried to shut the door on him. The door hit the toe of Noel's shoe but he never felt it because he was so shocked at her black eye and her animosity towards him.

'What are you talking about?' Noel was bewildered by her words.

'I'll call the police! They'll put you away!' she cried and turned and ran down the communal hallway to her flat. She closed the door just in time and Noel gently rapped on that door. 'Lucy, please explain – ' he started to say when he realised his double had done something bad to his former girlfriend.

'They'll do you for rape and assault!' said Lucy, and Noel heard her put on the bolt and safety chain.

Noel's throat closed up for a moment with fear, and then he opened the letterbox of the door and shouted: 'Lucy! Lucy, listen – it wasn't me – it was my double! I can't explain how but you've got to believe me! You know I wouldn't harm a hair on your beautiful head!'

'I'm phoning the police!' Lucy told him, then burst into tears and Noel could hear the telephone's rotary disc as Lucy dialled 999.

Noel panicked and ran out of the house and got back into his car. He drove to the Islington café and there was Maurice, reading *The Daily Telegraph* with a plate of untouched eggs and bacon at his elbow on the table. There was also a paper napkin spread out on the table with lines of strange symbols scrawled upon it.

'What have you done?' Noel seethed, and his startled friend looked up from the newspaper. He seemed to be in a daze and had a glazed look – as if he'd been drinking. He folded the newspaper and said: 'I know it hasn't gone to plan yet but he's a bad one Noel, it's never happened before. Don't let him see you or he'll try and kill you. I was only trying to help you.'

Noel's face went red with rage as he graphically recalled Lucy's black eye. 'That – that thing raped and battered a former girlfriend of mine and heaven knows what it will do next!'

'I'm really sorry – ' said Maurice.

'Sorry? Sorry? Is that all you can say?' Noel clenched his fist and drew it back as if he was going to plant it in Maurice's face. 'You'll have to send it back!'

'I've tried and it won't go back,' said Maurice, and with a tremor in his voice he stammered, 'ra-rape you say? Oh, what can we do?'

'I don't bloody well know, Maurice – you brought this thing into the world and you'll have to damn well get rid of it!'

'If we could get it into a pitch-black room with a mirror at each end – ' Maurice was saying, when Noel grabbed him by the lapels of his jacket and hoisted him out of his chair.

'Come on! You can talk while I drive!' Noel said, pushing Maurice to the door. He slapped down a fiver on the counter to pay for Maurice's uneaten meal, and then he roughly escorted his friend to the Triumph

Herald.

'Where are we going?' Maurice asked Noel, and the latter said, 'To the factory! It's already sitting in my chair!'

As soon as they reached the factory on Greenland Street, Noel posed a question which gave Maurice quite a start.

'Could a gun kill this thing?' he asked, getting out of the car.

'Yes, it could – why?' Maurice replied, 'You're not suggesting - '

'I've got an old shotgun,' said Noel, 'just need some cartridges. It wouldn't be murder would it? You said these things aren't human.'

'Yes, but explain that to the police when they find a man who resembles you with a few gaping holes in him,' Maurice replied, and he hurried after Noel across the car park towards the gloomy, forbidding building.

Noel and Maurice entered the warehouse and gingerly ascended a narrow stairwell at the back of the building that was rarely used. They tiptoed along the corridor leading to Noel's office. Noel peeped through the window in the door and was astonished to see his unearthly twin lying on top of the secretary Mrs Donders – who was sprawled out on the desk on her back. He had opened her blouse and he was kissing her bare bosom.

'I wish I had that shotgun now,' whispered Noel, his face pressed against the side of Maurice's head as the latter looked in at the office through the window in the door.

'She seems to be enjoying it,' remarked Maurice, his tongue and better judgement loosened by the whiskies he'd had an hour ago.

Noel turned his face and glared at Maurice. 'What a sick thing to say! That thing is a rapist, and it's going to pay, believe me,' Noel's voice sounded very firm.

'What are we going to do?' Maurice wondered out loud.

'Maybe I should just call the police,' said Noel, and he gave a harsh sidelong glance at Maurice and added, 'and you'll have to tell them the rest – and explain how you conjured this thing up.'

'They'd never believe me Noel and you know that,' said a fearful-looking looking Maurice, 'so let's do something practical instead of griping about the situation.'

'I think we should get that thing out of here first, lure it out into this corridor – there *are* two of us,' said Noel, but he sounded as if he was trying to convince himself. 'You're not scared of a bit of fisticuffs are you, Maurice?'

'I'm a bit tipsy but no, I'm not scared of scrapping,' said Maurice, 'so the idea is to knock him out?'

'Yes, that's the idea, Maurice, and then we can tie him up and you can do that thing you mentioned with the mirrors in the pitch-black room.'

'It might not work and the room has to be of a certain length,' muttered Maurice.

'Maurice, open the door and shout at him; tell him to come out, and then I'll lie in wait round here,' Noel pointed to the corner near the stairwell.

'Right, okay,' Maurice took a deep breath, and as Noel took up position around the corner, Maurice pushed the door of the office open and immediately he saw the living carbon copy of Noel Peake get off the secretary and zip up its trousers. Maurice yelled: 'Hey! You! Get off that woman and get out here!'

As the poker-faced doppelganger hurried towards him, Maurice backed out into the corridor. His back hit the wall and suddenly the hands of the sinister double were thrust out and they seized Maurice by his neck before the Occultist could even think of throwing a punch. There was a mighty clang as Noel struck his flesh and blood counterpart on the back of his head with a large red fire extinguisher. The replica of the company director staggered backwards, but recovered quickly, and it pushed Noel through the doorway of his office with such force, he almost landed on top of Mrs Donders, who was sitting up on the desk, confused by the violent proceedings. The double then delivered a hard punch to the solar plexus of Maurice Pickering which winded him, and as the "fetch" ran down the stairwell, the Occultist started to throw up.

Noel's dangerous duplicate used his car to travel to his house. It took the shotgun and drove off. It embarked on a string of assaults and even a robbery. It transpired that Lucy had not called the police that day when Noel called around, and if she had it would have been hard to prove that Noel had assaulted her physically and sexually – for Maurice dusted the phone in the factory office and discovered what he had long suspected – the fingerprints of the double were reversed versions of Noel's prints. The police were not yet using DNA samples forensically – all of that was sixteen years away in the future, and they would not be able to work out how the fingerprints of Noel and his doppelganger were mirror images. There were telephone calls to Noel's house in the dead of night –

probably made by the deadly twin to establish if Noel was at home – so Noel had to leave his house and live in a room over a shop on Bold Street – among as many people as possible, because he was of the opinion that there was safety in numbers as long as he remained the quarry of the psychopathic dead-ringer. On two occasions he was almost run down by his own Triumph Herald, and then the double started to empty his bank account. Dr Spinnery, was told about the weird delusions of Noel believing he was being stalked by his mirror image by Mrs Peake, Noel's mother, and the doctor was almost considering having the company director sectioned – just to prevent him becoming a danger to himself and members of the public. Then one afternoon as Noel was walking up Bold Street, he heard a familiar voice behind him say, 'Hello Noel.'

Noel slowly turned and came face to face with his living mirror image. The face was the same one he had first seen looking back at him from the mirror in his toilet – and that face was so like his own and yet the eyes were dead and emotionless. It produced a knife from its inside jacket pocket and it lunged at Noel, who jumped out the way.

'You don't belong over here!' Noel shouted at the double, more out of nerves than anything. He was ready to run.

'Stay still so I can kill you!' the cold-hearted alter ego told him, and swung the blade of the knife at him again, missing Noel's face by an inch.

'Oi!' shouted a policeman who had been on his Bold Street beat. He took his coat off and wrapped it around his forearm and then he bravely parried the doppelganger's attempts to stick him with the knife.

The policeman was no stranger to blade crime and had his own effective knife-defence skill. At one point in the confrontation the policeman seized the knife-wielding hand of Noel's look-alike and twisted his wrist until he let go of the weapon. The double then ran off with Noel in hot pursuit, but as it crossed Berry Street it was hit by a Scania freight truck. There were screams, and the double was thrown onto its back by the impact. The huge broad tyre of the braking truck went over the head of "Leon", and the double was looking at Noel at that moment with a blank expression. Its eyes popped out with the violent compression and the head was crushed as if it was a melon, with white and grey brain matter and blood spraying quite a distance. The unturning wheel skidded onwards and a horrified Noel saw the crushed jawbone of his metaphysical foe embedded in the road tar. The body of the doppelganger was riddled with nervous spasms and the leg was kicking. Noel turned away, wanting to throw up, and he held a handkerchief to his mouth as he saw the policeman who had saved his life coming towards him from Bold Street.

'Is he – ' the policeman was asking when Noel looked down - and received another shock.

There wasn't a trace of the doppelganger; no crushed jaw and skull fragments, no brains, eyeballs or blood – nothing whatsoever. Perhaps the corpse had returned to the enigmatic Altern Void. Noel Peake was put under psychiatric supervision for a while at a hospital, and he was visited by Lucy – and she told him she had talked to Maurice and now believed the story about the doppelganger, Noel told Lucy that he felt he had caused the whole strange incident by mentioning his soul-destroying job to Maurice, but she told him it wasn't his fault at all, and she later married Noel. The mirror was no friend to the retired company director for quite a few years. Whenever he shaved, brushed his teeth, or sat in a barber's chair, he always avoided looking too closely at his reflection – just in case...

# AS RARE AS SUMMER SNOW

In the merry month of May 1935 – May the 17th to be precise, and five weeks before midsummer – PC Bennett of Wavertree Police Station collared 10-year-old Jimmy Williams at 8am as he rode a bike along Childwall Road. He sprang out from the corner of Thingwall Road and a startled Jimmy fell off the bike. He said he'd found the bicycle, and PC Bennett said, 'Aye, found it before it was lost you mean!'

Jimmy started crying as the constable helped him to his feet. 'Save your tears for the judge, Williams,' said PC Bennett, tongue in cheek, 'this bike was stolen from old Mr Almond's backyard yesterday.'

Feeling thoroughly sorry for himself with a lump in his throat, Jimmy accompanied the policeman as they set off for the station on Wavertree's High Street. The boy walked beside the bicycle with his head bowed, wondering what his mum and dad would say when they were told that their son was a thief. Jimmy had told his father he had borrowed the bike from his friend Timmy O'Brien. As the schoolboy and the policeman neared the Wavertree Lock Up (a historic stone building once used to detain locals as well as for keeping sick people in quarantine), PC Bennett halted, and Jimmy looked up at him, puzzled. The copper was looking straight ahead with his mouth open, and he had a look of utter surprise upon his face.

'Don't say a word,' the lawman whispered to Jimmy, hardly moving his lips, 'but look at that!'

Jimmy followed the line of the policeman's hard gaze. It led to a boy in odd green clothes who was sitting on the fence surrounding the Lock Up. He had his back towards Jimmy and the copper, and was singing some mournful song. Jimmy recalled that part of the lyrics of the song went something like: 'All of the good ones are gone, and we won't see their likes again, oh I feel sorry for all you young 'uns, you never knew Mary Delane!'

'Who's that?' Jimmy asked, and in a barely audible voice Bennett replied, 'A leprechaun!' and while he made his reply he never took his eyes off the singing figure.

Jimmy contorted his face and said, 'I think I'm going to sneeze.'

'You make so much as a sound, laddie,' said PC Bennett through gritted teeth as he unconsciously made a fist, 'and I swear I will mark you for life!'

'I can't help it, it's me hay fever.' complained Jimmy, and the policeman seized the boy's nose between his finger and thumb and squeezed the nostrils shut. That seemed to do the trick. Jimmy now had no urge to sneeze, but his nose hurt.

The policeman took the bike from the boy and slowly laid it down, and then he crept up on the figure, and when he was about three feet from the alleged leprechaun he grabbed him by the arm.

'What the bloody – ' the diminutive person exclaimed and turned to see who had grabbed him.

Jimmy saw the 'boy' had a man's face, and he smiled as he looked up into the sky and pointed to a cloud. He said, 'Look at that angel!'

Jimmy looked at the cloud in question but the

worldly wise policeman didn't. He knew the little man was trying to distract him. His old grandmother had told him about the devious tricks of the leprechauns when he was a boy.

'Ha! Got you, leprechaun!' shouted Bennett, 'And I know you want me to take my eyes off you for a second so you can escape. Keep your eyes on him Williams!'

'There's your late grandmother Peggy with the devil!' the leprechaun told Jimmy but Bennett reminded the boy it was a diversionary trick to get him to look away.

'How did you know my grandmother was named Peggy?' a baffled Jimmy asked the leprechaun.

'Three wishes, come on!' the policeman laughed as he leaned forward and gazed into the leprechaun's green eyes.

'I'll tell you this for nothing mister police constable, trying to pull the wool over your eyes isn't easy,' sighed the leprechaun, 'but alright, fair is fair, let me grant the three wishes. Now, the first one is the boy's!'

'No, they're *my* wishes!' objected Bennett.

'And you an officer of the law and that;' said the leprechaun in a condescending tone to Bennett, 'you both found me, so the boy gets one wish and you get two. That is the law, and the law must be obeyed!'

'Well let me have my two wishes first then!' the policeman pleaded.

'The law of the leprechauns states categorically that youth precedes position, so stop being a spoilsport and let the boy have the first wish!'

Jimmy smiled and said, 'I wish it was Christmas!'

Straight away the temperatures dropped and heavy snow fell, and the early risers of Wavertree laughed.

Within minutes the snow was inches deep. As Bennett loudly demanded his wishes, a snowball, thrown by some little girl, hit him in the face, and when he opened his eyes, the leprechaun had gone.

'Where did he go?' Bennett asked a bewildered Jimmy, and he seized him by the lapels of his school blazer and shook him as he yelled: 'I told you not to take your eyes off him!'

'I couldn't help it,' said Jimmy, scared at the sight of the policeman's eyes, which were bulging out of his red face. 'I looked at you getting that snowball in your face and when I looked back the little man had gone!'

'I will have you thrown in jail for robbing that bike you little good-for-nothing – ' the policeman was threatening Jimmy when another snowball whacked him in the face. This one had not been thrown by anyone human on this occasion because it had literally come out of mid-air - so it had to have been thrown by that leprechaun.

Jimmy ran off into a blizzard and when he got home he asked a visiting uncle how he could go about joining the Foreign Legion. His uncle shrugged and Jimmy made himself a couple of jam butties, wrapped them up in brown paper and ran out of the house and into the out-of-season snowscape. He had no intentions of going to jail and decided to go on the run. He lasted till lunchtime and went home, where he expected a posse of policemen to be waiting for him, but no one ever came to arrest him. Jimmy started to suckhole around the man he had 'borrowed' the bike from: old Mr Almond, and this old man had a great book collection. He got Jimmy interested in reading and the boy later won a scholarship because of those books.

The snow that fell in that May of 1935 stopped the Dunlop golf championships at Southport (where a poor caddie collapsed from hypothermia at the third hole) and the races at Haydock were also abandoned. The fog-bell on the River Mersey sounded its mournful chant as thin ice formed on the waters, and gardens that had been in bloom hours before were covered in ivory blankets of deep snow, reminiscent of the traditional scenes on Christmas cards. Only the day before the bizarre snowfall, the weathermen had stated that the temperatures in Lancashire were more like those of August than May. The meteorological mystery remains unsolved to this day - 1935 was the year December arrived in May – and only little Jimmy Williams and PC Bennett knew why.

# NAN'S RETURN

One of the strangest stories of local witchcraft I heard concerned a girl from Walton. She told me the following story many years ago when she came to one of my book-signings.

On the sunny afternoon of Friday 13 June 2003, a 20-year-old Walton girl named Eve Coggins was sitting beside her boyfriend Ollie in his vintage Triumph Vitesse two-door saloon as it travelled down Hope Street when she suddenly had the overwhelming feeling that something was wrong with her beloved Nan, Eleanor. Eve had no idea why she felt her Nan's life was in danger – but the bad feeling suddenly swelled up into a panic attack and she told Ollie about her premonition.

'I'm not going to your Nan's, Eve,' he said sternly, pulling up near the junction of Falkner Street, intending to visit a newsagent to get some cigarette papers. Ollie couldn't stand his girlfriend's grandmother; he found her to be a weird and sinister person; there was just something about her he couldn't take to and his feelings towards her had triggered many arguments with Eve since he'd started dating her two years back.

'I'll go on my own then,' Eve said, taking off her seatbelt and reaching for the door but Ollie reached over, locked the car door and was about to start a row when Eve started fumbling with the lock but she was unable to make it budge.

'You haven't got a penny to get a taxi or a bus, Eve, stop being a martyr,' said Ollie, 'put your belt back on.'

The window in the front passenger door was down with it being such a warm day and Eve reached out through the open window and with her palms placed on the roof of the car she eased herself out backwards through the window as Ollie swore and threatened to call it a day on the relationship. 'You get your way too much with me and this time I'm not giving in!' Ollie shouted.

Eve fell, but turned quickly in mid-air and landed on her feet. She ran off in tears and took the first corner to get away from her boyfriend, which led her onto the cobbled road of Falkner Street. She ran as fast as she could, and there were dozens of students walking along, looking at the sprinting girl as she sobbed with mascara running from her eyes and down her face in watery black streaks.

All of a sudden, Eve felt odd. She felt light-headed, and thought she was going to faint for a moment. Her stomach then somersaulted as she felt herself being lifted into the air. She saw the street below fall away at an incredible speed and realised she was somehow flying through the air. Having a chronic fear of heights, the girl closed her eyes and froze in terror. The next thing Eve Coggins knew, she was on Walton Hall Avenue – about twenty yards from the house of her much-loved Nan. The girl's legs gave away as she recalled the flight through the air at what seemed to be hundreds of feet, and she crawled along on her hands and knees as bemused people passed by, probably assuming she was drunk or on drugs. Eve eventually got to her feet, staggered to her grandmother's house, and knocked hard on the door. Eve was surprised to see her older brother Ken answer; he normally had no time for his grandmother. He seemed very pale, and behind him, Eve saw her mother with a handkerchief to her mouth.

'Mam, what are you all doin' at me Nan's?' Eve asked, and as she passed Ken she said, 'You won't believe what just happened to me.'

'Keep your voice down,' a sombre-faced Ken told his sister and gently closed the front door.

Eve went into the living room and there was her Nan stretched out on the sofa, her head propped up by three pillows.

'Nan, what's to do?' a worried Eve asked and rushed to her side.

Eleanor's huge green eyes looked at her granddaughter and the old woman said something to Eve in a very faint voice which astounded her. 'I brought you here,' she said softly, 'because I wanted to see you one last time, love.'

'What do you mean?' Eve asked in shock, and she felt her Nan's small hand grab her hand. In that moment, Eve felt something pass from her grandmother's hand into her hand – it felt like an electric tingle.

The old woman smiled, closed her eyes, and quietly died. Eve couldn't accept the death of her grandmother and she kept shaking her now limp hand and asking, 'Nan? Nan you okay? Nan, wake up.'

Eve's mother extricated her daughter's hand from her mum's hand and gently led her away from the sofa.

Eve started to cry, and she went upstairs amid the confusion in the hallway as people debated whether to ring for an ambulance or to ask the telephone operator if there was someone else who should be notified – perhaps the police or someone at a mortuary.

An hour later, Eve's boyfriend Ollie arrived at the house and when Eve heard her mother admit him downstairs, Eve hurried down to the hallway and laid into him. 'Why are you here?' she yelled to Ollie, 'You didn't even like my Nan! Get out of here!'

'Aye-aye!' Eve's mother intervened, positioning herself between her fuming daughter and a red-faced Ollie. 'There's no need for all that when someone's just died!' she told Eve and eventually calmed her down and took her and Ollie into the kitchen. 'Put that kettle on, please Ollie, said Mrs Coggins, and Ollie grabbed the Russell Hobbs kettle and filled it under the tap. 'You need hot sweet tea, you're in shock, love,' Mrs Coggins told her daughter, placing each of her hands on the girl's shoulders. She guided Eve into a chair at the kitchen table.

As they all waited for the ambulance personnel to turn up, Eve told her mother about the strange incident where she was lifted into the air and somehow transported almost two miles across the city, but the girl's mum just gave a soft smile and grasped her daughter's hand – as if she thought that Eve was just coming out with the strange story as a reaction to the shock she'd received at seeing her Nan die before her eyes.

'When you ran round that corner,' Ollie suddenly said to Eve (and she refused to even look at him as he spoke), 'I ran after you – and I was about five seconds behind you – but when I turned the corner you'd gone. These women passing by said they saw you disappear.'

'She'll be alright when she gets all that sugar into her system Ollie,' Mrs Coggins told the young man.

Four years later, Eve was sitting in the flat she shared with Ollie on Mount Street (off Hope Street) one sunny afternoon, reading a beauty magazine when an odd scene suddenly came into her mind's eye: a sunlit field in Ince Blundell – the scene of many picnics she'd enjoyed with her Nan when she was a child. Eve tried to put it out of her mind and turned her attention back to the magazine but the sunny rustic scene once again materialised in her mind, and she developed the urge to go to the spot. Ollie was at work and he'd left the car behind today because he was going to a pub in town after work to have a few drinks with his brother because it was the latter's birthday. Eve had been having driving lessons and had driven Ollie's car once; she had a lot to learn about reading the road and she was a very nervous driver, and yet the overwhelming urge within her was telling her to get into that car and drive nearly ten miles to that picnic spot in Ince Blundell. If she got a single scratch on Ollie's vintage 1966 Triumph Vitesse – an 18th birthday gift from his late Uncle Matty – there'd be blood on the moon, but Eve was so consumed and utterly compelled to make the journey to Ince Blundell, she found herself taking Ollie's car keys from the dresser in the bedroom and within minutes she was starting the car on Mount Street. She had only a provisional licence and was uninsured to be on the road, so if Eve attracted the attention of the police she'd be in big trouble. She started the car, took the handbrake off – and mistimed the clutch. The car rolled backwards down the incline of Mount Street. She stepped on the brake pedal and recalled the hill start procedure Mr Thompson her driving instructor had drummed into her, and the car eased forwards and turned into Hope Street. As she waited in an anxious state for the traffic lights to change near the Philharmonic Hall, Eve noticed a policeman standing on the corner of Myrtle Street and Hope Street, and he was looking straight at her. It was possible that the police officer's attention was merely directed towards the vintage car Eve was in – but she was feeling paranoid because she was breaking the law. The lights changed and Eve was still eyeing the policeman when the motorist behind her sounded his horn. She stalled the car, then cursed the impatient driver – who was now overtaking her – and then she successfully started the car and the policeman watched her pass by.

Eve wondered how on earth she'd get to Ince Blundell, as her local geography was abysmal, but as she drove along Mount Pleasant towards Brownlow Hill, she felt herself fall into what she can only describe as a trance state. Eve felt as if she wasn't driving the car at all; she felt as if some professional driver was operating the wheel, pedals and gear lever through her, and whereas she'd normally be nervous in bumper-to-bumper traffic, she remained calm as she inched along in a queue of slow-moving vehicles. She travelled ten miles until she reached the rural lane in Ince Blundell, and she pulled over, got out of the car, and placed her face in her hands. Everything felt so unreal. The trance lifted and now Eve felt so nervous.

She wanted to call Ollie on her mobile and tell him about the bizarre situation but she knew he'd be furious and he'd have to leave work to come and get her and it would also ruin his plans for a birthday drink with his brother. As she stood there at the side of a field in the shadow of an old oak tree, Eve just knew that her grandmother had somehow guided her to this place – but why? As she had these thoughts, Eve noticed the approach of a group of women. They came across the field from the distant woods, and the gaggle of people drew nearer, Eve could see that one of the women was holding the hands of a small child who walked besides her in a pale blue dress. From the looks of their attire – long flowing floral dresses, strappy sandals, beads and headbands, Eve thought there was something "New Agey" and hippyish about the women. They halted a few feet in front of her and one of the women said to Eve, 'We have someone here to see you, sister.'

And this woman looked down to the little girl in the blue dress.

An uneasy Eve smiled out of politeness and looked at the face of the little girl – and she saw something which made her recoil in shock. That child was her late grandmother. She had the same large green eyes, the same features, except she was about four or five years of age. The eyes of the child locked onto the eyes of Eve, and then the woman who had directed Eve's attention to the little girl said, 'It's Eleanor. She's come back to us,' and she stooped and said to the cherubic-faced child, 'this is Eve – do you remember her?'

The girl nodded and said to Eve, 'Hello love.'

Eve felt weak with shock when she heard the little

girl greet her in this way, for her phonation sounded very similar to her late Nan's voice.

The women said they were a group of witches – a coven – called Sisters of the Moon, and Eleanor had been the head of the coven until a few years before her death, and she had told the members of the coven that she would return. Not long after the death of Eleanor, one of the witches became pregnant, and she had somehow known she was carrying the reincarnated leader of the coven. Eve hugged little Eleanor and the two of them cried, but the tears turned into tears of joy. The woman who would serve as the head of the coven until Eleanor turned sixteen, asked Eve to join them, and after much thought and consideration, Eve did. She never told Ollie she'd joined the coven at first, but he eventually found out when he found Eve's ceremonial robes one day and when she confessed to being a witch he told her she'd have to choose the coven or him, as he was dead against witchcraft and had been brought up to shun anything connected to the supernatural and the Devil. Eve chose the coven, and she is still a member of it today. She has told me that the little girl she believes to be the reincarnation of her grandmother is becoming more and more like her Nan every day.

# ODDTALES SOUP

When I was a child I had an eccentric uncle who often told me weird stories – and most of these yarns had no point or parable about them – and my uncle used to say, 'Let's open a can of oddtales soup,' – a play on "oxtail soup" – before he would start to weave a strange tale or two – often a morbid miscellanea of creepy stories - and now I'd like to open a can of these oddtales for you. Let us start in the Eighties...

On the Saturday night of 24 March 1984 at 7:10pm, 61-year-old Lucinda Fenwick was making a pot of coffee for her 65-year-old husband Jack at their semidetached home on Allerton's Booker Avenue when she happened to glance through the kitchen's faux leaded-glass window at the tall three storey house opposite. It was there again – the weird silhouette of a little head and shoulders in the square of yellow light that was the top lit window of the redbrick Victorian house. Lucinda shooed the cat out the way and hurried in to Jack with the coffee and he turned away from *The Price is Right* game show on the telly and asked, 'Where're the Viscount biscuits?'

'Jack, that thing's there again!' said Lucinda, wide-eyed with raised pencilled-in eyebrows.

'Oh, not all that again,' said Jack in a descending tone, 'I've told you, it's a cat!' He shook his head gently and turned his attention back to Leslie

Crowther on the telly. His wife poured him a coffee and then went back into the kitchen. The "little man" had gone from the window. She brought Jack the milk and sugar and a plate of chocolate biscuits wrapped in orange foil and then she went back in the kitchen. During the commercial break, Jack noted his wife's absence and he went into the kitchen – and found the light switched off in there. He clicked it on and his wife whispered, 'Turn it off!'

She was crouching slightly in front of the aluminium sink, looking through the window with a pair of 8x30 binoculars.

'You're going worse, Luci,' Jack told her, 'that's just a cat you're looking at but you won't have it – making a mystery out of nothing.'

'Jack, my eyesight's better than yours and I could see the thing,' said Lucinda, lowering the eyepieces of the binoculars from her face as she looked through the window into the windy March night.

'An old man lives in that place,' said Jack leaning over the sink to look at the illuminated window of the house under observation, 'and he must be knocking eighty – he's lived there since I was a kid. There's nothing spooky going on – '

'Look!' Lucinda noted the appearance of the mysterious black head and shoulders at the window. She trained the binoculars on the window fifty yards distant and there was a sharp intake of breath. 'Oh my God, I'm right, it's some type of doll! Have a look!' She thrust the binoculars to her husband. Jack heard the return of *The Price is Right* theme and the audience clapping on the TV in the lounge and he shook his head and lifted the binoculars to his eyes, but then he had to hold the eyepieces away from his eyes by about two inches.

'Hurry up slowcoach! Before it goes!' hissed an impatient Lucinda.

Jack saw that his wife was right. It was some sort of doll with an almost globular pale head with painted-on hair and a deadpan face. It looked like a ventriloquist's dummy and it seemed to be scanning the street from its window. It darted away from the window after a few seconds and then the light in the room the thing was in went out.

'Did you see it?' Lucinda asked, and she could tell from her husband's baffled expression that he had, and she gave a nervous laugh and said, 'That was no cat was it, eh?'

'Luci, will you pipe down? It's someone messing about with a puppet. They'll know people are looking at it; it'll be a kid operating that, out of sight under the windowsill. Puppets don't move on their own, love; I think you're going into your second childhood.'

'It's not a kid doing anything Jack; I've seen that thing for a fortnight now and I even saw it at six o'clock one morning.' Said Luci, and she followed her husband into the lounge, talking to the back of his head as he went. Jack sat down and unwrapped the Viscount biscuit and dipped it in his coffee as he watched the game show. Lucinda sat in her armchair and reached for the pack of More brand menthol cigarettes on the coffee table. She withdrew one of the long dark-brown cigarettes and lit up, then looked at the television screen for a few moments before getting up to go into the kitchen again. There was a faint light in that window across the road, but now the wind was rocking an overhanging tree branch that kept dipping down to obscure the window. Lucinda looked through the binoculars and saw that the hazy luminance in the window was coming from some open door in that room which was allowing light in from a landing – and then she received quite a shock when she saw the doll peeping at her from the right side of the window. She sensed that the thing had noticed her watching it, and this sent a cold sensation through her abdomen.

'You're going to miss *TJ Hooker*! He's on in a minute!' Jack shouted from the lounge, and then he shouted at the cat and grumbled about dropping a Viscount in his coffee.

'It's not on till eight!' Lucinda shouted back to Jack. She put the binoculars down and she closed the venetian blinds on the kitchen window and turned on the light. Jack came out to the kitchen and when he saw the blinds closed, his eyes travelled slowly to his wife's grey eyes and he saw fear in them. 'It's not like you to close the blinds,' he remarked.

'You don't know who's knocking round on these nights,' Lucinda replied, puffing on her cigarette as she started to head for the hallway, 'anyone can see right into this house from the street.' She put the front-door bolt on and went back to the lounge and sat there looking at the TV but her mind kept drifting back to that enigma across the road. At 8pm as *TJ Hooker* was starting on the telly, she lit another menthol cigarette and tried to be logical. She thought about what she had seen in that window across the road. *Was* it just some child messing about with a puppet? If that was the case, he or she was going to an awful lot of trouble over two weeks, and they were being ever so careful not to be seen at the window.

At 9:15pm that evening, Jack sat sipping a Scotch and soda as he watched Torvill and Dean in the World Figure Skating Championships from Ottawa, and Lucinda, meanwhile, was upstairs looking for a book she had mislaid when the telephones in the hallway and bedroom started to ring simultaneously. Lucinda's friend Anne often called at this time, usually out of boredom, but when Lucinda picked up the handset she heard a male voice – a strange childlike voice which said, 'I saw you spying on me.'

'Who is this?' Lucinda asked, and there was a long silent pause at the other end of the line. 'Hello? Who is this?'

'Horse, pig, dog, goat, you stink, I don't!' said the young voice, and then he giggled.

'If you ring me again I'll have the police on you!' Lucinda warned, and firmly put the phone down, and seconds later it was ringing again. She picked it up and there was silence on the line. 'Is that you again, you idiot?' she asked.

The mischievous boy suddenly broke the telephonic silence: 'Roses are red, violets are blue, onions stink and so do you!'

'Stop ringing me you idiot or I'll report you to the police!' Lucinda was so angry at the pest, she could feel her heart pounding.

The annoying boy said: 'If you keep spying on me, I'll come over to your house and they'll find you with a knife in your back in the morning, you nosy old bag!'

'Spying on you? What *are* you talking about - '
Lucinda was asking when she suddenly realised with horror that she was talking to that *thing* that she'd been

watching in the window opposite. She was stuck for words and she went cold.

'A big hole in the ground, and you and that man you live with shall go down it,' said the boy with so much anger in his voice, 'and the worms will eat you and him as well and you'll know you're dead and all your insides will turn to poo and jelly! All the dead people know they are dead and they can't move and it's really horrible and it won't be long till you and that man go down the big hole!'

'Oh!' Lucinda recoiled at the dreadful words and she slammed the handset down in the cradle and she left the bedroom and hurried down the stairs to tell Jack about the boy.

'They call them nuisance callers Luci,' said Jack, hugging his wife in the lounge with one eye on the televised World Figure Skating Championships, 'he won't even know who you are; they just get a kick out of upsetting people.'

'He *did* know who I was, Jack; he said I was spying on him and I was, with the binoculars; it's *him* - that thing in the window.'

'If you go on like this my dear you are going to have to get something off the doctor for your nerves,' Jack told her.

'How does he know our telephone number, Jack?' Lucinda asked with a worried look as she glanced at the closed blinds in the kitchen, 'There's something very odd about all of this.'

'You're joining the dots up wrong, dear,' Jack told her in a calm assuring voice, 'you're connecting two unrelated things: a child messing about with some puppet across the road and a pest who telephoned this house at random. The spying thing he mentioned was just something daft he came out with to provoke you. Now, why don't you just relax and read that book? You said you were enjoying it.'

'I can't find it or I would try and read it,' said Lucinda, and Jack smiled and said, 'I think I saw it in the bathroom on the chair; you must have left it when you had a bath last night.'

'I think you're right,' said Lucinda, and she headed for the door of the lounge, then halted and looked back. 'So, you think it's just been some idiot phoning people at random?'

Jack closed his eyes and smiled as he slowly nodded. 'Now go and read that book and calm down, Luci.'

As Lucinda crossed the hallway on her way to the bathroom, the telephone on the half-moon table started to ring, startling her. Jack came out into the hallway and said, 'Go on, answer it – it'll be Anne.'

'It might be - *him*,' Lucinda said, looking at the ringing telephone with her hand to her mouth.

'For heaven's sake – ' Jack picked up the phone, listened, then raised his eyebrows and said to his wife: 'Anne.'

'Oh!' Lucinda placed her hand on her bosom and sighed with relief. 'Really did think it was him, then,' she whispered.

'Fear is a great inventor,' quipped Jack, and he went back into the lounge.

Lucinda told Anne about the strange goings-on at the house across the road; she felt embarrassed telling her about the thing which looked like a doll peeping at her through the window but she had to tell someone, as Jack didn't believe her. Anne had never known her old friend to lie, so she was intrigued by the 'peeping doll', and when Lucinda told her about the threat she'd received earlier on the telephone, Anne advised her to go to the police.

'I can't Anne,' Lucinda told her friend with great resignation in her voice, 'they'd think I was nuts, and I can't say I'd blame them either. The whole affair doesn't make sense and I know I shan't get much sleep tonight.'

'Shall I come round tomorrow?' asked Anne, 'Jack goes fishing with his friend on Sundays doesn't he?'

'Oh yes, I forgot about that;' replied Lucinda, 'oh thanks Anne, I'd really appreciate your company. Otherwise my nerves will be shot through when Jack's out the house.'

That night, Lucinda lay in bed for a while, trying to sleep. Jack usually snored when he was lying on his back but he didn't upon this night, and the noise would have been welcoming to Lucinda, just to distract her from her preoccupation with that thing across the road. She heard a sound at the garden gate around 2am, but would not even go to the window to see what it was because she knew she'd look over at that window and see something. She lay there, still, and was relieved to hear the sound of cats crying like banshees at one another. She drifted off and snatched half an hour of sleep but it was shattered by a nightmare of the doll. In the dream it was tapping on her bedroom window and she was trying to get out of the room but the door wouldn't budge. Lucinda awoke just after three with her heart palpitating. Hearing Jack snoring now, she smiled and turned over and went back to sleep.

At 10:30am Anne called around. She brought a bouquet of flowers and a bottle of wine, and she also brought a photo album which featured many old snaps of Lucinda and herself from their schooldays to the present day. Jack left the house at 11pm and got into his friend Richard Inglewhite's car with his fishing gear. Lucinda waved at her husband as he belted up in the car but she snubbed his friend. She did not approve of Inglewhite, a man who had served time for burgling a number of high-class homes in Cressington ten years ago. The car moved away as the two men headed for Mostyn. They weren't due back from their fishing trip till around seven in the evening.

Lucinda and Anne sat in the lounge drinking coffee and nibbling Mr Kipling cakes as they caught up on one another's lives. It wasn't long before Lucinda gave a detailed blow-by-blow account of the weird "doll" she and Jack had seen peeping out the window, and now, in broad daylight, Lucinda felt brave enough to go outside onto the path and point out the window concerned. There was nothing there now, just a black square, because the curtains of that room were wide open.

'Isn't that odd?' muttered Anne, turning over what Lucinda had told her in her mind as she eyed the window. 'Wonder what it is?'

'Well Jack said a child was behind it all,' said Lucinda with an uneven smile, 'that some kid was larking about, acting like a puppeteer to frighten us.'

Ann gave a puzzled look and shook her head, 'Nah, you'd see him wouldn't you? I tell you what Luci, that house actually gives me the creeps. There's just something about it. Who lives there?'

Lucinda shrugged as she looked at the house. 'Jack said there was an old man who lived there when he was only a kid, so whoever he's talking about must have died. Jack's sixty-five, as you know, but he thinks he's about forty; he forgets time moves on; I was talking about Mrs Jones, our neighbour the other day, and how nice she is and Jack said, "They're the salt of the earth, old people," but Mrs Jones is fifteen years younger than him!'

Anne smiled and asked, 'So you don't know who lives over there?'

Lucinda shook her head. 'No, it's funny, I know most people round here but I call those houses over there Sleepy Hollow because you never see anyone going in or out of them; it's always quiet over there.'

'It's probably my imagination,' said Anne, squinting in the harsh spring sunlight, 'but I could have sworn I saw something at that window then.'

'Oh, let's get in then,' Lucinda said, and gave a false trembling laugh. As she passed the telephone in the hallway she told Anne, 'Jack said the person who gave me all that abuse last night on the phone was some prankster who had called me at random, but I think it's got something to do with that thing across the road, Anne, I really do.'

Anne closed the front door behind her and went into the lounge for more coffee. Lucinda started looking through the old photo album when she suddenly brought one of the pages close to her eyes. She put the book down, located her reading specs on the coffee table, and put them on. She looked at the photograph again.

'Who are you looking at?' Anne asked her with a

smile.

'Anne, where was this taken?' Lucinda asked, 'That's the house across the road isn't it?'

'Let's see,' Anne got up and angled her head as she looked at the snap from about five feet away. 'Hey yeah, it is,' she said, 'that's my younger brother Eddie and our cousin Julie – '

'Anne – oh my God – look at the window – you won't believe it,' Lucinda passed the photo album to her friend with a trembling hand.

Anne saw it straight away – a little grey and slightly blurred image of the head and shoulders of something resembling a little man – or a *doll* at the very window the women had just been looking at outside. Anne had to hold the photograph at arm's length because of her far-sightedness.

'What year was that taken?' asked Lucinda, and she took a gulp of coffee because her throat had dried up.

'I'd be about thirteen so it must be around 1936,' said Anne, and she reached out with her right hand to Lucinda. 'Can I just have a look through your specs?'

Lucinda eagerly handed her glasses to Anne and watched her scrutinise the area of the black and white photograph taken with an old Brownie camera almost fifty years ago.

'You know what it looks like Luci? And you'll think I'm nuts saying this – ' said Anne. Her large blue eyes were magnified to almost comic proportions by the glasses.

'No, I won't think you're nuts, go on,' Lucinda assured her.

'It looks like Morph – ' said Anne with a faraway smile, 'that little man on Tony Hart's art programme.'

'Who?' Lucinda asked, and then, in a flash she recollected the character Anne was referring to. 'Oh yes! Yes, I remember him now; that's what he looks like – like the thing's made of plasticine.'

'Luci, what in God's name is it?' Anne wondered out loud, and she took the glasses off and handed them back to her friend. 'If that thing's been around since 1936 – well, it doesn't make sense. This is really creeping me out.'

'You're alright Anne, you can go home later,' said Lucinda, trying to smile, 'I've got to live here facing it.' Lucinda put her glasses back on and looked at the photograph before flipping through the rest of the pictures to see if there were any more snaps of the house across the road – but there weren't any more – just that single photo.

At 6:30pm, Anne said she'd have to be making tracks back home. She'd left her son-in-law – a trainee chef – in charge of the kitchen but she didn't think he was capable of making the tea. 'Anne, you've been great company today – ' said Lucinda, faltering as she tried to finish the sentence in the hallway, but Anne interposed jokily, saying, 'Even though I gave us the creeps with that photograph.'

'Well, yes,' laughed Lucinda, and Anne offered to give her the photograph so she could show Jack but Lucinda knew it would only scare her even more once Anne was gone and she politely declined. The two women went outside and already twilight was falling. There wasn't a single person about and the bourgeois emptiness of Booker Avenue hung in the chilly March air. As Anne put her hand on the garden gate, ready to open it, an old 1930s Rolls Royce Wraith came gliding along the avenue – and it came to a silent halt outside the red brick house facing Lucinda's home. The chauffeur gracefully left the vehicle and opened the door of the stately vehicle to let out a very old lady. She was dressed in a long dark fur coat and she wore a cloche – those close-fitting helmet-like hats Anne and Lucinda had not seen since their childhood days. The chauffeur opened the gate to the house and he and the lady went to the front door.

Lucinda and Anne watched the proceedings with great interest, and Anne stepped back from the gate. 'That car must have cost a few bob,' she said.

'That's an old Rolls Royce,' whispered Lucinda, watching the chauffeur bring the ornate black knocker down on the front door three times with some force. No one answered so he knocked again. The old lady then bent forward and pushed the flap of the letterbox open and she shouted, 'Aubrey! Aubrey! Open the door!'

Anne suddenly let out a sneeze, followed by another one, and the chauffeur looked across the road towards her – then said something to the elderly lady. He and his employer then came across the road. At close quarters the woman's face was heavily lined and she looked even older. She said to the two women: 'My brother Aubrey hasn't telephoned me for two weeks, and it's not like him to do that. I was wondering if you might know if any of the neighbours have a key. I am concerned about him as you can imagine.'

'No, I haven't got a key I'm afraid,' said Lucinda.

The lady held her hand behind her ear and said, 'You'll have to speak up dear; what was that?'

'The lady does not have a key ma'am!' said the

chauffeur in a loud and well-spoken voice.

'He's just turned one hundred, Aubrey,' said the old lady, and she smiled and produced a handkerchief to dab tears welling in her eyes. 'I'm ninety-seven,' she added, and paused with a smile.

'Oh, you don't look it,' said Anne, 'what's your secret?'

'No, everyone knows, it's not a secret,' said the old lady.

Richard Inglewhite's car pulled up a few feet away and Jack got out and eyed the Rolls Royce, then looked at the old lady and the chauffeur standing at the gate of his home. 'Hi,' he said to the strangers, and Lucinda told him how the lady was worried about the well-being of her brother in the house facing and how she could not gain access. Jack turned and had a word with Richard Inglewhite – the former burglar of well-to-do homes who had supposedly now turned over a new leaf and secured employment in an insurance company. Richard got out of the car and told the old lady he'd try and open the door if she'd allow him to try. His offer was relayed to the old woman via the chauffeur because of the woman's difficulty in hearing. A few minutes later, with his back turned to the old woman, her driver, and Jack, Anne and Lucinda, Inglewhite whistled as he rattled something – possibly a skeleton key – in the lock of the red brick house's front door. There was a click. Inglewhite then pushed the door open, turned, bowed to the old lady – who seemed very unsteady on her feet all of a sudden. She grabbed the arm of Lucinda and said, 'I do hope my brother hasn't died. He's just turned one hundred. I wouldn't be able to live without Aubrey.'

Lucinda accompanied the old lady into the dark hallway, and the chauffeur switched on the light. There was a mound of unopened letters and junk mail behind the door – which didn't look good.

'Aubrey! Are you there, dear?' the old woman shouted in a trembling voice.

'Come on, let's go in with them in case someone's turned the place over,' suggested Richard Inglewhite, adding, 'they might still be on the premises,' and he walked into the hallway, followed by Jack and Anne. The living room had an aroma of damp mould, and Anne noticed mildew on the heavy purple drapes. There was wood and coal in the grate of the fireplace but it had not been lit. Despite her age, the old lady ascended the stairs quickly and seemed to be dragging Lucinda with her. Jack, Richard, Anne and the chauffeur hurried after them, and as soon as they saw the old woman and Lucinda go into what turned out to be the master bedroom, there was a scream that echoed throughout the house. It was the screams of the old woman and Lucinda.

There, lying on the bed, was the naked decomposing body of a man. He lay on his back, and he looked skeletal. The flesh of his face was gone, as if something had torn it off, and the genitals were absent – with a red crusty hole in their place. The putrid aroma in the bedroom turned the stomach of everyone, but the old woman started ranting. What she was talking about was hard to understand. She started searching for something, and began by opening a battered-looking trunk at the end of the bed. There was nothing in it but old biscuit tins and bundles of documents. The old lady swore, looked under the bed, and her searching hand pulled out an old-fashioned sword in a scabbard. The woman unsheathed the sword and then, just as Anne took Lucinda out onto the landing as the latter was overcome with the stench of decomposition, the elderly but sprightly woman sneaked up to the wardrobe, hesitated, then pulled open the door. Something resembling a doll made of some semitransparent gelatinous substance, was crouched down at the bottom of the wardrobe with its arms in a defensive posture. The head was perfectly round and the eyes of the thing were two black button-like discs. The mouth was bloodstained and there were sharp triangular teeth in the head of this unidentified being which looked as if they were made of clear glass.

'You killed Aubrey! You bastard! You killed him!' the old lady screeched as she brought the blade of the sword down on the thing. It hissed as the blade went into the small body, yet the creature was able to run from the wardrobe, and Lucinda and Anne screamed as it flew past them and fell down the stairs. It got to its feet in the hallway and ran off on all fours straight through the open front door.

'Oh Aubrey!' the old lady said, dropping the sword as she staggered to the bed where her brother's mutilated corpse was lying. She stumbled and fell forward, landing on the chest of the corpse. Her hands went straight through the chest of the cadaver and grey, greenish and red matter oozed out. The woman then fell face down in this vile gunk, and her eyes widened and her mouth opened wide. She collapsed and slid off the bed. The chauffeur and Jack knelt at the side of the woman and the driver tried to feel for a pulse, but shook his head and in a clear loud solemn voice, he announced, 'She is dead.'

Lucinda started to scream again and Richard Inglewhite tried to console her, but she ran down the stairs, followed closely by Anne. Jack went down into the hallway and noticed a telephone on a table stacked with directories. He called the police.

The official version of events was that Aubrey had suffered a stroke after he had lain down on his bed after a bath. He had died not long after and as his body decomposed, rats had entered the house from the cellar and made their way up to the bedroom to gnaw at the corpse, eating the most tender part of the mortal remains – the soft flesh of the face and the genitals. Lucinda mentioned the unearthly diminutive "thing" in the wardrobe to the police, and her testimony was backed up by her husband, his friend Inglewhite, as well as Anne, but for some strange reason, the chauffeur said the thing had been a large rat. The police found his version of events much more credible.

A year after the mysterious incident, Lucinda had a mental breakdown after receiving chilling telephone calls in the dead of night. The voice sounded exactly like that caller who had telephoned her that Saturday night on 24 March 1984. Most of the messages from the unknown pest were about Lucinda lying in her grave as worms and insects ate her, and how, as she aged, she was sure to succumb to a terrible disease. When Lucinda finally recovered from her breakdown, Jack sold the house and took his wife to a new home in Heswall. The anonymous calls from the sinister telephone pest were received at the new residence for a few weeks, but then they suddenly stopped. Lucinda passed away years later in the late 1990s, and, according to her wishes, she was cremated. I have received many letters and emails about the house on Booker Avenue where the bizarre entity was encountered, and whatever it was, it seems to have been active at the house as far back as the 1920s – but just *what* the thing was remains an unfathomable mystery.

Let us now move backwards thirteen years from 1984 to 1971 for another serving of oddtale soup, with perhaps a little pinch of autumnal pumpkin spice...

In October 1971 a 40-year-old Liverpool bachelor named Mike Stephens was made redundant, and he decided to leave his house in Clubmoor and move into a flat atop the 22-storey tower-block of Entwistle Heights on the borders of Edge Hill and Toxteth. He made this drastic move because he wanted to get away from the old scene of his neighbourhood and make a brand new start. His friends were all in nine-to-five jobs and wanted him to continue on that treadmill – a routine he had known since he had left school, but Mike had privately decided – for once – to have a rest from the rat race and take stock of his position in life. He really had reached a mid-life crisis at forty, and he actually signed on for welfare. His friends started to regard him as a 'sponger' who had savings, yet was content to live off the state, and Mike had told his judgemental associates that he wasn't getting the type of big bucks the Royal Family was receiving from the Civil List. That's when the break took place and Mike Stephens felt as if he had taken a brave step away from his humdrum level of existence. He also started looking for a different type of girl to date – someone like him who wanted to reach beyond the claustrophobic confines of working class mentality.

Mike was a very practical mechanically-minded man, good with a soldering iron and a wizard with tools and machinery, and after reading a Pelican paperback called *Revolution in Optics* by Samuel Tolansky, he decided to build his own high-powered Schmidt-Cassegrain telescope, and he actually invented a mirror that could amplify light by feeding an electronic high-frequency signal through its silvered layer. Mike had excelled at science at school and his science teacher Mr Prescott had strongly advised Mike's parents to get him to university, but the advice fell on deaf ears and Mr Stephens would often put down his son's ideas by saying, 'You never thought of that Michael; you're not clever enough.' The boy therefore developed a sort of inferiority complex.

What Mike saw through his super-telescope was breathtaking from the twenty-second floor flat; pin-sharp images of Blackpool Tower, Snowdon, the craters and mountains of the moon, the rings of Saturn, the icecap of Mars – as well as something *very* strange. One evening Mike trained the scope on the 11-storey Belem Tower, just under a mile away, and he clearly saw an old lady in her kitchen washing dishes at the sink. A tall man in black came into view and stood behind the old lady and placed his hand on the left shoulder of the woman and she immediately collapsed. That man then literally vanished; he was there one moment and gone the next. Mike rushed from his hi-rise flat and went down to a public phone-box to anonymously call for an ambulance. He told the emergency services operator that she should direct the ambulance personnel to go to the third floor of Belem Tower, where the woman had collapsed. He then rode a taxi to the tower – and subsequently saw the ambulance men arrive and later bring the woman's body out. He later learned from a newspaper report that the old woman had died from heart failure. Mike Stephens was certainly not a man who had any belief in the supernatural, and he often mocked people who read horoscope columns and also classed himself as an atheist – yet he could only reason that the man in black he had seen in that old woman's kitchen was some type of personification of death; in other words – a Grim Reaper – and this take on things was hard to accept because of a lifelong scepticism towards the paranormal. Just over a month later, Mike was trying out a new eyepiece lens – salvaged from an old pair of binoculars – on the telescope, when he saw that sinister figure in black again. On this occasion, Mike had trained the telescope on a maisonette on a housing estate half a mile away, and he could see right into a living room. It was 9.25pm and darkness had fallen on Liverpool. The living room was lit by a bare single tungsten bulb and a woman was sitting in an armchair looking at an out-of-sight television. Mike could see the woman in side-profile, and the bluish glare from the TV was flickering on her face. He saw the same man in black he had seen in the kitchen at Belem Tower *come through the wall* into the living room. Mike swore under his breath and sucked hard on a Player's cigarette as he saw the apparition make its eerie entrance. It stood there looking at the woman, and Mike could see that the entity's face was as white as snow, and the eyes looked like small black buttons.

That woman in the armchair suddenly leaned over the right side of the chair's armrest and picked up something that glinted. It was a huge carving knife. She held its handle with both hands, turned the blade to face her bosom, and then she firmly pushed the blade into her chest. She threw her head back and her mouth opened as if she was yawning, and Mike's stomach felt as if it was falling down a lift-shaft. 'Why?' he cried, 'Oh no, why?'

The woman slumped forward. The black-clad figure crouched slightly and smiled as he looked the woman in the face, and then he straightened up – and stepped backwards, vanishing through the wall.

Once again, Mike found himself making a hasty descent from his hi-rise home to that red telephone call box, and this time there were two teenager messing about in it. Mike swore at them to get out of the phonebox and grabbed one lad by the arm and threw him into the other one. 'I'll get my dad to duff you up you 'arl bastard!' cried one of the boys.

Mike dialled 999 and gave vague directions to the maisonette where the woman had stabbed herself, but the operator told him he'd have to be more specific. 'I don't know! It's on a housing estate by – oh for Christ's sake – I don't know where it is!'

'Sir, how did you witness this incident?' asked the emergency services operator, and Mike went ballistic. He smashed the telephone receiver against the wall of the call box, then stormed out and returned to Entwistle Heights as the two teens he had handled roughly watched him before running off to tell their dads what he had done.

Mike was so shook up by witnessing what must have been an act of suicide, it played on his mind and he hardly slept. He kept seeing that woman sticking the knife into herself. He went to drown his depression in a local pub called the Spekeland two days later, and as chance would have it, he overheard one of the drinkers talking about a woman who had stabbed herself to death. Mike went to the drinker and asked why she had killed herself.

The drinker said, 'She was only thirty, and a real beauty she was, but she had a brain haemorrhage and it paralysed the left side of her face, and then she started getting really bad eye infections in her left eye so they had to sew her eye shut, and well, you know, people started to stare at her, and you know how cruel some kids can be, calling names and that. They reckon that's why she topped herself. Did you know her mate?'

Mike had tears in his eyes as he shook his head. 'No, I didn't know her,' he said, and he left his drink on the bar counter and headed for home. On the way, he saw an old priest walking up Tunnel Road, and he startled him by saying, 'Excuse me father, but I have a question.'

The priest halted, looked at him nervously and said nothing in reply.

'Is there such a thing as the Grim Reaper? Now, before you dismiss me as some crank, I'd like to tell you that I'm as level headed as the next man – but I have a very valid reason for asking this question.'

In a well-spoken kind-sounding voice, the holy man said: 'Well, there is a mention of a Pale Rider in the Book of Revelation; he personifies death, and there's also a Destroying Angel who is sent out to kill the enemies of the Israelites. But you mean that *thing* with the scythe don't you?'

Mike was surprised at the priest's reply as well as the clergyman giving him the time of day, for way back in his teens, Mike had given up on the Church because they seemed to be more interested in passing the collection plate around rather than addressing the cruel and unjust ways of life.

'Yes, that's exactly who I mean,' Mike replied.

'The Hindu scriptures speak of *Yajarah* - a Lord of Death, and the good old Ancient Greeks had Thanatos, a merciless bringer of death. This city is mostly Celtic, and the Celts believed in Ankou – the henchman of Death; he goes about collecting the doomed souls.'

'It's just that, well – ' Mike started, but changed his mind; he thought the priest wouldn't believe him. 'Anyway, father, from a lapsed Catholic – thank you.'

The priest smiled with a knowing look in his faded grey eyes, and walked on, saying, 'Bye now.'

Mike walked on in the opposite direction and was startled to hear the priest shout, 'Hey! If you saw that man in black, you'd better start taking an interest in the living again, or he might start noticing you.'

This comment really jarred the mind of Mike Stephens, and before he could think of a response, the priest had turned a corner to walk down Spekeland Road. Mike walked home, realising that the old priest had probably encountered the "reaper" he had been seeing; after all a priest often administered the Last Rites and was often called upon to comfort the sick and dying. But the warning the priest had issued naturally bothered Mike; he had advised Mike to start taking an interest in the *living* again – or receive a visit from that harbinger of death. Mike decided he'd dismantle the accursed telescope, but somehow, a morbid curiosity took hold of his mind, and he decided to have another look through the glorified spyglass on the following evening. He began scanning the nightscape of Liverpool at 7.15pm, and two hours passed – during which he saw nothing vaguely supernatural. He made himself a coffee, watched some TV, then found himself drawn back to the telescope around midnight. He focused on the second-floor bedroom window of a Georgian house on Grove Street, less than half a mile away. The curtains were partly open and Mike could see a young lady lying in bed in a nightie reading a book. She looked right at him, but she could not see Mike, she was merely gazing out the window, possibly at the full moon that was hanging in the sky that night. Feeling like a sex-starved Peeping Tom, Mike was about to swivel the telescope away when a black-clad figure came into view in the young lady's bedroom. He put a black gloved hand over her face and there was a struggle. The bedroom intruder had on what seemed to be a balaclava but he was moving about too quickly for Mike to take in any clear details. He got on the bed and started to rip off the woman's night dress, and already, Mike intended to go down to that call box to alert the police, and this time he had an idea where the house was on Grove Street, but then came the twist: the young woman was smiling and apparently laughing as the masked man in black pulled off his balaclava. He began to kiss her, and then he rolled sideways off the bed, only to return stripped to the waist. Mike guessed that the couple were merely indulging in some role-playing game, perhaps to spice up their sex life. He swore at them, and swung the telescope to the right, towards the campus of Liverpool University. He decided that, come the morning, he would take the telescope apart and move out of the block of flats. That advice the priest had given him echoed in his mind: *'...you'd better start taking an interest in the living again, or he might start noticing you.'*

The next individual the telescope homed in on was a security guard in a squat university building. He was reading a copy of *Melody Maker* and the image was so clear, Mike could see the photograph of Paul McCartney's new band – Wings – on the cover, and he could even read the print.

And literally in a split second *that* ominous figure in black appeared – the one that had been present when the old woman had dropped dead in her kitchen and the same ghoul that had smilingly inspected the dying face of the woman who had knifed herself to death. His face was ghastly, white and smooth as putty, and where the eyes should have been white they were pink, with large black irises. The guard obviously couldn't see the weird entity. The sinister figure slowly placed his palm on the top of the guard's head – and the young man slumped forward onto a desk. The eyes of the guard opened and then they rolled up into the forehead, and that pallid abomination kept its hand on his head as it began to shake him. It smiled as it shook his head, and Mike saw blood pour from the guard's nose and his mouth opened and the tongue flopped out. Saliva ran from that tongue onto the yellow plastic tabletop and the shaking went on for about thirty seconds. The bringer of death then went to the window and he looked out – straight at Mike, and this time Mike knew that he really was being observed – from almost a mile away. He went ice cold and felt nauseous as the dark eyes seemed to burn into him. He pulled the telescope away from the window, closed the window with such force he cracked one of the large panes, and then he drew the curtains. He switched on the TV, the radio, and he fumbled for his packet of Player's Number 6 cigarettes, but couldn't find his lighter. He went into the kitchen, used the push-button igniter to light a gas ring and lit his ciggie from the blue flames. He was convinced that the death entity would pay a visit, and he felt the goosepimples rising on his arms. He shuddered and swore and thought about leaving the tower block, even at this late hour, just to be among the living – even amongst the many prostitutes in the local red light area – but the nicotine got into his blood and his addicted brain released dopamine as a reward for satiating its craving and he started to calm down.

There was a loud bang at the window behind the curtains which made Mike jump, and he went into the kitchen, took a bread knife from the cutlery drawer, and then advanced to the curtain, which was slowly moving – but when he swore and threw the curtain aside he saw the noise had merely been caused by him not closing the window properly, and a gust of wind had frayed his nerves. He turned the handle, making sure the window was closed, and did not even look at that distant point of light that was the window where the guard had just died – just in case he saw something. Mike then did something that even surprised him. He found a pair of scissors and from a piece of cardboard he cut out a cross – a Christian cross, and he nailed it to the wall. A strange thing for an atheist to do, he told himself.

He smoked six more cigarettes and downed four cups of coffee, and he sat writing about the sightings of the "reaper-man" (as he called him) in a Silvine exercise book which he titled "Deathwatch" in a block shadow-letter font drawn with a felt-tip pen – and then around half-past four, he went to bed and slept in his clothes with that cardboard cross on his bedside table.

On the following day, Mike Stephens walked into the city centre and went window shopping. He sat in a café and got chatting to a young lady and managed to get her telephone number. He put on a bet at William Hill and then he went to see *Where Eagles Dare* - a war film featuring Richard Burton and Clint Eastwood – at the Odeon on London Road. It felt good to be taking part in life, not observing it like some detached voyeuristic outcast of society. When Mike left the cinema in the evening he decided he'd start going to the Job Centre each morning.

That evening, Mike looked at himself in the full length mirror of his wardrobe. He needed some decent trendy clothes if he was going to start dating again, and a new haircut. He got the shock of his life as he looked at his reflection because *he* stepped out from behind him. Mike swung around and felt an electric shock cross his chest. He backed away from the figure, which was much taller than it had looked through the telescope. 'Get away from me in the name of Our Lord!' Mike yelled, and he backed into the edge of the open door, which hit him in the spine, but he was so afraid, he didn't feel a thing.

The figure walked silently across the room, took hold of the telescope and smashed it against the wall. Its mirror cracked and the white metal tube of the instrument was stamped on by the ghostly-looking being. It picked up the tripod and swung it at Mike, who ran into the hallway and tried to open the front door – but it would not budge. He turned the brass knob and fiddled with the catch but he could not open that door.

The reaper-man came into the hallway holding the "Deathwatch" journal rolled up in its chalk white hand. 'I *will* take you if you pry into my business!' he hissed – then vanished in an instant.

Mike tried to open the door again and this time the knob turned and a catch clicked and the door opened effortlessly. Mike ran down the stairs of Entwistle Heights, convinced that the reaper would be waiting for him as he reached each dark landing. He felt ill as he listened to his footsteps; they seemed to go on forever until he at last reached the ground floor. He burst through the swinging door and out onto the pavement, gasping for breath. He never returned to his flat, and he moved in with his brother in West Derby. A month after this, Mike moved into a flat with Sue, the girl he had met in the café, and he had nightmares about the reaper-man for years and never looked through a telescope again.

From 1971 we next trace fourteen orbits of this earth through space and time to another serving of our oddtale soup; this one is a real *soupe de mystère* too, seasoned with some very unearthly goings on. Before I ladle this one into your bowl, let me start by putting the story into context with a basic prologue.

Thanks to all of the data from the space probes over the years, we now know the basic materials needed for life are out there in the universe, but alien biology might incorporate sulphuric acid, methane or ammonia in the way water is used as a solvent on earth. Some unearthly life form was allegedly at large on earth – in St John's Shopping Centre of all places – in 1985. It was seen mostly by children, and was described as a 9-foot-tall spindly black humanoid with a globular grey head which opened up like the rosette of a cabbage. I mentioned the "thing" on a local radio programme years ago and was afterwards deluged with letters and emails from listeners who had either encountered the being or heard of it. Jamie and Charlie were both aged twelve when they decided to play truant one April afternoon in 1985. They visited St John's Shopping Centre and dared one another to steal things from shops and toy stores until they were chased by a guard. The truants then went to get chips and gravy and a meat pie from the shopping centre's chippy. It was around then when Charlie noted the weird grey globe, the size of a beach ball, on one of the ceilings of the precinct near a store that was possibly called Treasure Island. The ball slowly inflated and deflated, and made a snoring noise which made the boys laugh. Jamie had a box of matches and he took two of them out, held them together as he struck them, and hurled them up at the strange sphere – and it sprouted a pair of long thin black legs and two black arms. The boys grinned and looked about, thinking it was some sort of Jeremy Beadle (of TV's popular show *Game For A Laugh*) type of stunt, and when they pointed the thing out to passersby, the lads realised only they could see the oddity. The ball and its arms and legs fell to the floor and the terrified lads ran off. They looked back and saw a giant black silhouetted figure with a head like a cabbage of unfurled leaves was chasing them, and it was so tall it had to stoop to prevent knocking its head against the ceiling of the shopping centre. During the heart-stopping chase, Jamie felt the thing's long bony fingers grab his shoulder and he screamed, tripped, and fell down the escalator, knocking Charlie over. When the boys looked up the moving stairs they saw the weird attacker had gone.

No one believed the lads but their description of the gangly stalker matches the description from many other children who encountered the shopping centre's bogeyman - but what it was and where it originated I do not know. I mentioned Jamie and Charlie's story on the *Billy Butler Show* and naturally assumed Billy would think it was all far-fetched, but he asked around a million of his listeners if they had heard of the strange story or knew anything about the alleged 'bogeyman' of St John's Precinct and the telephone switchboard was soon lighting up as quite a few people called the radio station. As I mentioned earlier, I received a lot of emails and letters about the spindly "thing" – and a high percentage of reports were from people who had heard about the entity second-hand, but Billy also put a few people through to me on air, and they all said that they had seen something very creepy in the shopping centre. One caller, named Rob, said he was fourteen in 1985 and had often hung around St John's Shopping Centre when he "sagged off school" (played truant). He recalled one morning in October 1985 when he was dreamily looking in the window of Tandy (an electronic goods retailer and Hi Fi store) at a CB set when he heard two girls around his age scream behind him. Rob turned and the girls, who were clinging on to one another, were looking at something above Rob with expressions of fear on their faces. Rob naturally followed their gaze and looked up – and he saw an abnormally long black arm with a hand of three fingers and one thumb, reaching for his head. This arm was protruding from a long thin gap in the ceiling just inches away from the Tandy shop front, and Rob jumped back reflexively. The long thin black arm retracted back into the narrow opening in the ceiling. He stood there for a while with the girls, but the arm stayed put inside that ceiling and it really played on Rob's mind for years. A woman named Rita, who served in a well-known clothes store in the precinct, also called me on air to say how she and other members of staff would see something dark darting about in the store, but whatever it was, it could only be seen out the corner of the eye; 'If you turned to try and look at it,' Rita told me, 'it flitted away, but sometimes we could see a dark blurred object on security footage of the store that had been recorded by the closed-circuit TV cameras when the place was empty.'

Another store owner at the shopping precinct named Ian called me on air at BBC Radio Merseyside and said he had been working late one night, unpacking stock and transporting items into the store room when an air-conditioning panel fell from the ceiling in the middle of the store, and something resembling a long black snake fell out of the air-conditioning duct in the ceiling and dangled there, writhing. Ian stepped into the stock room and peeped out at the weird wriggling 'snake' and saw it go slowly upwards, back into the ceiling. He heard thumps and noises up there and a weird ghastly noise which sounded like a nest of squealing rats. Ian got the air-conditioning engineer out the next day and he climbed a ladder and shone a torch into the space above the shop and swore. Ian asked him what the matter was, and the engineer said, 'It's full of cobwebs up here, and they're hard, as if they've been starched or something. They're dead hard to break. I've never seen anything like it.'

Ian and the engineer then detected a strong aroma which they both described as ammonia which seemed to be coming from the air-conditioning ducts. The engineer brought out a few colleagues and they never got to the bottom of the hardy cobwebs nor did they ever trace the origin of the ammonia. Was something truly 'otherworldly' at large in the air-conditioning and ventilation ducts of the shopping centre? Could the thing – whatever it is – still be about?

From a possible extraterrestrial being living in the crawlspaces of a 20th century shopping centre, we next go back through the fogs of time to the Victorian age for a small but nevertheless weird serving from our pan of oddtale soup. It concerns a rather ominous harbinger who once held Wavertree in a grip of fear...

I have files bulging with the forgotten bogeymen – and bogeywomen - of bygone Liverpool, from "Nellie Longarms" – a weird old North Liverpool woman with extendable arms, to "Stripey"- a bald white-painted man in a black-and-white striped suit who rose from his grave in Toxteth Park Cemetery after dark to chase girls. The other day I noticed the file on "Coffin Jack" – an eerie harbinger of death who carried phantom corpses of those who were about to die. He terrorised Wavertree in the 1890s, and at first, people dismissed the early reports of the coffin-carrying ghost as a weird rumour – until late one August night in 1894. Drinkers at a pub on Lawrence Road called the Salisbury Hotel heard a man sing: 'I carry the good and the bad, in this box upon my back! All must come to death's door, young and old and rich and poor, and they call me Coffin Jack...'

The singer was coming up Tabley Road, alongside the Salisbury Hotel, and the moon was full upon this night, so the silhouette of the morbid minstrel was visible on the blinds of the establishment – and the shadow presented was of a man crouching forward with a long box on his back – the size of a coffin. A young man – against the wishes of the pub landlord Georgie Tomkinson – lifted the blinds – and saw crooning Coffin Jack in the glaring moonlight as he crossed Lawrence Road, and there was a woman stretched out on the coffin the oddity was carrying. Another drinker, a plumber by trade, looked out the window and recognised the corpse as that of his sister Lottie. The stunned drinker tried to get out of the pub to 'rescue' his sister but the landlord, a very superstitious soul, locked the door and a fight broke out. Three days later, the plumber's sister came down with a strange fever and died within hours. A week later there was a broad daylight encounter with Coffin Jack as he came up Callow Road, singing more deathly ditties – and this time he carried a female corpse everyone knew – the beautiful red-headed teacher from the local school. Before the ghoul had even reached Lawrence Road, a nauseating aroma of decay had reached the grocers and the butcher's and large weird-looking black flies with orange-red eyes buzzed the carcasses and the fruit and vegetables. A 'carriage and pair' had to halt on Lawrence Road to let Coffin Jack cross, and some ran into shops in fright, but some stood their ground, although they had heard that anyone attempting to obstruct Jack would invariably drop dead or be attacked by his swarm of flies. Up Granville Road he went – towards the cemetery on Smithdown Road, his long black hair stirred by the breeze. Sure enough, the teacher died days later after a short illness. The last encounter took place in the following year during a thick fog when Mrs Annie Broxton and her daughter almost walked into Coffin Jack on Egerton Road. Like that other bogeyman, Spring-Heeled Jack, this Jack vanished back into obscurity and the tales surrounding him became exaggerated – but will Coffin Jack return to haunt the streets of Wavertree again one day?

And now for our final serving of oddtale soup – and this one's a light but tasty summer pub soup – all chopped spring onions, knob of butter, splash of olive oil, courgettes, fresh vegetable stock, mint, trimmed watercress and Greek yoghurt – and served to you in a pub – a certain pub in the south end of Liverpool in the summer of 1974. The soup will cost you 20p and a pint of Harp lager just 16p in Seventies money.

Liverpool was baking under a clear fresh alpine blue canopy of sky that August afternoon in 1974, and at a certain off-the-beaten-track Threlfalls pub in the south end of the city, a tall black 20-year-old university student named Neville Joplin was standing between two beautiful fellow students named Magenta and Abigail, and they were pleading with him to sing the Lobo hit *I'd Love You To Want Me* as they thought he had a heavenly voice, and he acquiesced, but when he got to the third line of the song, Neville became distracted by the sight of a naked man standing in the sunny street outside. His voice faltered and he peered through the arabesque swirls etched into the pub window and said, 'There's a fellah in his birthday suit standing in the middle of the road.'

'Where?' asked an excited Magenta, but she could see nothing. Neither could Abigail or their friends Mike, Chris and their girlfriends. Neville went outside and saw that the naked man looked very off-colour – almost grey, and then the student realised he was a ghost. He'd been seeing them since he was a child, and occasionally he still did but usually said nothing, as his 'talent' scared people away, and it had taken him so long to attract all of the friends around him. Magenta and Abigail stood smiling on each side of Neville as he gazed at something they could not see, and they really did think he was having them on. 'You can see me?' said the wide-eyed ghost of the nude man. He was about 5ft 7 inches tall and had brown hair styled into the popular 'feather cut'.

'Yeah, who are you?' Neville replied as the girls giggled. He really didn't want to acknowledge the ghost but sensed the presence was desperate.

'I was in a car crash with my brother. He's dead but I'm in a coma at the Royal Infirmary,' said the man, 'and my name is Ronnie Hailsham.'

'Oh, so you're still alive then,' whispered Neville, 'I've never seen a ghost of the living before but my Nan used to tell me about them.

The phantasm of the living nodded eagerly and said: 'I came here because a girl I loved used to drink here. Her name is Lindsay Ross.'

'I know her – she's real pretty with red hair,' said Neville, 'haven't seen her in the pub for a while though, Ronnie. Where does she live?'

'She's moved,' said the ethereal projection, 'and I went to her house loads of times but she's never there. If she could just hold my hand at the hospital, I might be able to come back. There are horrible things after me that are trying to take me to Hell. They already took my brother. Here they are now!'

The apparition cried out, looked at something which Neville could not perceive, and then it vanished.

'Okay Neville this isn't funny anymore,' complained Abigail, but Neville went back to the pub and with great sincerity he told his friends about his unearthly gift – how he could see ghosts – and what had just happened. Perhaps because his friends were in varying states of intoxication, they smiled and accepted Neville's claims. They had never known him to even tell a white fib, so they all believed him, and Abigail asked, 'Okay, so you're psychic – what next?'

'Good question,' Neville told her, and then he smiled and said, 'we have to turn detective – we have to find this Lindsay Ross and get her to the hospital while this Ronnie bloke is hovering between life and death.'

'You're not John Shaft,' joked Neville's best friend Chris, 'but seriously, if there's a chance – however slim – of us saving this fellah's life, we'll have to put our feelers out and find this Lindsay – but where do we start?'

'Ask Tony the landlord,' suggested Magenta, nodding to the middle-aged bald man behind the bar reading the *Daily Mirror*. 'He knows everyone. He's a good start.'

The landlord said he didn't know much about the girl in question but he knew someone who did: a regular named Mrs McGarrick who worked in the laundrette up on Myrtle Street. She had often been seen drinking with Lindsay at the pub and in another boozer called the Caledonia on Catharine Street. Neville went to the laundrette with Abigail and they found Mrs McGarrick. The woman was naturally suspicious when Neville asked her if she knew where he could get hold of Lindsay Ross.

'What do you want her for?' Mrs McGarrick asked, looking Neville up and down in a condescending manner.

'Well, we need her because someone's life is possibly depending on her,' answered Neville.

'Yer what?' the laundrette worker asked with a lopsided smirk.

'A man named Ronnie Hailsham,' said Neville, 'he's in a coma at the hospital and the doctors said that if Lindsay could talk to him – '

'He was violent towards Lindsay,' interrupted Mrs McGarrick, 'that's why she left him. They were always fighting like the Kilkenny cats. He struck her once in front of me.'

'Oh,' recoiled Abigail, and she glanced at Neville.

'She hit Ronnie on the head with a hairdryer first like, but he shouldn't have hit her,' Mrs McGarrick told the two young people, 'like chalk and cheese they are, so I don't know why they want Lindsay to see him in a coma – they should go and get his mother.'

'We really need to see Lindsay, Mrs McGarrick,' said Neville, but as he talked to the woman she turned her back and went to help a customer to operate one of the washing machines. She came back to Neville and said, 'Lindsay wants a bit of peace. I heard about him being injured in that car crash but it's no great loss to the world. Ronnie was trouble.'

'So you're not going to tell us where we can find Lindsay?' Neville asked in a resigned tone.

'No!' Mrs McGarrick stated firmly.

Neville and Abigail left the laundrette – and there coming towards them was Lindsay Ross; Neville recognised the redhead immediately.

'Excuse me,' Neville said to the girl as he raised his hand and almost waved, 'are you Lindsay Ross?'

The girl said nothing for a moment, and her eyes travelled from Neville to Abigail and back again to the tall black student. 'Why?' she asked.

Neville told her the whole apparently far-fetched story, and expected Lindsay to dismiss him as a crank, but instead, his account of the visit from Ronnie as he lay in a comatose state in a hospital bed brought tears to her eyes.

'I still love him, despite what we've been through,' Lindsay sobbed. 'I heard he'd been in a crash but thought he was just in the hozzy because of his injuries. No one said nothing about a coma.'

'Lindsay, shall we get a taxi to the hospital now?' Neville suggested.

'I haven't got a light on me,' the young lady told him.

'Don't be daft, I'll pay,' said Neville, and he waved frantically at the hackney cab coming up Myrtle Street.

During the journey ride to the hospital on Pembroke Place, Lindsay clung on to Abigail, who kept assuring Lindsay that Ronnie would be alright. At the hospital, Lindsay was the only one who was allowed to visit the bedside of Ronnie Hailsham. A doctor warned her he was unresponsive and he said any chance of recovery was exceedingly slim. Lindsay pulled a chair to Ronnie's bedside and she held his hand. There was no response. About ten minutes later, Neville saw the doctor in the corridor outside the small ward and he asked him about Ronnie's health. 'I'm not allowed to say as you're not a relation,' he was saying to the student when they heard Lindsay shouting something beyond the green doors leading to the ward. The doctor rushed into the ward and Lindsay cried, 'His eyelids are flickering!' She still held his hand as the doctor took a close look at Ronnie's face.

Ten minutes later, Ronnie Hailsham opened his eyes. Most people in comas have no memory of anything – not even the imagined blackness some picture death as – but Ronnie recalled a very strange place which, when he reflected upon it, seemed to have been some other level of reality. He had spent a period of time – it had seemed like months – moving about devoid of any clothes in some valley of death with steep slopes of grey stones with overcast skies above, and shadowy, squirming entities resembling vortexes of black smoke which were always chasing him. He'd had the awful impression that these whistling whirlwinds of darkness were demonic in nature. Two of them had taken Ronnie's brother off into the distance and pushed him into some pit where he'd heard people shrieking and groaning. He'd imagined the pit as an entrance to Hell. Ronnie had wandered out of the valley, across a bleak monochrome plane and crossed a low-lying moist expanse of some type of salt marsh until he had come to the misty glades of a forest. Still he was pursued by the vortexes but he had caught sight of an enormous rainbow, and below it were green hills overlooking some idyllic village where people were dressed in white and pale blue robes. There was some huge golden archway with a gate, beyond which ran a path which led to the halcyon village of sleepy cottages. As Ronnie looked upon this vision, he yearned to run to the Arcadian community, and he saw a man in the distance, dressed in one of the flowing robes the people over there wore, and this man shouted, 'Come to the yat!'

Ronnie was puzzled by the cry, and thought the man was saying, "yacht" but it sounded as if it rhymed with "cat". It could have all been a product of Ronnie's comatose mind, but *yat* is an Old English word for "gate", and is still used in some English place names such as Symonds Yat in Herefordshire.

As Ronnie got ready to run to the man in the robe, he heard a discordant harmony of whistling sounds behind him and this time he saw three of those dark vaporous spinning hunters closing in. He ran in a curve, back to the plane of misery, shadows and solitude, and he became very distressed. He thought of the woman he had loved most when he was in the sorely-missed land of the living – Lindsay Ross – and became very choked up. He wished himself back to the life he had known and for limited amounts of time he had found himself back on the streets of our everyday world where no one seemed to see him – except for one Neville Joplin. Now all the memories came flooding back, and Lindsay hugged him and they both cried. Ronnie thanked Neville and he eventually made a full recovery. Ronnie later married Lindsay and Neville was the best man.

# THE DOORS OF TIME

In the Summer of 2012 a 28-year-old woman named Keeley was diagnosed with fibromyalgia, a very disruptive long-term condition – now classed as a disability - which is characterised by widespread areas of tenderness – specific points on the body where chronic pain is often felt, and these points may become tender at any moment without warning, but they are just one of the numerous symptoms of this mysterious medical condition. Fibromyalgia also makes you extremely tired, and will sometimes be associated with restless leg syndrome, numbness, tingling and sharp pains that come and go in places from your toes to your armpits. The condition also affects the bladder, intestines and can really dampen the spirit, causing depression and insomnia; I personally know a person who is suicidal with fibromyalgia. Keeley's doctor told her that the cause of her condition was still unknown, and that a cure was still a long way off, but he suggested a change in diet and regular exercise. The young lady bought a bicycle and eventually built up the confidence to cycle from her Gambier Terrace flat to Brownlow Hill, where a student friend lived, but as she reached the traffic lights outside the Philharmonic Hall on Hope Street, a car lunged through a red light and ran into her – knocking Keeley from the bike. This accident was witnessed by quite a few people, and all of them, Keeley included, saw that the vehicle – now stationary – was very futuristic-looking with a Mercedes logo. A stunned and naturally enraged Keeley rapped on the driver's window – only to see that there was no driver at the wheel. Puzzled, she looked at the two young blonde ladies in the passenger seats and saw one of them swigging from a large bottle of champagne – and the other one looked as if she was snorting a narcotic from the arm rest of a sleek-looking white padded seat. These women – who both looked as if they were in their twenties - seemed oblivious to Keeley and appeared to be drunk. The driverless vehicle then moved off up Hope Street, driving over Keeley's bicycle, and it swung left into Caledonia Street, where it collided with a car moving out from a disabled parking spot – before vanishing in an instant. The driver felt the "ghost car" as he referred to it - actually hit his vehicle – and yet a subsequent examination revealed that there wasn't a mark on his car. The driver said what looked like a bank of pink LEDs on the back of the car spelt out the word "SLOW" as it vanished – and he could see the blonde heads of the passengers in the rear of the vehicle before it 'just *went* like a light being switched off'. A policeman was in the area that day and he too saw the ethereal car. He told me – off the record – that this car had been seen before by colleagues and members of the public on various roads in the city centre. The policeman – like me – believes the car is not a ghost but a vehicle of the future – possibly some variation of a Mercedes-Benz F 015 research car – but why is it being seen well in advance of its release? And who are the high-living blondes seen in the back of this time-hopping car? Yet another possible mystery of the timeslip phenomenon. It's an account I had to include in this volume of *Haunted Liverpool*, because, as most of the readers of my books and many newspaper columns will know, one of my longstanding interests within the sphere of the paranormal is the timeslip. I was the first investigator of the paranormal to document the Bold Street timeslips back in the 1990s on the *Billy Butler Show* on BBC Radio Merseyside, and now the accounts of those slippages in time have travelled the world and have even been featured in numerous documentaries broadcast on European, American and Australian television. I am still actively investigating timeslips and now have specialist equipment, as well as electronic devices I've invented myself which seem to detect timewarps. One device I constructed is a type of interferometer which uses a simple laser that bounces (via electronic mirrors) a beam up and down the insides of two long tubes set at right angles. When some (but not all) timeslips occur, gravitational waves pass through the immediate area. These waves send ripples through what we perceive as empty space (actually the very fabric of spacetime) and these waves affect the laser beams by distorting the space they travel through, and the way the waves of the affected beams recombine at a photodetector along with the resulting change in laser-light intensity allows me to measure the gravity wave. In other words, the device measures localised warping and slipping of spacetime. Other devices I use are ultrasensitive chronometers – usually about ten of them – and they are all triggered simultaneously by an infra-red remote control switch. I put these devices in a wide circle (typically with a 15 foot radius) at a location where timeslips have occurred – and sometime two or more of the chronometers lag behind the others, because time is running at a different rate in different spatial areas during a 'slip' – so that the timeflow in say, a kitchen, might be one hundredth of a second behind the time in the hallway. Once timeslips are fully or even partially understood, it will probably be possible to recreate them – and this could open the door to time-travel – a way of actually visiting the past and future.

I believe that we have been visited by time-travellers from the future (and perhaps even from the past) on many occasions down the millennia. The background to one possible visitation made the front page of the *Liverpool Echo* on Friday, October 27 1978. That day, just before 1pm, a terrific bang shook Merseyside, and shockwaves from the mysterious blast blew in windows and shook the foundations of houses on both sides of the river. The *Echo* article, written up by a reporter named Geoff Barnes, was headlined: 'Mystery Bang Rocks Merseyside' and this article ran thus: 'What caused the Big Bang that shook many parts of Merseyside just before one o'clock this afternoon? Doors were blown open in Wallasey, Windows cracked in Upton and Crosby, and furniture jumped about in Bromborough and Greasby, but more than an hour later Merseyside Police reported that they were as baffled as the rest of Merseyside.'

Concorde and supersonic military jets were ruled out – and a curious rumour later circulated about a sphere made of some clear material - with a woman inside of it – that had been seen rolling down Formby beach at a tremendous speed. I interviewed three witnesses to this purported event on the *Billy Butler Show* and they said the giant ball burst, and a red-haired woman in a white one-piece suit clawed her way out of a globe of jelly-like substance in the disintegrating sphere and she ran off, vanishing among the Formby sand dunes. Was she a visitor from the future? Well, there have been many reports of strange visitors from elsewhere dropping in on us; some might have been from any of the countless inhabited worlds of space, and some may have been from another time – most probably the future, where the problem of time travel will have been cracked at some point. In 1954, the Japanese authorities detained a man trying to enter the country with a passport that revealed he was from an unheard-of country named "Taured". A thorough check was made by the customs officials to see if there was such a place anywhere on Earth, but they drew a blank. The stranger refused to throw light on the whereabouts of the mysterious nation of Taured and quickly left Japan. Occasionally, people have encountered the futuristic city of Taured, and some have written to me about it. One Liverpool couple visiting Spain once told me how the plane landed at Taured Airport, which was located somewhere between southern France and northern Spain, close to the Pyrenees. When the couple later returned to the city, it had vanished. In 1851 another possible time traveller - a strange man calling himself Joseph Vorin - was found wandering in the German village of Frankfurt-an-der-Oder. When the German authorities asked the man where he was from, Vorin told them that he was from Laxaria, a country on the continent of Sakria. This baffled the authorities because neither of the places existed anywhere on their map of the world and the place Vorin pointed to on the map was a stretch of water in the South China Sea – but of course, today, Subi Reef, one of the many artificial islands created by China, exists there. There's been a surge in the construction of artificial islands – particularly by the governments of China and the United Arab Emirates. One can foresee developments in the near future where giant robotic construction units will tirelessly create enormous new islands for use by the military, the tourism industry and of course, the unnatural islands will ultimately be a way of dealing with the planet's population explosion. We may even have to create artificial continents with vast forests to combat global warming, and I wonder if Joseph Vorin came from one of these future synthetic continents – which will perhaps one day be called Sakria.

One of the best documented reports of a possible visitant from another world – or future time period - came from the little French town of Alençon, which is situated about 30 miles north of Le Mans. The town is nowadays famous solely for its fine lace, but over two centuries ago, Alençon became renowned for something far less mundane.

At around 5 a.m. on June 12th, 1790, peasants watched in awe as a huge metal sphere descended from the sky, moving with a strange undulating motion. The globe crash-landed onto a hilltop, and the violent impact threw up soil and vegetation which showered the hillside.

The hull of the globe was so hot that it ignited the surrounding dry flora, and a grass fire quickly broke out. The peasants rushed up the hill carrying pails of water, and within a short time, the fires were extinguished. A large crowd encircled the crashed globe, and some of the more adventurous stepped forward to touch the hull of the unearthly craft to discover that it was quite warm. A physician, two mayors from nearby towns and a number of officials also turned up to see what had descended from the morning sky, and these important witnesses arrived just in time to see something sensational.

A hatch of some sort slid open in the lower hemisphere of the globe, and a man in an outlandish, tight-fitting costume emerged through the hatchway and surveyed the observers with an apprehensive look. He started mumbling something in a strange language and gestured for the crowd to get away from him and his vehicle. A few people stepped back, at which point the man ran through the break in the circle of spectators and fled into the local woods. Some of the peasants also ran away, sensing that something dangerous was about to happen and the remainder of the crowd decided to follow suit. Seconds after the last members of the crowd had retreated from the sphere, it exploded with a peculiar muffled sound, creating a miniature mushroom-shaped cloud. The debris from the craft "sizzled" in the grass, and gradually turned to powder.

A police inspector named Liabeuf travelled over a hundred miles from Paris to investigate the crash, and he quizzed many of the witnesses, including the mayors and physician who had been present at the strange spectacle. The inspector organized a thorough search of the woods where the oddly-dressed man had taken refuge, but the hunt resulted in nothing. The stranger seemed to have vanished as mysteriously as he had arrived.

In the report to his superiors, Inspector Liabeuf put forward the suggestion that the man who had landed in the globe could have been "a being from another world" - but the higher authorities in Paris dismissed the intimation as "a ludicrous idea".

Closer to home – right here in Liverpool - we have the curious case of one "Holly Clarke" – a pretty slim woman in her early twenties who called at the West Derby home of a 40-year-old secretary named Janet Hughes one evening in 1932. She wore a strange one-piece pink suit and odd shoes made of a white waterproof fabric that adjusted themselves. Holly said her husband was out to kill her and she had travelled from Scotland to hide from him. Janet told the girl to go to the police, but Holly said she had done that and they had advised her to go home and seemed to doubt her story. Janet, a religious spinster, took Holly in and listened to her convoluted story about her husband – Drake Clarke - being insanely jealous of her and falsely accusing her of adultery. Janet got Holly a job as a hotel receptionist in Mossley Hill and she told the young lady that she was welcome to stay in her home till she felt safe enough to leave and get a place of her own. One evening Holly started drinking a bottle of wine she'd brought home from the hotel where she worked, and she became tipsy and told Janet she was from the year 2039, and that she'd fled from her husband because he was a serial killer known as the "Backstabber". Janet thought it was just bizarre drunken talk and Holly later claimed it was just that, and Janet then started to suspect that her guest's peculiar story was possibly true, because the pink one-piece suit (or a "onesie" as we'd now call it) – seemed to be made of a satin-like material that never got dirty, and Janet had also seen the fabric change colour. She also wondered about the shoes with the self-adjusting bands that Holly had swapped for a pair of women's two-tone Oxfords. Furthermore, Janet had noticed that some of the slang words Holly came out with were unintelligible. One Saturday morning, some three months after Holly had entered the life of Janet Hughes, the two women went shopping in the city centre of Liverpool, and by 1pm they were in Coopers Café on Church Street having lunch, when Holly seized Janet's arm and said, 'That's him!'

She was looking, wide-eyed at a tall dark man who had just come into the café.

'Who is he?' Janet asked, and she could see the fear in her friend's face.

'My husband,' whispered Holly, and she picked up her chair and slowly turned it, then sat back down at the side of the table with her back presented to the stranger.

The man looked about at the other diners, and then he fixed his gaze on the back of Holly, and came over to her. 'Holly?' he queried in a deep rich voice, and when Holly failed to turn around, he walked around the table and smiled as he saw her. 'What are you doing here, love?' he asked, and seeing his face now at closer quarters, Janet could plainly see that the husband of Holly was wearing make-up and even his eyebrows looked as if they had been plucked into shape. His lips also seemed an unnatural colour – a shade of cerise pink.

'If you lay one finger on me I'll have the police on you!' Holly warned her husband and rose from the chair. She drew back and the legs of the chair squealed across the wooden floor. People stopped eating and drinking on the other tables in the café and looked at the disturbance.

'They won't find us by the time they get here you little whore!' seethed Drake Clarke, and he rushed around the table and in one swift movement he had Holly in a headlock. Janet screamed and men rose from their tables and one of them said, 'Oi! Let go of her!'

Drake dragged Holly across the floor and pushed her through a door leading to a stairwell. Three men burst through that door – and saw only an elderly lady coming up the stairs. There was no trace of the couple.

'Excuse me madam,' said one of the vigilantes to the old lady, 'but did a man and a woman just pass you on these stairs?'

'No,' replied the lady, gasping as she gripped the stair rail, 'no one went past me.'

The three men went down the stairs and looked for the man and the woman on Church Street, but they were nowhere to be seen. The trio returned to their girlfriends and wives shrugging with bafflement, and Janet Hughes asked them where Holly and her brute of a husband had gone, and one of the men said, 'Vanished, like ghosts – honest. There one second, then gone. Who are they?'

Janet paid for the half-eaten lunches and went to search for her friend – a young lady she had started to almost regard as a daughter – but she could not find

Holly and her husband and she never saw her again. What's tantalizing about this case is that the self-adjusting shoes and the one-piece suit belonging to Holly Clarke remained at the home of Janet Hughes until she went into an old folk's home. Her relatives then cleared out the house, along with what might have been tangible evidence of a possible time-traveller. If Holly Clarke was indeed from the future and her story of being on the run from a serial killer is true, I wonder what became of her? Did Drake kill her? Perhaps in the future someone will read about this account and will be able to prevent the murders.

In Liverpool, the hotspot for timeslips is Bold Street, and over in Wirral I've noted that Grange Road (and Grange Road West in particular) has a high incidence of timeslips. I've also noted a number of time-slippages on Old Chester Road, and one in particular stands out. It came my way when I was a guest on a Pete Price Phone-in radio programme many years ago. I was talking about the paranormal and a listener named Stephanie told me her son had actually gone back in time twice whilst travelling along Old Chester Road, and she had thought the incidents were somehow linked to the Devil because she was very religious and believed some force was responsible for the baffling occurrences. I visited Stephanie at her Wirral home on Bedford Road and thoroughly interviewed Ian, her 30-year-old son. He was re-interviewed six months later and did not add any further details to his story or embellish it in any way. I found Ian to be a very down-to-earth man and not the sort to have fanciful flights of imagination. His sole interest in life seemed to be his motorbike and his mother said he constantly had his nose in magazines about motorcycles and books on motorcycle maintenance and restoration. In June 1999, Ian (then aged 25) had been travelling up Old Chester Road on his motorbike to visit a friend named Chaddy in Holborn Hill, but as Ian reached the junction of Downham Road – near Mersey Park – he felt strange. Everything seemed to be slowing down and he felt a weird depression come over him – and then he saw that all of the cars on the road looked vintage, and the pedestrians were dressed in flares and sported long hair. Ian pulled over and looked about, and he realised that the June sunshine and unbroken blue skies had now been replaced with low grey clouds and it was noticeably cooler. He drove off to his friend Chaddy's house and told him what had happened, and then the incident was eventually forgotten. In early September 1999, Ian was once again travelling up Old Chester Road on his way to his sister's house, and this time the sky was overcast and minutes into the journey a thin rain started to fall. Ian wore an open visor and was annoyed because the rain was coating his sunglasses. Just before he reached the junction at Downham Road, the skies turned blue in an instant, and once again he saw Ford Cortinas and some of the cars looked as if they dated back to the 1960s. Ian also saw a young and very pretty blonde lady walking along the pavement to his left. He slowed his bike and then in a flash he recognised her. It was Allison, his babysitter from the 1970s. She turned into Downham Road and he drove after her, thinking she was some ghost – because she had tragically died from what we now term sudden arrhythmic death syndrome around 1979.

The girl looked around nervously when she saw Ian follow her on his motorbike. He shouted her name and she stood there with a baffled expression. He took off his sunglasses and she still didn't recognise him. He told her his full name and said, 'You used to babysit me,' to which she said, 'I'm only eighteen – how could I have babysat *you*?'

She smiled and seemed to think Ian's remark was some joke, and she stood there, perhaps waiting for the punchline. What she heard frightened her. Ian said, 'Allison, I told you I loved you when I was three. I was jealous of your boyfriend Rob.'

'Who *are* you?' she asked, her smile evaporating, and Ian said, 'Come with me Allison; they might be able to fix your heart.'

Allison backed away, then turned and ran into her house and moments later she came out with her big brother, George. Ian drove away, confused and beginning to doubt his own sanity, and when he reached Old Chester Road, he found himself back in 1999, and he also found himself in tears. He drove to his sister Melanie's home and told her what had happened and although Melanie could not believe what her brother had told her – that he had met a girl who had died twenty years ago – she could plainly see that he was very upset and later told her mother about the incident. Melanie suggested that the family doctor should be informed, but Ian was furious at the suggestion and told his sister and mother he had not been seeing things. About a week later, Ian's friend Chaddy said he had been walking his dog up Old Chester Road and had seen old fashioned cars passing by for a few moments, as if he had been looking back into the past. Ian had never known Chaddy to tell a lie and believed him, and his friend's experience reassured Ian that he had not hallucinated the timeslips – but of course, the questions about the nature of these timeslips remain unanswered; what causes them? Does time sometimes loop back on itself? If that were so it would mean that all time is eternally present; the events of the past are still going on and are still there. Just as your eyes travel along the words of this book in a linear fashion, your consciousness would also move along a 'timeline' with everyone else at a rate of sixty seconds per minute. Once you have read this sentence it still exists and you can go back and reread it, and time may be the same; if you could travel through time right now you could go back to 12:15 p.m. on 16 October 1793 and see the guillotine blade take off the head off Marie Antoinette – and you could see this as many times as you wanted – it would not be a replay of the kind you see on a DVD when you playback a scene – the execution would always be 'live'. Your conception is happening right now at a certain point on the timeline and your burial or cremation is also happening now a little further along the timeline – so all of your life and the entire history of the universe is – and always will be – in existence. I think it's highly likely that the methods to visit the events in the past and future will be discovered one day, but in the meantime we will have to be content with timeslips provided by what seems to be Mother Nature.

Years ago at a book signing I met a Mr Clarke, a retired history teacher with a very strange tale to tell. In 1969 he was teaching at a school in Halewood and noted the drastic behavioural change in a 14-year-old pupil named Helen, a quiet girl and frequent truant who was, according to Mr Clarke, 'not particularly bright'. She wrote an essay about a visit to Speke Hall one day which intrigued Mr Clarke. The teacher had been covering the Tudor dynasty and so he had asked his pupils to visit the Tudor manor house of Speke Hall and to try and sketch it and find out as much about the place as they could. Helen wrote about her visit to Speke Hall and she also described how she'd found 'a hole in time' by the 16th Century building which gave access to the future. Helen had befriended a gang of teens named the Arrawaks. Something terrible had happened to the world in the future, and everything was in ruins and the weather was tropical. The "big cathedral" (presumably the Anglican one) had sunk into the ground 'because they'd been drilling for gas' and most of the people in Liverpool had emigrated. The Arrawaks had moved into Speke Hall and there was a moat around the place to keep the other gangs out. The gang had two fearsome robot dogs named Snapper and Brutus and all the gang members were armed and wore body armour. The gang leader, "Scar" wore a weird medieval helmet, and he had fallen for Helen and initiated her into the Arrawaks. They wanted to come into 1969 but couldn't for some reason. Mr Clarke and the pupils noticed that Helen had streaks of colour in her hair – very unusual for 1969 – and the usually introverted girl started to bully people at the school and often used slang no one had heard before. When something was good, Helen would call it 'dandy' and she would play a game in the playground called 'hittermiss' where the opponent – male or female – had to guess what hand

Helen held a stone in. If they got it wrong they got a very hard slap and if they guessed correctly, Helen would French kiss them. Helen's best friend, a girl named Julie, told Mr Clarke that Helen was always going to Speke Hall, and she seemed to vanish for days when she went there. Helen had told Julie she was going to marry Scar and stay with him. Clarke drove to Helen's house to have a word with the girl's parents but saw Helen walking along Old Hutte Lane. Clarke followed the girl in his vehicle. She went to the grounds of Speke Hall. Clarke parked up and followed his mystifying pupil – and he saw her walk behind a tree. When the teacher went to that tree Helen was not there. He heard strange deep humming sounds that made his head vibrate and he felt very dizzy at that spot. When Clarke stepped back a few feet, the sounds and painful vibrating sensation stopped immediately. The teacher went back to his car, puzzled at the disappearance of Helen and perplexed by the weird sensations he'd felt near that tree. He felt a migraine coming on as he drove off, bound for Helen's home. He mentioned the strange goings on to Helen's parents, but they didn't seem to care. Helen's father just said, 'Oh, she'll be back for her tea,' in a very nonchalant manner and read his newspaper, and from the doorway of the kitchen his wife nodded with an inane smile and echoed, 'She'll be back for her tea.'

The girl was not seen for a fortnight and her parents still didn't seem to care. Mr Clarke reported the girl's absence to the police and several officers searched the grounds of Speke Hall and nearby fields, all to no avail. Helen then turned up at her school on a Tuesday morning and told Helen she'd killed someone. A gang called the Nazis had attacked Scar's gang – the Arrawaks – and one of them had tried to shoot Scar's friend Dutch so Helen had fired a crossbow at him and the bolt had gone through the gang member's eye. He'd fallen down dead, and Scar and the Arrawaks had howled with laughter and they later carried Helen on their shoulders as they cheered on their way back to the Hall.

'Oh no, Helen, that's murder,' said a shocked Julie, 'you'll go to jail.'

'No, it's in the future, so it doesn't count,' said Helen, and then she added: 'I'd do it again. I'd do anything for the Arrawaks.'

'The police have been looking everywhere for you,' Helen informed her friend, 'with you being gone so long. Your teacher told them you'd gone missing.'

'Mr Clarke?' asked Helen with a knowing look, and Julie nodded.

Helen went into the history classroom during lunch-break and caught Mr Clarke sitting at his desk with a cigar in his mouth, ready to leave for the staffroom.

'Where in God's name have you been?' Clarke asked.

'Never you mind Mr Clarke,' said Helen, 'you are going to ruin things for me if you keep reporting me to the police when I go off to – ' and then she stopped speaking and her eyes turned to the windows.

'Go off *where* Helen?' asked an intrigued and highly curious Mr Clarke, 'Because I'd dearly love to know. I followed you to Speke Hall a fortnight ago, and you seemed to vanish into thin air when you walked behind a certain tree.'

'Oh!' Helen huffed and shot a frustrated look at the teacher. She yelled something which sounded like:

'You're a real hook nose namesclop!' And then she ran out of the classroom and went missing again – this time for almost a month. When Helen returned to school she had become very outspoken and violent, and was expelled from the school after she punched a teacher. A few weeks after Helen was ousted from the school, Mr Clarke visited the girl's home out of curiosity and Helen's parents told him that their daughter had left home and they had no idea who she was staying with or where she had gone. Two years later Helen's mother received a telephone call saying she was now married to "Scar" and that was the last anyone heard from Helen. Some thought the girl was just a fantasy-prone attention-seeking teenager but others – such as her teacher Mr Clarke – wondered if the girl had been telling the truth, and had actually somehow gone to live in some other century in the future. Most people who find themselves in a timeslip find the experience rather short-lived, but in Helen's case – if she was telling the truth – then time displacement has lasted years. One wonders if the 'hole in time' is still there in the vicinity of Speke Hall near one of the many trees that dot the grounds of the 16th century manor house.

Sometimes when a person enters a timeslip, he or she will suddenly feel depressed, or they will feel strange, and they will often feel unreal - but there have also been many instances where the person walking into the timeslip has felt nothing at all and was not aware they had entered another time period until they notice that the people around them are wearing outdated clothes or the buildings surrounding the subject look decidedly old fashioned. A case in point concerns the late stage, film and television actor (and brilliant farceur) Patrick Cargill, the star of the popular TV comedy *Father, Dear Father* (1968-1973).

One foggy November afternoon in 1960 the 42-year-old actor was walking up Liverpool's Ranelagh Street after a visit to a friend in the Adelphi Hotel. Patrick was in the city because he was appearing in a play called *Border Incident* at the Royal Court, and he decided to spend the little free time he had visiting the shops. As he passed the newspaper seller at the gates of Central Station, the actor heard him shout, 'President Kennedy shot in Dallas!'

Patrick had never heard of a President Kennedy – Eisenhower was still President at that time. He bought a copy of the *Liverpool Echo* out of sheer curiosity and showed it to the cast when he got back to the Royal Court. 'It's one of those joke newspapers,' said a stagehand, 'like *Billy's Weekly Liar*.'

'If it's a practical joke, someone's gone to an awful lot of trouble producing it,' said Patrick, flipping through the *Echo's* pages. He saw several shows in the TV listings he'd never heard of – such as *Doctor Who*, *The Telegoons* and *That Was The Week That Was*. The peculiar newspaper was eventually mislaid and of course, three years later – almost to the day – President Kennedy was fatally shot in Dallas – so how had a newspaper featured the assassination of the American president back in 1960?

A year after this, another 'premonition' of a murder was received, this time in a dream. Ellen Brown, a 32-year-old Tuebrook housewife, was lying on her sofa, recovering from the flu, when she had a vivid dream of a spectacled man walking towards a house in a fog.

The man knocked at the door, which was answered by a woman who threw her hands to her face when she saw the caller. The man then stepped into the hallway and produced a knife before closing the front door behind him. Ellen then saw the woman being stabbed repeatedly in a lounge with balloons and decorations hanging from the ceiling, and after the murder she saw the killer burst the balloons, then leave. This nightmare was replayed in Ellen's mind almost every night for a week. Then in the following month, just before Christmas, Ellen read of the shocking "Knotty Ash Murder" in the newspapers. The killer had called at the house of Maureen Ann Dutton on Thingwall Lane, Knotty Ash and stabbed her to death with fourteen thrusts of a long-bladed knife. Ellen had seen the face of the killer in her dream and wanted to go to the police but her husband said they'd laugh at her.

In the summer of 1962, Ellen and her sister were shopping in the city centre of Liverpool when a familiar man caught Ellen's eye; it was the killer from her dream. The sisters followed him, and lost sight of the spectacled man on the campus of the university. He seemed to know he was being followed, but Ellen never saw him again after that day. Ellen had the feeling the sinister man had worked at the university, and the strange thing is that the murder victim Maureen Ann Dutton had worked at Liverpool University in the veterinary department before taking maternity leave. How a Tuebrook housewife had been able to see into the future and witnessed a murder that had not yet happened, remains a mystery. It's as if the brain, when it enters a certain state – perhaps through some specific neural oscillation (of the type associated with gamma or alpha waves) - can free the mind to focus on events further along the timeline. Many physicists today say there are eleven dimensions – one of space and ten of time, and they are using complex theoretical frameworks – such as String Theory - to try and fathom just what time is – but what if someone has already worked out what time is and learned how to look into the past or future? Many scientific inventions have come along before their time, only to be lost, vanishing into obscurity before being rediscovered, sometimes centuries later. Take, for example, antibiotics; we tend to think that the antibiotic penicillin was first discovered by Alexander Fleming in 1928, but 2,000 years before Fleming was born, the antibiotic tetracycline was being taken by the ancient Nubians who had a kingdom located in modern-day Sudan, just south of Egypt. The tetracycline these ancient people took (to cure all manner of ills) was made palatable by infusing it into beer and the substance is still being found in the bones of the Nubians unearthed by archaeologists. The inventions of that gifted Renaissance polymath Leonardo da Vinci – the tank, parachute, helicopter, submarine, bicycle – and even a robot - were mostly confined to his sketchbooks and no one took the ideas any further for hundreds of years. In 1755 a far-sighted Frenchman named Du Perron presented King Louis XVI with a machine gun, but the monarch branded the invention and the inventor as enemies of mankind and the machine gun and its blueprint were consigned to the dustbin of history. It was the same with the first steam engine – not the one James Watt improved upon in 1776, but the steam engine Hero of

Alexandria made sixteen centuries before. No one could see any useful application for the model of the steam engine and it was dismissed as a mere novelty.

Another invention that has allegedly appeared – only to be lost again in the mists of time – is the so-called "Camera of Past Events" – a device which allows scenes from history to be captured as a snapshot or a movie. The origins of photography can be traced back to an Italian alchemist named Giambattista della Porta, who invented the pinhole camera in 1550, and when the image projected by this crude camera was made permanent by projecting it onto light-sensitive chemicals in the early 19th century, the resulting photographs were viewed as a kind of time travel – the freezing of scenes from long ago. Then some scientists allegedly discovered that certain crystals housed between mirrors could also produce strange images of the past and future, and the secret of the camera that could photograph images from other times was discovered, but both the Vatican and the Church of England suppressed the device because it supposedly made a mockery of religious and political history. The time-camera has surfaced now and then only to be lost or banned. In December 1966, a young policeman named Barry was on his beat in Huyton one snowy evening, and his mind was concerned only with his job – keeping a keen lookout for anything amiss on his beat of course – and the lovely hot mug of cocoa and bourbon biscuits he always enjoyed at the station during his midnight break. Barry was a very down to earth man who bore a strong resemblance to that late man of many talents, the TV presenter Roy Castle. Upon this freezing night, his mind was on his duty and he did not have any thoughts about anything remotely supernatural. Around 10pm, Barry saw a pretty spectacled woman across the road waving frantically at him. He went to see what the matter was and she said she'd seen a man with a gun near Cartmel Road. She then looked at her watch, and there was an almighty crash as a car slid on black ice and skidded onto the pavement across the road – where Barry would have been walking if the woman hadn't called to him. Barry ran to the car – which had impacted into a lamp post – and when he glanced back he saw the woman in glasses running off. He had the sneaking suspicion she had known the crash was going to happen and had saved his life. Barry later saw the mysterious woman in February 1967 as he was on his evening beat. He followed her as she walked down Primrose Drive with her border collie dog, and as she reached her home on Blue Bell Lane he tapped her on the shoulder and asked, 'Did you see any more of that man with the gun?'

The woman, named Barbara, pretended she couldn't recall the incident at first but Barry was determined to find out the truth and sternly asked, 'Did you foresee that car crash?'

Barbara invited Barry in and told him a bizarre story. She was a widow, and her husband, a research physicist, had invented a device that could focus on scenes in the future and the past and show them on a monitor. After her husband's death, Barbara had kept his discovery secret for she knew it would be misused by the military. She showed Roy the "time-scanner" in a garden shed, and the young policeman was bewildered by all of the equipment and the consoles and monitors lining the interior walls of the shed.

'You're right, Barry, I *did* see you killed that night by that car, and recognised the location as Fairclough Road, so I prevented it with my cock and bull story of a gunman. It was the only way to make you move from that spot where the car would have ploughed into you.'

'Thankyou,' Barry replied, seeming stuck for words. He looked around at all of the electronic paraphernalia and said, 'This could revolutionise crime detection.' He looked at the twinkling red, green and yellow indicator lights on the consoles and screens displaying dancing Lissajous curves. Lacking the words to express his marvelment, he gasped, 'It's incredible.'

'Yes, it is, but the military people and the intelligence service would use it to predict what the enemy was going to do and then they'd also use it to control their own people, so I'd appreciate it if you kept all this a secret for now,' said Barbara. She then gravely announced: 'Around the 21st of this month, a lorry will crash into a bus shelter at the junction of Longview Lane and Liverpool Road and kill twenty people. Not sure what time it happens but from the position of the sun it looks like it could be in the morning.'

'So, wait a minute,' said Barry, trying to get his mind around the strange concept, 'you're telling me that the future we see on these TV screens is not set in stone? We can change it?'

'Yes, that seems to be the case,' said Barbara. 'I don't know exactly how that works, but my husband said something about changing the course of time to some other parallel world – some other track. I really wish I would have asked him more questions.'

'How did your husband – pass away?' asked Barry, deliberately avoiding the word 'die'.

'Heart attack, ' said Barbara, with great sadness welling in her eyes. 'If only he had seen his own end, he might have been able to get medical help.'

Barry and Barbara went to the concrete bus shelter on the predicted day of horror. They tried to scare people away from the bus shelter that morning with a story about a bomb threat and some walked away, but most ignored them. A lorry then collided with a van near Hillside Road and came hurtling towards the shelter – Barry and Barbara jumped out of its path and the lorry smashed into the shelter, injuring 14 people – but no one was killed. Barbara still felt as if she'd failed in her mission, but Barry reminded her that twenty people had *not* died as a result of their intervention.

Barry ached to tell his best friend and colleague Ron about the incredible early warning invention but knew the news of the device would soon get out if he did and it would fall into the hands of military minded individuals who would use the time scanner to turn Britain into a totalitarian state. One afternoon at the shed, Barbara treated Barry to a cup of tea and some biscuits, and he asked her how the device worked. She hesitated for a moment, tapped her lips with the top of her ballpoint and said, 'It uses a component called a time crystal. All crystals – even diamonds – are made up of a repeating structure called a lattice, and their lattices are in 3 dimensions, but the crystal in the time scanner extends into the fourth dimension – the dimension of time. A number of closed circuit cameras are focused on the time crystal at different angles, each on a different facet of the crystal, and the images come through straight from the fourth dimension.'

'Oh,' said Barry, but he didn't understand a word. He watched the hypnotic Lissajous curves morphing smoothly into soothing patterns on the oscilloscopes and monitors. Every now and then, images would appear on the screens – mostly images of people walking along streets, but sometimes scenes of fires, muggings and car crashes appeared on the monitors, and Barbara would look at the complicated readouts on the instrument panels and work out the rough time and date of these future events. Then she and Barry would try their best to prevent the tragic events from happening. They prevented a fire which would have killed a family on Huyton House Road, a murder in Jubilee Park, and a domestic row between a husband and wife in which the wife stabbed her husband to death.

'The way things are going with my crime clean-up rate, I'll be the head of the CID in a few years,' quipped Barry. Whenever he was on the Blue Bell Lane part of his beat – and often when he was off duty – he'd call at Barbara's home and she'd brief him on the latest crimes and accidents that were due to happen locally. Barry's colleagues at the police station thought it was odd how he always happened to be at the scene of these incidents before they took place but put it down to coincidence.

And then one evening when Barry called in at Barbara's shed, he watched her adjusting the controls of her late husband's machine, when a shocking image came on the screens: Barry and Barbara were standing side by side outside of a church – it looked like St Michael's - in a little blizzard of multicoloured confetti.

They'd obviously been married. The image vanished after about five seconds into a fuzzy pattern of interference – and a hard silence materialised in the shed.

'That – that can't happen – I'm a happily married man,' said Barry in an uneven voice. He looked at Barbara, who gazed at the floor. She seemed stuck for words for a moment, and then she said, 'I don't see how it can happen either, but it must have happened in the future – but just how far in the future I don't know – I didn't get a chance to measure the signal strength.'

'My Auntie Flo was in the background, and my best mate Ron,' recalled Barry, 'but – wait a minute – does this mean something's going to happen to my wife?'

'I don't know,' said Barbara, looking very uncomfortable. She turned dials and pressed buttons on an instrument panel but the screens were still streaked with interference patterns.

'Do you know something and you're not telling?' Barry asked Barbara, 'Are you keeping something from me? Is Jean going to die?' Jean was his wife of three years.

'I don't know!' yelled Barbara. 'I'm as much in the dark about this as you are.'

'Look, Barbara, you're a very attractive woman, and a really lovely person too, but I happen to love my wife an awful lot,' said Barry, and then he looked at Barbara apologetic, 'I'm sorry the way that came out but this is a shock,' he said. He took his police helmet off and fidgeted with it. 'If Jean died, I'd never bother with anyone ever again; I've been with her since we were both at school.'

Barbara said nothing. She seemed hurt. Barry left the shed confused about his feeling towards Barbara. He liked her but he was a married man. He walked through the moonlit night, and for the first time, his mind was not on the job; he was too distracted by that image of the marriage outside of Huyton Parish Church.

It was hard to do – because he loved her company – but he forced himself to stay away from Barbara for four days, and then one afternoon he returned to her home. There was no answer, and a neighbour told him she had moved. Barry went into the garden, opened the shed – and found it completely empty; just a few wires lay on the bare floorboards of the shed. Forty days later, he received a letter with a Brighton postmark. It was from Barbara but she had not included a return address. She told him she had seen his wife having an affair with his best friend, Ron. She told Barry that Jean would become pregnant by Ron and that Barry would knock his friend clean out during the resulting violent altercation. Barry would then divorce when Jean stuck by Ron. Barbara said she had also seen intelligence agents visit her at some point in the future to seize the scanner, so she had left before it could happen. Barry ended up divorced. He left the police force, moved in with a relative in north-west Norfolk, just to get away from the painful memories of his wife's betrayal – and the loss of Barbara – when something quite unexpected happened. Barry had turned to drink by the summer of 1969, and on most evenings he tended to ramble along the Norfolk coast towards The Wash, his sad eyes surveying the stretches of sand and low cliffs as he thought of the loss of his wife and also the tragedy of losing Barbara, for now he realised he *had* loved her, and had he met her before Jean he would have surely married her. She had struck him as a very caring woman, and he bitterly regretted those days he had stayed away from her shed. One night as he walked along the beach with the full moon rising from the sea's horizon, he had heard a dog barking, and then he had seen a border collie running towards him. Further up the beach was the silhouette of a woman. As she came hurrying after the dog, Barry saw to his utter surprise that it was Barbara. At first she didn't recognise Barry because he had a thick beard, and she called to her dog because the collie recognised the former policeman and was yelping and jumping up at him. Then she saw who it was, and Barry said, 'Barbara, how are you?'

'Barry, what are you doing down here in Norfolk?' she asked.

'I was trying to forget the past – how about you?' was his reply.

She told him she had destroyed her late husband's invention and burned all of his notebooks because she realised that – sooner or later – the scanner would fall into the wrong hands, and she felt that the human race was not ready for such a device yet. The couple got back together, and later married and settled down in Lincolnshire.

Barbara mentioned a crystal with a four-dimensional lattice as being the heart of the time scanner, and I thought this sounded like something out of a *Doctor Who* episode, but I was shocked to learn that such crystals do indeed exist and are known as space-time crystals and were first seriously proposed by Frank

Wilczek, a Nobel Prize-winning professor at the Massachusetts Institute of Technology in 2012 – some forty-six years after Barbara mentioned such a crystal to Barry. The space-time crystal officially became a reality in October 2016 when one was created at Maryland University – and as Barbara explained to Barry in the 1960s, the crystal's architecture is four-dimensional. Most scientists will not yet stick their necks out and state that such crystals could be used to probe time, but these crystals are like the laser – they hold a lot of promise and could be used to tackle a variety of problems in the world of physics – including the challenge of time travel.

The first alleged time traveller I discovered in the history books when I was a child was the mysterious Count St Germain, a chameleonic individual who was seen throughout many time periods and may still be around today. Let me tell you a story about him. The mighty Wheel of History turns perpetually and the same people and attitudes come round again. Today, most young people are suspicious of their own government, and they question consumerist values, and oppose all military overtures – and it was the same in 1967 during the so-called Summer of Love; The Beatles were at the height of their powers and Liverpool was the Athens of the counterculture with people from around the globe making pilgrimages to the city – even immortals, it would seem. An elegant, aristocratic woman named Christabel once told me how, in May 1967, at the age of twenty, she had come up to Liverpool from the sheltered existence of her high-class Mayfair home in London to join a group of artists and poets. She lived over a Bold Street shop in a two-room flat, and one afternoon, as she was painting in oils on a canvas she was, to use her own words, "beguiled by sitar music echoing down the communal stairway."

Christabel wondered who was playing the beautiful Indian music and she left her canvas, went out of her room and slowly ascended the stairs until she came to an attic door. She knocked, and the music stopped. An exceedingly handsome long-haired hippie in flamboyant psychedelic clothes answered, and when she looked into his eyes, all time seemed to halt. Feeling hypnotically drawn to the stranger, Christabel went into the attic as he stepped aside. He closed the door behind Christabel and without looking at her he sat on a Turkish divan. The unknown musician plucked at a swarmandal – also known as an Indian harp. Lost in the heady scent of joss sticks and stirring music from the harp, Christabel felt as if her creative mind was rising from some cellar dungeon to a sunlit attic. She had read about these euphoric peak experiences – often arrived at with hallucinogenic drugs – in the books of Aldous Huxley and Abraham Maslow – but now she was directly experiencing one and it felt overpowering and oceanically overwhelming. The attractive musician sat cross-legged as he played, framed by a Persian-blue velvet map depicting the twelve signs of the Zodiac. He was surrounded by occult paraphernalia – crystal balls, Ouija board, wands, indigo candles and a Tarot pack. Christabel wanted to remain there forever, but as soon as the man stopped playing the harp, her mood reverted to the usual humdrum state.

'Who are you?' she asked.

He put down the Indian harp and looked up at her. 'My name is Simon Fairbrother,' he told her, and she detected the slight inflection of French in his speech.

'Are you from France?' Christabel asked, and he nodded. Christabel told him her full name and soon afterwards she began an affair with Simon. He never discussed his background, however hard Christabel pressed him, and she worried he was hiding some criminal past at first, but as she got to know Simon she realised there was something very unusual about him, but what this was she could not really say. "There was just some incredible aura around him," she told me, "and he was the first real love of my life – and possibly the only one."

Christabel was an able artist, and when she showed a sketch of Simon to her grandmother Rachel, the old lady shot a peculiar look at the drawing. She then fetched an album of photographs and pointed to a familiar face. It was of Rachel and a well-dressed man, taken at the Café Royal, London in 1910. 'Simon Welldon,' said Rachel, 'we were engaged for a while. He died in the trenches.'

'That's him!' Christabel gasped, for it was, without a doubt, her lover Simon Fairbrother, but her Nan told her granddaughter her boyfriend was merely a dead ringer for *her* Simon. Christabel showed the photograph to Simon and he denied it was him at first, but then a tear welled in his eye and he said he was an immortal man known by many aliases: the Count St Germain and Count Welldon amongst others, and he had personally known many of the great personages from history, from Plato and Christ, to Robin Hood, Henry VIII and Marie Antoinette. Simon said the

Beatles would change the world and evoke a mass shift in the consciousness of most of the human race, and he also told Christabel in a very solemn manner that the Age of Aquarius was about to Dawn. A new religion based on "The Flower of Life" was also coming, which promised eternal life and happiness. He told Christabel: 'I have to leave you now, my love; I have to keep the human race on track. We *will* meet again one day and know forever in your heart that I will always love you.'

Before a shocked Christabel could protest at his intentions to desert her, she dozed off, and when she awoke from a deep dreamless sleep, the attic was empty – and Simon was gone.

Christabel immediately looked into the aliases her lover had gone under, and when she saw the 18th Century etching of the Count of St Germain, she was really shaken, because he looked exactly like Simon. She asked me if he was in league with the Devil, as many occultists believed, and I told her that, in my humble opinion – and I have studied the Count for decades – he was a traveller in the realms of time and space – a type of renegade Timelord of the kind depicted in the long-running television series *Doctor Who*. The Count is not a legend – he is an actual historical personage and if you take time to delve into the history books and the hundreds of old newspaper reports and entries in the diaries of men and women from the last three centuries, you will find references to him. People have tried to rationalise the whole affair by asserting that the Count of St Germain was many different people in different periods, possibly even a father and son who bore strong resemblances to one another, but even if that was so, someone would recognise them and identify the charlatans – but the Count was never identified by anyone, and furthermore, we cannot explain the Count's incredible wealth, his unheard of expertise in chemistry and the curious way he enlarged diamonds to enormous sizes. He spoke all of the European languages as well as Arabic, Hebrew and Classical Greek. He was a friend of the Shah of Persia, Catherine the Great, the Kings of France, Marie Antoinette, and was welcomed in every Masonic lodge and royal court on the Continent. To those he trusted, he told them how he had been in the company of Jesus of Nazareth and his disciples, and once ruefully remarked, 'I had always known Christ would meet a bad end.' He was also an intimate confidante to Marie Antoinette, and warned her about the approach of the French Revolution, which he described as 'gigantic conspiracy that would overthrow the order of things' – and Marie later regretted not taking the Count's advice in her diaries. He was on the European scene from circa 1710 to 1821, and never grew old – he always looked as if he was about forty-five, and many believed he had discovered the fabled Elixir of Youth – a mysterious tasteless medicine which restores the length of telomeres in human DNA and keeps a person alive for as long as the medicine is periodically taken. After 1821, the Count was rarely seen until World War One, when he was captured by two Bavarian soldiers at Alsace. He told them there would be another world war and described to his bemused captors how 'a man with an ancient symbol' (the Swastika) would plunge the globe into an even fiercer conflict that would end with a new age of destruction – a cryptic reference to the Atomic Bomb and the beginning of the Cold War.

And where is the enigmatic Count today? He could be anywhere – or perhaps he has gone to some other period in the long corridor of history – he might have even returned from whence he came – to some future age where time travel is commonplace. I have a strong suspicion that we will hear from the Count again in the near future.

I continually receive reports of timeslips from readers and I also have a large 200-page book of newspaper cuttings which details some amazing slippages in time. Here is just one example from that book of clippings – taken from a very intriguing article in the *Liverpool Echo*. Derek Whale, who passed away many years ago, was an incredible local journalist, and the author of the popular books, *The Liners of Liverpool* and his knowledge of our city's history was unrivalled. On 31 October 1978 in his "Merseyscene" column, Derek wrote an article entitled, "Was it the ghost of Liverpool past?" in which he wrote: 'Seeing ghostly people is not uncommon, but seeing an area of Liverpool which existed centuries ago must be rare. And yet, two independent witnesses claim to have seen this same sight – in Tithebarn Street. Mrs Olwen M. Exell of Penmaenmawr, formerly of Woolton, recently broadcast her story of how, when walking from Old hall Street along Tithebarn Street, just beyond Exchange Street East in January 1948, she saw an 18th Century house with a cobbled forecourt. This lasted only a few seconds and the scene returned to normal. Now, here is corroboration of her story. In 1958, Mrs Mary Hansen (formerly of Anfield) but now living in

Mostyn Street, Llandudno, was walking along Tithebarn Street, making her way to Moorfields, when (she writes) "I suddenly found myself in a deserted, cobbled courtyard, with passages on all sides. I remember thinking, in bewilderment, that I must have taken a wrong turning, and I stopped for a second to get my bearings. Realising that the way out was across the courtyard, I hurried ahead. I also remember thinking that cobbles wouldn't be doing my stiletto heels much good! Upon reaching the other side, I looked back and found, to my amazement, that Tithebarn Street was back to usual." Mrs Hansen also recalled a strong musty smell at that time. Mrs Exell stated, "I was delighted to hear from Mrs Hansen, because her story lends weight to mine. She did not know that I too had been walking from Old Hall Street. I was particularly struck by her reference to the cobbled courtyard and passages. This must surely refer to the heys and alleys still to be found in the city centre, which were features of the old Liverpool. Both experiences happened in the middle of the day when the street was busy. I can only guess that we each travelled back in time - about 200 years in my case."

The 'phantom' cottage the two women encountered near Tithebarn Street has been seen many times, and when I discussed the subject of timeslips on the *Billy Butler Show* on BBC Radio Merseyside some years ago, three people telephoned the station and mentioned seeing what seems to have been the very same cottage in the 1980s. One woman saw the quaint old dwelling in 1981, whereas a businessman in 1988 actually passed the cottage and took it to be a real solid dwelling - until it vanished before his eyes – and in 1989 a young man on his way to sign on at the unemployment office at Silkhouse Court one May afternoon saw the cottage slowly appear – and then disappear as he walked along Tithebarn Street. He too – like Mrs Hansen thirty-one years before – also detected a musty smell in the vicinity of the spectral cottage.

And now for a very intriguing timeslip in which the time glimpsed was not the 17th or 18th Century – but some era possibly dating back to the Pleistocene Epoch – around 2.6 million years ago.

George is 77 at the time of writing, but back in 1964 he was a 22-year-old conductor on the buses, and he recalls a very frightening yet intriguing incident he and four other people witnessed on a Number 44D bus as it was travelling along Walton Hall Avenue, Norris Green early one Saturday morning, bound for the city centre. George was a bit nervous on this route because only a week before a fellow conductor had been attacked by youths on the bus, and as a result of the serious injuries sustained in the assault, representatives of bus crews and officials of the Passenger Transport Department had met to discuss a withdrawal of services. Hundreds of passengers ended up stranded by the resulting suspension of services, but now things were returning to normal. There was a girl of about sixteen on the bottom deck, two young men on the upstairs deck, and of course, the driver, Alan, a close friend of George, and all of these people were about to witness something quite extraordinary. As the bus travelled along Walton Hall Avenue, it became enveloped by a fog within seconds. This fog cleared and sunlight poured through the windows of the vehicle again, but now Walton Hall Avenue was no longer there; instead, the bus was in an immense field of deep snow that stretched for miles, and in the distance were either giant glaciers or snow-covered mountains, and in this arctic-like wilderness there were giant birds with huge fearsome-looking beaks walking about. The teenage girl looked at the bizarre scene beyond the windows of the bus, and then she looked at George, as if he would explain what was going on. Alan the driver then had trouble driving in the deep snow and the bus stalled. The temperatures plunged and one of the huge birds which George estimated to be about fifteen feet in height came creeping over to the bus. At the sight of what looked like some feathered dinosaur, the girl started screaming and clung on to George. The oversized bird tried to get into the bus but was too large. It poked its head in, looked at George and the hysterical girl, opened its massive beak and let out a screech which left the conductor with a ringing in his ears. The girl fainted, and George heard the two lads on the top deck coming down the stairs but warned them to stay put. Seconds later, the birds and the glacial landscape outside vanished and the familiar streets of Liverpool came back into view. Did time slip back to some ancient ice age as the bus moved along Walton Hall Avenue? Later that day when George and Alan got back to the depot, they made the mistake of discussing the timeslip nightmare. 'Me and Alan were in the canteen,' George told me, 'and Alan mentioned the weird incident to one of his hoppos, and this blabbermouth then told everyone and someone said to me, "You and your driver want to keep off the ale when you take the buses out mate," and I almost came

148

to blows with him. We were the butt of many jokes after that and I never even told my wife what had happened.'

Timeslips have brought back other long-vanished lands from the remote past. How it does it is still a mystery, and come to think of it, entropy – the manner in which time wears us all down – is also an enigma. Time devours all things, and it does it relentlessly and silently like a diamond-encrusted file that makes no noise as it erodes. Time topples all civilizations in the end, and we only have to look at the Colosseum or the Acropolis of Athens to remind us of the fall of the once-great Roman and Greek empires. Nearer to home we have many lost villages in England; places like Radley (often mistakenly called Raleigh) in Nottinghamshire, which vanished without a trace in the 12th century, and there are other places which have mysteriously disappeared off the face of the earth in the North West. Kilgrimol once existed between Lytham and Blackpool in the 12th century, and was either submerged by some type of tidal wave or perhaps simply buried by the constantly inward-drifting sands. The most fascinating lost land in the North West has to be the arboreal kingdom known by occultists as "The Realm" – this is an immense dominion which existed a long time ago – long before the Roman Invasion – probably about five thousand years ago. The Realm was a territory which stretched from modern-day Meols to Formby, and was mostly made up of an immense forest that stretched to its southern border. Mirage-like apparitions have not only been seen of this long-vanished kingdom, I have also received many accounts of people who have physically entered it over the years through some timeslip anomaly. The vestiges of the ancient forest of The Realm, can occasionally be seen at Dove Point, Meols, between the slipway and the groyne, if you'd care to check it out for yourself. Alas, the only traces of the forest are petrified stumps of ancient oaks. In August 1983, two old friends, Martin, a doctor, and Ken, a retired Lever research chemist – both aged 62 – left their homes in Hoylake one sunny afternoon and went to call on a mutual friend at Meols, but getting no answer the men went to walk along Meols Parade to get some sea air in their lungs. As Martin and Ken walked along, they noticed what they assumed to be a dark cloud on the beach, but could not see any fire. They then noticed a thick wooded area which went right up the beach and onto Bennet's Lane. The presence of this heavily wooded area naturally baffled the two men, and they went to explore the wood. Other locals saw the trees too, Ken recalled, but he and Martin were the first to enter the bizarre out-of-place wood. Ken thought there was something very strange about the whole affair and told Martin they should turn back, but the latter was filled with rampant curiosity and said, 'They must have planted all this as a sea-defence type of thing,' and Ken shook his head and replied, 'Defence from what? Let's go back, Marty.'

The inquisitive doctor took no notice and marched on through what seemed to be a sprawling forest of oaks and huge ferns, and it struck Ken that the place was looking more like the rainforests he had seen on the TV nature programmes rather than a humble wood. After walking for about ten minutes, Ken once again tried to talk Martin into leaving the baffling forest. He said, 'Marty, we must be about half a mile out now, and the tide might come in!'

'We'll go back in a minute,' said Marty, looking at the floor of the forest, 'can't see any sand – this is all soil – it doesn't make sense.'

Ken then noticed a tall standing stone, similar to the ones seen at Stonehenge, only a bit smaller, and as he set eyes upon it, a blinding light radiated from the tip of the stone, and it became surrounded by a halo of various colours. 'What in God's name is that?' Martin asked, startled by the luminous stone. Suddenly, to the right of the stone, a tall figure, well over six feet in height, stepped out from behind the massive trunk of a tree. It was someone dressed in a silvery suit of armour with a fearsome mask of metal built into the helmet. Ken was a keen birdwatcher, and straight away he saw that there was an engraving of an oystercatcher on the breastplate of this menacing knight. The armoured figure was resting his gauntlets on the pommel of the sword's handle, and the tip of the blade was impaling the soily ground. The knight said nothing, and to the left, the standing stone was still giving off light and making a crackling, electrical sound. Martin also noticed a second stone about twenty feet away, and that too was glowing. A beautiful red-headed lady in a blue satin hooded robe came from behind a tree, and with her was a huge panther-like cat, only it was white as snow. She said something to the knight in a language Ken and Martin did not recognise, and the armoured man immediately lifted the sword above his head in a threatening manner, and at the same time the huge white cat growled and came over to the frightened men. Ken and Martin turned and ran, and they could hear the growling big cat closing in and the clanking sound of the knight giving chase. The men expected to be cut down by the huge sword or savaged by the cat any moment, but seconds later, they found themselves running across the sands of a beach. They looked back, and saw that the forest had vanished.

Phantom lands brought back to life by the mysterious workings of the tides of time and space is one thing – but it would seem that we also have a couple of forgotten seas in this region as well, and every now and then they return from their bygone age and superimpose themselves over modern terrain. Take the sea that once existed in Britain just after the last ice age. It stretched from Southport to Wolverhampton and covered most of modern-day Manchester, St Helens, the outskirts of Liverpool, the Cheshire Plain, and Crewe was totally submerged by it. This sea was over 80 miles along its north-south axis and over 40 miles along its east-west axis. It was caused by a melting glacier ten thousand years ago. This sea eventually drained into the bowels of the earth and what was left partially evaporated leaving marshlands – but a pilot flying from Manchester Airport in the mid-1960s and many of his passengers were almost blinded by the glare caused by the noon sun reflecting off the ancient sea as it suddenly reappeared for a few minutes. Another forgotten sea lies hidden beneath the streets of Bootle and would make an excellent tourist attraction if someone could explore and survey it first – perhaps via a submarine drone. I am referring to an immense body of freshwater that exists under Bootle and extends beyond Ainsdale. The *Liverpool Echo* publicised the existence of the subterranean sea in a very informative article dated 12 July, 1989. Most of the evidence for the hidden sea comes from a chart given to Bootle Council many years ago by W. H. Williams, a retired water engineer, who, as a boy, worked at the old Bootle Waterworks in 1888. Bootle once had over 2,000 water springs and was renowned far and wide as a provider of high-quality drinking water. Liverpool was highly dependent on Bootle spring water for many years, but no one really gave any thought about the source of the water. In 1950, Bootle Fire Brigade was investigating possibilities regarding an emergency water supply when several exploratory drillings were made into massive sandstone caverns beneath Bootle. It was eventually ascertained that a gigantic sea of fresh water extended under Bootle, Litherland, parts of Liverpool, and it seems to extend into Lancashire for many miles. Entrances to the secret sea have been found in places as diverse as the civil parish of Kirkham near Preston, Southport, Church Road, Litherland (in the form of a well), and of course, numerous places in Bootle, including a cellar in a house near the appropriately-named Well Lane. I wrote about Bootle's best kept secret in one of the *Haunted Liverpool* books some years ago and told a story, dictated to me by a Bootle man who once played truant in the 1950s when he was a child. He explored part of the sunless sea in a relative's dinghy (which he boarded in a waterlogged cellar). Many other locals in Bootle have explored parts of the eerie sea over the years and talked of seeing strange old ships drifting about in still waters beneath the stalactites of a vast sandstone firmament. Others who have gone down to explore this Lovecraftian sea have spoken of their encounters with strange aquatic creatures, many of them blind in the absence of light, but still no systematic exploration of the forgotten sea has ever been launched. Perhaps it is time for some brave explorers to shine a light on this murky Bootle mystery.

There is yet another timeslip concerning a forgotten subterranean wonder of the old world – and this baffling throwback in time concerns the Lost Mersey Tunnel.

On Tuesday 31 August, 1971, a hole being dug by a gang of Wirral Water Board workmen in a private road in Thurstaston suddenly caved in – and revealed an old smugglers' tunnel. The workmen had been laying a new water main off Station Road, near Thurstaston Church, when the surprise discovery was made. A young lady named Rita Howell, who was working on her father's farm near the site of the intriguing excavation, crawled sixty yards into the tunnel and later told newspaper reporters, 'The air was very pure down there and the passage was carved expertly out of the sandstone. It seemed to run in the direction of Thurstaston Hall and could have come from the ancient Dee port of Dawpool.' Miss Howell added that there had always been talk of secret smugglers' tunnels under the area but most thought they were just local legends. Like Liverpool, Wirral is criss-crossed with unchartered subterranean passages in quite a few areas, and some tunnels are vaguely known to the public – such as the ones under Bidston Hill and the Tranmere tunnels - but have never been thoroughly explored and accurately mapped. The most incredible local legend about a secret passage is the one concerning the Lost Mersey Tunnel. Around 1967, on Birkenhead's Church Street, just a stone's throw from the Priory, there lived a 48-year old Liverpool-born man named Arthur who was something of an eccentric but a brilliant engineer who had worked on the tunnels in Gibraltar in World War Two. Arthur was having an affair with Helen, a beautiful 25-year-old blonde lady in a nearby street. When Helen's husband – a wheelchair-bound man in his forties - heard about the alleged affair he literally kept his wife locked up most of the day in her home. Because of his wheelchair, the husband could not go to the cellar of the house, and Helen went down there to bring up coal now and then. One day, Arthur said to his friend Barry, 'There's an old proverb: "Love can go through stone walls" – well so can I!'

'How do you mean?' Barry asked, and Arthur smiled, then mimed a man digging with a spade as he sang *There's a Hole in my Bucket*. 'We dig dear Barry, we dig!' said Arthur in a well-modulated voice full of bright optimism, 'Now let me have half a tumbler of neat whiskey; I find it focuses my powers of concentration. You having one, old boy?'

'You can't be serious?' Barry gasped, but Arthur was deadly serious, and he poured himself a scotch and he went into his cellar and later in the evening with pickaxes and shovels he and Barry started to dig a tunnel to the cellar of the house where Helen was being kept a virtual prisoner. The two men reinforced the tunnel with wooden stanchions and had to make a few diversions to avoid gas and water pipes. During the excavation, a nest of rats was disturbed and they all swarmed over poor Barry, squeaking and squealing and the young man almost passed out from shock as Arthur roared with laughter. After almost three weeks of digging, with Arthur continually consulting his compass by torchlight, he and Barry broke through the cellar wall of a house forty feet away. Helen heard the breaking through of the cellar wall that night and went down to see who it was with a lamp and a cricket bat – when she saw Arthur standing there besides a grimy faced Barry with a wide smile. She was flabbergasted when she saw what Arthur had done – all to be with her, and he later asked her to desert her husband but she refused, as she said she just couldn't coldly abandon her husband because she feared he would commit suicide. Arthur, being a perfect gentleman, accepted Helen's decision, and he decided to extend his tunnel to the cellar of Barry's home, just out of boredom, for Arthur was a man who wasn't happy unless he had something practical to do. During one of the subterranean trips to Barry's cellar, a section of the tunnel fell away to reveal a passage which was illuminated by burning torches secured in sconces carved out of sandstone. Barry was told about the discovery and he and Arthur went down the illuminated sandstone tunnel with flashlights. According to Arthur's estimations, the passageway led to an area behind the Royal Hotel (now called The Swinging Arm) – where part of a graving dock had been filled in. Here, the men came upon an amazing sight – inside of a cave with stalactites hanging from the ceiling, there were chests filled with gold coins, various gold crosses, including a giant cross embedded with rubies, emeralds and pearls. Two more passages ran from this cave – one which must have run towards nearby Birkenhead Priory, and the other towards the Mersey. Barry had very keen hearing and he told Arthur he could hear the sound of crashing waves echoing down the tunnel which was headed for the river. Two hooded figures, dressed in the attire of monks, suddenly came down the passage from the Priory, and seemed completely unaware of Arthur and Barry's presence. The monks took hold of one of the chests of gold items and carried it slowly to the tunnel leading to the east – which must have led to a subterranean passage under the Mersey. Barry exclaimed, 'Jesus Christ!' and the ceiling of the cave started to fall in. A huge boulder crashed through the ceiling of the tunnel and hit one of the monks on the head. The holy man lay there with his head flattened to bloody pulp under the boulder. The ensuing blast of thick dust blew out the torches on the walls and Arthur pulled a blinded and panicking Barry back up the passage towards their own tunnel. 'Calm down, Barry, we're safe now!' Arthur cried, trying to reassure his terrified friend. They coughed as they escaped and made it back to Arthur's cellar.

'They must have been ghosts, Barry,' said Arthur, pouring a scotch for his trembling friend. When the men later returned to the tunnel they saw it lit up again, as if nothing had happened, and they saw a monk looking up the tunnel towards them – and then, that tunnel caved in. Arthur talked about tunnelling for that gold he had seen but decided it would be unlucky to take that which belonged to the Benedictine monks of Birkenhead Priory. It is an old legend – that long ago, during the Dissolution of the Monasteries, the psychopathic henchmen of Henry VIII were sent to take the gold and valuables from the Priory, but the monks, unable to transport the gold by ferry over to the monks of Stanlawe's monastic Grange in Aigburth for safekeeping, decided to use a tunnel they had been working on for many years – the very first Mersey Tunnel – but there was a tragic cave-in, and somewhere beneath the bedrock of the river, there lie the skeletons of the monks and what would now amount to millions of pounds in gold – in the lost Mersey Tunnel.

Some timeslips seemed to be triggered when something old is disturbed, or – as in the case of the following tale – something from long ago with a secret history is put into a modern setting.

In the Summer school holidays of 2012, Gary Shaw, the divorced father of 14-year-old Chloe went into hospital for a serious operation, and the girl's Aunt Samantha was supposed to look after the teenaged girl but Samantha herself ended up hospitalised after a car crash in the Midlands. Chloe's mother had remarried years ago and lived in Spain, but Chloe thought she could easily look after herself at the palatial house on Prenton's Brancote Road, and she invited her best friend Mia to stay over with her until her father was discharged from hospital. Chloe was originally from Broadgreen but had lived in Prenton since she was ten and her father had spoiled her rotten since the day when she had been wrenched from all her school friends before the move to Wirral. Chloe used her father's credit cards to buy things for herself – mostly from the big online stores – because she believed in retail therapy – that buying things for herself would help her get through what she called, in all seriousness "the darkest days" of her life as her dad lay in hospital. She bought clothes, shoes, make-up, jewellery, vinyl records (a new craze of Chloe's) art supplies (she liked to draw and purchased over 200 Copic markers), and she had a habit of ordering pizzas almost every day for dinner and tea. Two days into Mia's residency at Chloe's house, the latter decided to play Slipknot's *Psychosocial* at full blast on the music centre, and minutes later the neighbour's 17-year-old nephew Matt came knocking on the front door. He was a stocky young man with spectacles and when Chloe answered he seemed shy and tongue-tied for a few moments, then in a low, monotone voice he said, 'Could you keep the noise down? My Auntie's in bed with a migraine.'

Chloe pouted, looked Matt right in the eyes and said, 'Oh, I'm sorry. I'll just go and tell my idiot friend to turn it down. Oh by the way, my name's Chloe,' the teen added, and thrust out her hand, startling Matt, and he went red as they shook hands.

'And you are?' Chloe queried.

'Matt,' came the reply, and then the flushed-faced young man slowly turned and walked away and Chloe shouted after him, 'Matt, wait!'

Matt turned, and behind his glasses his eyes were wide. He looked petrified.

'Do you know how to put a garden shed up?' was the random question from Chloe. It just so happened that Matt was a natural born DIY man who excelled at carpentry at school and loved building things. The offer to erect a shed was much more exciting to him than meeting a potential girlfriend. Matt and Chloe were soon sitting side by side at the kitchen table looking at the bigger garden sheds on the laptop's listings.

'Okay, don't laugh,' said Chloe, 'but here's my scatty idea. I want to open my own nightclub in the back garden, just like made of wood like a shed but huge, and I want to call it The 27 Club. I got the name from like -'

'Yeah, I know,' interrupted Matt in his monotonous voice, 'Amy Winehouse, Jim Morrison, Kurt Cobain, and all that.'

'Brian Jones, Jimi Hendrix, and Janis Joplin died aged 27 as well,' added Mia, sitting on the opposite side of the table.

'I think there are like restrictions – you can only have a shed so big or you need planning permission,' said Matt, and Chloe squeezed his hand and said, 'I'll deal with all that, I just want you to build a massive shed covering half the back garden.'

'It'll cost you a bomb,' said Matt, looking at the girl's hand clenched around his, 'but I mean, *I* won't charge for my labour.'

Chloe smiled and fanned her dad's credit card under Matt's face. 'Money eez no probleemo,' she said in a hybrid Scouse and Spanish accent.

'I think I'm in love,' Chloe told Mia on the following sunny morning as the girls watched Matt in his navy-blue bib and brace carrying planks and wooden panels into the garden. Mia rolled her eyes and warned Chloe: 'Your dad will go nuts when he sees how much you've spent on his card.'

'Oh stop bringing me down, Mia,' replied Chloe in

an aggravated high-pitched voice, 'my dad always said he'd give me his last just to see me happy.'

'It will be his last the way you're shelling out for things on his card,' Mia replied.

In the space of one week, Matt, working from 8am till 8pm each day, completed the gigantic garden shed, and even wired the place up so it had lights and outlets via a mains cable to the house. Huge speakers were also mounted on the walls. Chloe bought a disco lights laser projector unit and as a bizarre finishing touch she purchased (for £150) a huge vintage carpet off eBay which Matt laid down on the "club" floor. Chloe drew up a guest list for the opening night of her very own club, and Mia made a drinks list. At 10pm on the day the club was finished, the girls danced about to Metallica's old hit *Enter Sandman* and Matt played the role of DJ, when something very strange happened. About fifty weird figures of men (and a few women), dressed in 18th century clothes and white periwigs appeared. All of them wore Lone Ranger style masks, and most were seated on old-fashioned chairs. Many of these eerie outdated people had swords and daggers, and they were all watching Chloe and Mira dancing. The girls were too wrapped up in their dance moves to notice the ghosts, but Matt stopped the music and the girls stopped dancing – and then they saw the crowd of unearthly old-fashioned masked strangers. A group of the ghostly figures got to their feet and, armed with swords and daggers rushed at the girls. The teens ran out of the glorified garden shed and were relieved that the ghosts did not follow them out. When Matt ventured back into the shed some time later, there was no one there. It was then that he noticed the pattern on the old carpet – it depicted a group of 18th century men and women. The shed was eventually dismantled by Chloe's furious father after he had made a full recovery from his operation and the apparently haunted carpet was thrown into a skip. Chloe's dad Gary told me that he had heard a group of people singing some song in what sounded like French one evening – and it was coming from the carpet in the skip, and this really unnerved him and convinced him that Chloe and Mia had been telling the truth about the ghosts in old-fashioned clothes chasing them with swords and daggers. Gary contacted the seller of the carpet on eBay and he said he had obtained the old carpet from a dealer who had been clearing out an old house down in Kent. The eBay seller said he knew nothing more about the history of the carpet. It obviously had a sinister history, and the energetic dancing of two girls upon it might have somehow conjured up the spirits of the enigmatic masked people, or perhaps the carpet contained some time element of its history which was simply replayed like a projected hologram; it really is hard to say what caused the backdated people in masks to appear.

And finally, I must end this chapter now with a very strange story regarding the apparent reversal of time. I was talking about timeslips one afternoon on a local radio station and after I came off air, the station receptionist told me that a man wanted to see me in the reception area. It was a tall grey-haired man in his late fifties named Bobby. He told me how, at the age of 22, he had arranged to see a beautiful 18-year-old girl named Betty who worked as a typist at an insurance office in Liverpool in late August 1972. He had met Betty a few days before while they were on their respective lunch breaks and he had really hit it off with her. She had told Bobby she'd like to go to a quiet pub with him after work on Monday, and he had asked her what time she knocked off. 'Half-past five,' she had told him, and she asked Bobby to wait for her on Chapel Street, which runs from Tithebarn Street. 'What part of Chapel Street?' Bobby had asked, and Betty had told him exactly where to wait for her: 'Right by the church,' she said, meaning St Nicks', the Sailor's Church with the little ship at the top of its spire. Its official title was the Church of Our Lady and Saint Nicholas. Bobby worked at a paper warehouse in the area, and normally got off work by 5.15pm, but on this Monday afternoon he was delayed because an old man he worked with collapsed and had to be taken to hospital. By the time Bobby got to the rendezvous point on Chapel Street, he could see that the clock on St Nick's Church said 5:40pm, and worse still, he could see Betty walking away from him in the distance at the other end of Chapel Street with a red-haired young man. Bobby thought he'd blown his chance, and felt so sad. He looked up at the clock on the church and recalled his old grandmother saying 'Time and tide wait for no man,' and in his case it was a painful truth. We often wish we could turn the clock back and do things differently. Well, just before he intended to walk away and get on the bus to take him home to Kensington, Bobby glanced up at the church clock – and saw it go backwards. He could not believe his eyes; the black cast-iron hands of the clock moved slowly in an anticlockwise direction, and then they picked up speed and stopped at 5.20pm, settling on the roman numerals of the face.

Then, at exactly 5:30pm, Betty appeared, and she was accompanied by a tall gangly red-haired youth who looked as if he was around Bobby's age. She waved at Bobby and he came rushing to her. Betty grabbed Bobby's hand and then she said to the ginger-headed youth, 'Bye-bye Roy!'

She almost dragged Bobby along with her and she then explained that Roy was the office sex pest who was always trying to chat the girls up.

'Did you walk down Chapel Street with him about fifteen minutes ago, travelling towards Tithebarn Street?' Bobby asked the typist and she returned a puzzled look and answered, 'No, I've only just knocked off.'

Bobby decided not to tell Betty about the clock going backwards in case she thought he was nuts.

Intrigued by this story, I examined the archives of the *Liverpool Echo* and sure enough, there was an article which corroborated Bobby's story. When I got the article printed I sent it to him and he wrote back and said, 'That's incredible – it was actually mentioned in the local press. I will treasure this clipping forever, Tom. Betty became my wife and died a few years ago.'

The article that vindicated Bobby's weird experience was on page 9 of a copy of the *Liverpool Echo* that was dated Tuesday, 29 August, 1972, and it bore the headline: 'Time went backwards at St. Nicholas' Church' and beneath this the piece stated: "It was just one of those days when time seemed to stand still and then go backwards in Liverpool city centre yesterday. For mystified Merseysiders stood in disbelief as St Nicholas' Parish Church clock started to go backwards as fast as it had previously gone forwards. Father Bernard Elsdon said last night, 'We are having a new electric cable put in and this means that the power supply has to be cut off at frequent intervals. The only trouble is that instead of stopping, the clock has started to go backwards and we don't really know why. It's never done this before. We couldn't believe it at first, but there is nothing we can do until the cable is installed.'

Father Elsdon is then quoted as saying that clock-watchers should look at the nearby Liver Building clocks if they wish to know the correct time.

# BRIDE IN A SUITCASE

Mild-mannered insurance clerk Archie Bassett boarded the bus in Everton that Saturday night in October 1959, bound for a woman who would hopefully be Miss Right. He kept his spectacles in his inside coat pocket, as he thought he'd have more of a chance of copping off without them. Archie's hair was Brylcreemed, and his thrice-shaven face was as smooth as the visage on Michelangelo's marble *David* – except for the tiny piece of tissue still stuck over the razor nick on his cleft chin. The clerk wore his Sunday best suit, and not believing in colognes for men, Archie thought the faint carbolic scent of the Lifebuoy soap he'd used in the extra-long bath would make him smell as manly as the next hot-blooded male. The blind date had been set up by a cousin and he was to meet the lady at 7:30pm at the Vines on Lime Street. She would be dressed all in pink and would have a blonde beehive hairdo. Her name was Nancy and she was 22 and worked as a waitress in Reece's Restaurant on Parker Street. Archie had just turned 34 and he was worried about the age gap. According to Archie's cousin, Nancy looked like a very young Diana Dors. When she met him that night she denied being Nancy, even though a Teddy boy called her by that name.

'It's alright if I'm not your cup of tea,' said Archie, his heart broken, 'but can I get you a drink anyway? It'd be nice just having a friend tonight.'

'Oi!' the Ted positioned himself between Nancy and Archie and told the rejected date: 'Listen here Barney Boko, if you don't leave Nancy alone I'll get the Wilkinsons out and rearrange that ugly gob of yours.' The Ted imitated the carving movements he'd make with the flick-knife in the air in front of Archie's face. He smiled at the fear in the clerk's eyes and told him: 'So, Archie, piss off out of here and go and take a nice long leisurely walk off the landing stage!'

Archie could hear Nancy giggling as he left the pub. He wandered from pub to pub, and not one female looked at him. At eleven o'clock he went to an all-night coffee bar, and he felt like a living fossil because the place was full of young Teds and the jukebox was pounding out rock 'n roll. He just didn't fit in with the youthful Ted culture, so he went to catch the bus home.

As soon as he opened the door to his flat, his current best friend, Zebedee the cat ran along the hallway to him – but ran around him because he wanted to go out. Archie sat in the dark at the window of his flat and looked up at the eternal stars. Love's sweet old story had passed him by again. The neighbourhood was as quiet as the grave. He decided he should move to the city centre – maybe to a flat over a shop – some place where the bustle of life would make him forget he was lonely. He later found a flat that could possibly meet his needs – it was fully furnished and situated over a café on the busy thoroughfare of Leece Street, and he found the place via the *Liverpool Echo's* accommodation to let column. Archie paid the deposit on his new place, and made bus journeys back and forth as he took his belongings to his new pad. On the last journey, he packed a suitcase of all his shirts, then boarded the bus to town. During the journey his meandering stream of consciousness ran from "Would it always be like this? No one to love?" to "Will Zebedee get lost in his new neighbourhood?"

At last the bus trundled onto Lime Street, and most of the passengers on the lower deck got up with Archie. A drunk stinking of rum pushed him aside and needlessly instructed the driver to "Stop here mush! I wanna get off here, got that?"

Archie grabbed his suitcase from the luggage rack at the stop near the Adelphi Hotel and waited till the six people in front of him got off. He thanked the driver, stepped onto the pavement and walked a few feet from the bus when the suitcase he held in his left hand flew open with a violent jolt, and people waiting to board the bus and the few getting off the vehicle drew back in surprise as a wedding dress and veil – together with a bouquet and a pair of white shoes – sprung out of the suitcase - and they all went up the steps of the Adelphi, as if an invisible woman had the bridal dress on. The arms of the dress threw themselves around a young lady who had been coming down the steps, and she yelped with shock as the outfit flopped to the ground. The lady – named Jenny was more astounded than scared, and as an embarrassed Archie picked up the bridal dress, she said to him, 'Did you see that? It must be haunted.'

'I must have picked up the wrong suitcase,' Archie told her, 'that dress doesn't belong to me.'

'That's what they all say,' said a young man standing behind the insurance clerk, 'bet you've got knickers and suspenders on under those kecks!' Jenny giggled and picked up the shoes and handed them to Archie, who straightened up and turned to look at the bus pulling away. 'My suitcase with all my shirts is on that bus,' he said.

The young man who had joked about Archie wearing women's clothes said, 'I'll stop it!' and he rushed off, running parallel to the bus and the driver stopped the vehicle on Renshaw Street. The youth came running back with Archie's suitcase, and the clerk thanked him and tried to offer him half a crown but the young man refused, and as he panted from the dash back, he said, 'The driver asked all the passengers if anyone had a wedding dress in a case on the luggage rack but no one replied.'

'Oh, isn't that odd?' Jenny remarked.

'I'll put a notice in the *Echo*, see if anyone replies,' said Archie, 'but I won't mention the shoes in case someone dishonest just tries to claim the dress.'

'I'm dying to find out who the dress belongs to,' said Jenny, her eyes aglow, 'I love a mystery.'

'I'd get shut of it,' said the young man who had rescued Archie's shirts from the bus, 'it might belong to a ghost.'

Archie asked Jenny if she'd like to come to a café for a coffee, and she nodded and said, 'Yeah, okay - on the condition that you'll keep me informed about the outcome of the great wedding dress mystery.'

No one ever claimed that wedding dress and the

shoes. Jenny believed that it had perhaps belonged to someone who might have died – possibly a romantic lady – and she had seen a chance to play Cupid and find someone for Archie. In the summer of 1960, Jenny married Archie, and she actually wore the mysterious wedding dress and those beautiful size 6 ivory shoes on that special day.

# WITCH GAMES

For reasons of confidentiality I've changed a few names in the following strange account but otherwise the story is exactly as it was reported to me by many credible witnesses. In June 1974 32-year-old traffic policeman Mike Whittaker was cruising down Lodge Lane on his Norton Commando 850 motorcycle when he saw a man outside Blake's Van Hire waving frantically to him. He pulled over and the man pointed to an orange car, saying, 'There's no one in that Cortina!'

Mike shot a bemused look at the man and asked, 'You taking the mickey?'

The orange car in question – not a Cortina at all but a Hillman Avenger – went through the lights and almost knocked down two old women. Mike sped off after it and drove alongside the Avenger on Upper Parliament Street and it was plain to see there was no one at the wheel and no prankster hiding on the floor of the car. Mike radioed the registration of the driverless vehicle and was told it belonged to Georgina Keynes of 129 Mount Pleasant. This name sounded familiar to Mike. When he told HQ the car had no one at the wheel the operator jokingly replied, 'Have you been drinking?'

At 45mph the Avenger screeched and made a sharp right turn onto Grove Street, where it narrowly missed a child, and then it turned left into Falkner Square and peeled rubber as it picked up speed. Mike wondered if he could somehow drive alongside the deserted car, open its door, and take control of it – but then his bike would career off into people and traffic so he dismissed the possibility. He drove ahead of the Avenger on Canning Street and flashed his headlamp and frantically waved drivers to get out of the way, and the unmanned vehicle missed a queue of cars at the lights by inches and its tyres squealed as it rocketed along Upper Duke Street and turned onto Rodney Street where it scraped the side of an oncoming mini. Mike saw his colleague Bill Bradford coming towards him up Clarence Street – he'd come to assist him in a situation that had not been discussed at any police school. Bill could see that Mike was right – the car turning onto Leece Street had no driver. The Avenger eventually pulled over on Renshaw Street and a beautiful raven-haired lady – Georgina Keynes – got into it with her shopping bags. The policemen quizzed her and she smilingly reminded them that she could not be charged for Dangerous Driving because she had not been in the vehicle at the time of its dangerous transit across the city. Miss Keynes was subsequently 'let off', and Mike suddenly realised why she looked familiar; she'd danced with him at a nightclub a year ago but he had turned Georgina down when she asked him to take her home because Mike had only recently married and loved his wife. Had that woman been some revengeful witch? He had the sneaking suspicion Georgina was indeed a witch who had been playing some game with him that summer's day in June 1974, but of course, the law does not recognise the supernatural, but it did once acknowledge witchcraft.

In times past, bad harvests, the unexplained death of cattle, and any mysterious illness were often cited as the results of some witch casting a spell or exerting the dark power of the "evil eye". In 1542, Parliament passed the Witchcraft Act which stated that any person practising witchcraft would be sentenced to death. This severe law was repealed five years later but then it was restored by a new Witchcraft Act in 1562. Then a new law was passed on the use of witchcraft in the reign of King James – a monarch who had a personal interest in witchcraft and the occult. The new law transferred the trial of purported witches and sorcerers from the Church to the courts of the land. The last witch trials ended around 1717, and by then, around 500 alleged witches had been executed. In 1776 Parliament passed an Act to repeal the old witchcraft laws, but anyone claiming they could use spells and magic would still be fined or imprisoned, and that Act was finally repealed in 1951 with the introduction of the Fraudulent Mediums Act. This latter Act was in turn repealed on 26 May 2008 by an EU directive which prohibited unfair sales and marketing practices. Despite all of these laws against witches, they still thrived of course, and some witches continue to amuse themselves by toying with the 'mundanes' – non witches that is – as the following story hints.

Earth can seem like the most alien of planets when you're alone without a friend in the world, and 45-year-old Jim Tilbury felt as if he was on Mars as he stood at the bar of a pub on Great Charlotte Street, mechanically sipping his lager as he looked for love, but no woman noticed him. Jim had lost his mum to cancer six months ago, and just had to get out the house, away from the stifling loneliness. This was the summer of 2001, and the situation comedy *The Office* was showing on the television in the bar. A group of young men were watching the TV and one of them – a 30-year-old man named Ian – did a perfect impression of the comedy show's David Brent character, which amused his friends. After the show ended, Ian noticed Jim Tilbury and slyly pointed him out to his pals. Ian took out his comb and combed his hair over his head, copying Jim's comb-over, and then he stuck out his bottom lip, aping Jim's prognathism. All of Ian's mates giggled, and when Sophie – a girl Ian had tried to date for a few years – came into the pub, he tried to attract her attention by standing next to Jim as he clowned around. Ian noticed Jim's stammer, so he asked the barman for a lager with a put-on stutter, and then Ian said to Jim: 'You remind me of the lead singer of Human League; you know, the way your hair's combed over.'

All of Ian's mates laughed.

'Stop that,' a girl with long black hair told Ian. He thought she looked like a Goth in her black clothes and pale make-up. 'If the wind blows you might stick like that,' she said.

'It's just a bit of fun,' he told the girl, 'stop being a party pooper.'

Ian's skitting went on for some time, and at 10.40pm, when Ian went to the toilet, he tried to comb his hair back from the imitation comb-over – and clumps of it fell out. He also noticed that his bottom lip really was protruding now, and it felt swollen. Ian's best friend Luke came into the toilet and laughed at his friend's thinning, combed-over hair. 'How did you do that?' he asked, 'It looks dead real!'

Ian tried to tell him it *was* real and found he had a stutter. Luke roared with laughter. Ian panicked and ran out of the pub. He jumped in a cab at the rank on Great Charlotte Street and kept stuttering his address to the driver until he was understood. The cab driver insensitively said, 'Jesus Christ, you could have walked home by the time you told me that!'

For one long year, Ian was bald and he had a stammer. He bumped into Jim Tilbury in town one day, and saw that he had a full head of hair and was chatting perfectly to that 'Goth' – and she smirked at Ian and as she passed by she shouted to him, 'I told you you'd stick like that if the wind blew!'

Ian just sensed that there was something very sinister about the girl – and he thought she might be a witch. When he finally lost the stammer and his hair had regrown, Ian never again mocked anyone's appearance.

From the year 2001 let us fly by broomstick back in time to the year 1964 in our search for other bewitching ladies who have toyed with us mere mortals. I researched this story a long time ago and established that the intriguing lady referred to in the tale - who seems to have possessed an incredible talent for apotropaic magic – was encountered all over the country and as recently as 2011.

One foggy afternoon in September 1964, debonair gambler Simon Richards entered the type of pub that's so hard to find nowadays; no booming TV, no deafening jukebox and no plastic fittings. This pub was wood-panelled throughout with cosy snugs, an open fire, solid local ales on tap and stained-glass windows. Although it was a Saturday it was virtually empty except for the barman and an old customer. George the landlord found Simon behind the bar, removing the horseshoe.

'No wonder I've had so much blasted bad luck! This thing's on upside down!' Simon told the barman George, hooking the horseshoe back on the wall so it was oriented as a "U".

Simon ordered a pint of mild and sat studying the declared runners for the 1964 St. Leger in a quiet cosy corner of the pub. After about a minute, Simon heard the pub door squeak – as it always did when anyone came or went – and he happened to glance over the top of his newspaper to see who it was, and he noticed a beautiful lady enter the pub. A little of the fog swirled in with her, and now she stood there with her head tilted back slightly. She looked down her nose in what seemed to be a condescending manner at an elderly man who was sitting in the corner, playing Patience at a table diagonal from Simon. This woman immediately intrigued Simon. She had pallid porcelain skin, large Carolina blue eyes, cupid-bow lips and her dark hair, with tinsel strands of grey, was coiffeured in a short, elegant style. She turned her head and looked at Simon and he thought he saw her surrounded by a blue aura of dazzling stars for a moment. He squeezed his eyes shut for a second then opened them, thinking he was seeing things because he'd hardly slept last night (because of certain nagging financial worries). The lady standing before him still seemed as ethereal as the Milky Way – she just didn't seem to be a part of gritty reality. 'You have got to be an aristocrat,' Simon found himself saying, and she said a strange thing in reply. 'I am Fortuna – Lady Luck.' Her voice was

176

silken, well-spoken and clear as a bell.

'Really?' Simon lowered the newspaper, 'I could do with Lady Luck in my life. Enlighten me.'

She smiled and raised her eyebrows. 'I can't elucidate any further,' she said in a descending tone, as if Simon had asked a ridiculous question. 'I don't need to enlighten anyone – you either believe me or you don't,' she added.

'Endarken me then,' joked Simon, and then he rose from his comfortable corner seat and asked "Fortuna": 'May I get you a drink?'

'Oh, thank you,' she said with a hint of a smile on her perfect lips, 'I'd like one of those drinks – I think they call them Babycham.'

'Certainly,' Simon nodded and turned to the barman George, who was tackling a newspaper crossword spread on the bar counter. 'George? A Babycham for this lady, please.'

The charismatic visitor to the pub suddenly came out with something very random. She looked at the newspaper Simon had left on his corner seat and told him: 'That horse – the one named Indiana – it shall win the St. Leger tomorrow.'

'Indiana?' Simon queried with a polite smile and then, with a rise of his eyebrows he said, 'At long odds of 100 to 8?'

The woman nodded once slowly with a lazy assurance.

'Well, thanks for the tip,' said Simon Richards and he picked up the glass of Babycham from the bar counter and turned to offer it to the lady – only to find she had gone. He went cold. No one could have left the premises that quickly, and the door would have squeaked as it always did if she had opened it. Simon turned to George, who was chewing the end of a pencil as he looked at the crossword. 'George, she's gone!' Simon informed him.

George looked up. 'Who's gone?'

'The lady who was standing here a few seconds ago,' Simon replied, gazing at the ghostly fog beyond the windows. 'The one I bought the Babycham for.'

'She's probably gone to the toilet,' said George, and then he said, 'Here, you're good at words – what's the answer to this? Number 8 down – the clue is "For the seaside crystal gazer" and there's four letters in the first word and five in the second.'

Without hesitation, Simon said, 'Pier glass,' and looked at the spot where Fortuna had stood.

'A what glass?' George asked with a grimace of bafflement.

'Pier glass – a trumeau mirror,' Simon replied with impatience in his voice, and then the pub door opened with a squeak and in walked the young barmaid Anna. George looked at his 18-year-old employee and said, 'Do us a favour girl; go in the ladies and see if there's a woman in a blue dress in there.'

Without questioning the directive from George, Anna walked straight to the brown door at the end of the bar and pushed it open. She came back out shortly afterwards shaking her head. 'There's no one in there,' she said, and then she took her coat and scarf off and hung them in the little badly-lit cloakroom behind the bar.

'I told you,' Simon said to George, 'that woman disappeared – she was there one moment and then gone the next.'

'You trying to say she was a ghost?' asked George. He smiled but his eyes looked worried.

'All I know is that she seemed to just vanish,' shrugged Simon, and then a voice came from the other corner of the bar.

'She's a witch, that one,' said the old man playing Patience. Simon recalled how Fortuna had looked at him in a condescending manner shortly after she had made her entrance into the pub.

'A witch?' said George, 'It's getting worse, this,' he said, and gave a forced laugh, 'a ghost and now she's a witch.'

Simon picked up his newspaper, mindful of the tip the mysterious woman had given him, and then he walked to the old man in the corner. 'Why is she a witch?' he asked.

The elderly man gathered the playing cards and looked up. 'I'm eighty,' he said, and paused, 'don't look it do I?'

'No, you don't,' said Simon.

'No, I probably look ninety,' joked the old man, then he became serious and he said: 'I saw that woman in the blue dress in the Raven about twenty years ago. The Raven's an alehouse up in Low Hill. Anyway, she was with this fellah – he was a bit of a rogue – let's just leave it at that – and he came into an awful lot of money, and he started winning money left right and centre, on the horses, at poker – he fleeced me a few times – and they said it was because he was hanging around with Aggie.'

'Aggie?' Simon queried.

'Yeah, that's the name of that woman you were talking to,' said the old man, 'and I remember it because it was my 'arl lady's name. Any road, the lucky rogue's luck suddenly ended because he started seeing this girl, and he lost everything. His luck took a nosedive and he couldn't win an argument, and he ended up topping himself. He was a big man, and he put on a lot of weight. He tried to hang himself at a house in Kensington – tied one end of the rope round the top banister and then stuck the noose round his neck and jumped, and he was that fat, his head came off. A neighbour heard the bang next door, and her husband kicked the door in, and there was the body twitching away, and they said the blood was gushing out of the neck like a hosepipe on full blast – '

'Oh shut up, stop it!' cried Anna, from behind the bar, her hands over her ears.

'And if this was her – the woman I talked to, why is she a witch?' asked Simon, sitting down at the old man's table.

'Well there were rumours, like,' the old white-haired man replied, shuffling the cards, 'people said they remembered her years before, and she never got any older, and there was an old priest who said he remembered her back in the 1930s and I think she went under another name then, but she caused trouble then as well. I'm only telling you what I heard and what I remember and what I saw. That woman is the very same one I saw twenty years ago; she hasn't changed - not one wrinkle on her face.'

'People *love* mysteries, don't they?' George asked Anna, who was still imagining the headless suicide from her twisted expression. 'Look, all that's happened is this,' George said to Simon, 'you were talking to that woman, and she's gone out that door – and sometimes that door doesn't squeak. I've looked at customers in here, looked at the till and glanced back and they've vamoosed – some people dart about real fast. It's all in the mind all this ghost nonsense.'

'Are you trying to say I'm a liar then?' asked the old man, glaring at George.

'No, of course I'm not,' said George, his face blushing slightly, 'and I'm not saying what you've said didn't happen – I'm talking about Simon here, but look, it's like talking about religion and politics and sport isn't it? Everyone has their own views and it only causes people to argue.'

'There was something very odd about that woman's vanishing act, George,' said Simon, and he got up and headed for the door. The following day, the horse named Indiana won the St. Leger Stakes, and Simon had backed the runner out of curiosity. He told the publican George about the money he'd netted from the tip Fortuna had given him and the barman asked, 'Have you been drinking Bentox? You really think she was a ghost don't you? That old man was just a big Tom Pepper.'

On the following Saturday at the pub, the publican George was upstairs in bed with the flu, and only Anna was serving. George was standing at the bar, thinking, as usual, about his financial problems. Around 3pm, Fortuna walked in, and Simon saw her entrance in the reflection of the mirror behind the bar – and he froze for a moment. She looked solid unlike any witch or ghost he'd ever imagined. He turned and smiled at her, then thanked the lady for the horseracing tip. 'You left rather abruptly last time,' said Simon, 'may I get you the same again?'

'Oh thankyou,' said Fortuna, 'yes I'm sorry I left so quickly, but I thought I'd left my oven on.'

'And had you?' Simon asked.

A hard silent pause hung in the air.

'Er, no, I hadn't,' Fortuna said, and looked at her own reflection in the pub mirror.

Simon gave her the Babycham and this time she took the glass from him and sipped the drink. He walked with her to a quiet corner, and there he asked her if she really was Lady Luck. She nodded and told him in a very matter-of-fact fashion that she *was* a deity, but needed love and faith from a mortal to survive, as everyone had deserted the old gods. 'This is such an age of disbelief,' she said in a groaning voice, 'and the atheists – how I despise them; they know nothing whatsoever about this unending universe but they're so self-assured there's no Supreme Being. They are just as dogmatic as the Spanish Inquisition. I love to toy with them and puncture their little bubble world now and then. I have a wicked side you see.'

'And all you require is love – and acknowledgement?' said Simon, leaning in close to the extraordinary lady's face. He could see what looked like glitter in her pores; she seemed radiant.

'Yes, that's right – you're very perceptive – Simon Richards,' she said, with a smile that was the very essence of the feminine mystique to Simon.

'Ah, you know my name,' said Simon, a little taken aback.

She seemed to ignore his comment and went on about the gods and goddesses that once crowded the ancient world and 'the downfall of the theocracy' which she termed as 'the literal twilight of the gods'.

Fortuna and Simon ended up sitting in a quiet corner of the pub, and he could not get her drunk, even though he plied her with shorts for over an hour. One part of his mind thought she might just be a woman with delusions of being some deity, but he recalled the St. Leger tip and there was no doubting the otherworldliness of the lady.

'I will love you forever, Fortuna,' said a tipsy Simon after his sixth pint. She smiled and touched his nose with her index finger and whispered, 'Good luck be with you.'

Moments later she vanished as he staggered to the bar to get her another drink. Days later, Simon won £1,034 at the Top Rank Bingo Club on Prescot Road, and then his premium savings bond came up – and he netted £5,000. His debt problem was over, but he started placing fifty pound bets on the horses and he kept winning. He amassed a fortune, and decided to fly to Spain, where he met a beautiful young art student from a well-to-do family. Her name was Jacqueline Capel. He fell in love with the 20-year-old beauty, and lavished his newfound fortune upon her, and the couple decided they should live together. Jacqueline's rich uncle let her and Simon move into a luxurious home in Château d'Oex – a municipality in the canton of Vaud in Switzerland. One evening at his new home, Fortuna appeared to Simon, and he said, 'Fortuna, thankyou for all the good luck – you have even helped me to find something I had long given up on – a wife!'

'But you told me you would love *me* forever,' she told him in a broken voice, and seemed close to tears.

'I *will* always love you – ' Simon replied.

'Liar! Typical lying man! You're all the same!' she

cried, and threw her hands to her face as she sobbed.

'Is your name really Aggie?' Simon suddenly asked, and he posed the question to somehow offend her for trying to spoil his relationship with Jacqueline - but soon regretted asking it.

Her hands dropped from her face and a pair of eyes brimming with hate drilled through his very soul. 'What was that?' she asked.

'Nothing,' said Simon, 'look, let us remain friends – '

'Quiet!' she roared, and she seemed to stare at his forehead for a moment. 'You were told this by an old man, weren't you?'

Simon realised she had just read his mind.

'He said I was a witch,' said Fortuna, 'do you believe him?'

'Of course not, he was a silly old man!' Simon replied and wondered if she'd read his mind again.

'You believe him,' she said, 'after all I've done for you!'

'I don't believe you're a witch – you're Lady Luck!' Simon shouted, trying to drown out his own doubtful thoughts.

'That girlfriend won't be yours for long - I bring bad luck too!' she coldly informed Simon - and vanished. This time Simon witnessed the actual disappearance of the woman.

Sure enough, over the course of just a week, Jacqueline became very distant and eventually she told Simon she had met someone. Simon flew back to England and continued his gambling, but his luck ran out, and he lost all of his money to cards and horses. He returned to his favourite pub, and George told him a strange thing. A few weeks back, the old man who

184

had claimed the woman in the blue dress was a witch had cried out as he sat in the corner of the pub, and blood had gushed out of his nose. A blood vessel had burst in his brain, and as he lay there on the floor of the pub, George thought he had seen that woman – the so-called witch – standing over the old man. Simon Richards started to attend church and turned his back on gambling, and he eventually met and married a Southport woman. I have heard about the "lady in blue" many times since then – and she may very well be an immortal witch – it's hard to say, but what *is* her game? Does she amuse herself by toying with mortals (making them believe she's Lady Luck, for example), and is she really looking for love? If she is as old as some say she is, perhaps she continually finds herself needing new love when she outlives her lovers.

# WEIRD ABDUCTORS

One morning in early August 1963, a little girl named Mary left her home on Prince Alfred Road and ran across Wavertree Park, headed for her auntie's home on Rathbone Road. Mary was ten today and Auntie Marjorie always gave her money and had a big cake with pink icing and lit candles waiting for her on her birthday. Halfway across the park, the girl heard a voice behind her cry out, 'Mary! Mary! Quite contrary!'

The girl stopped and looked back. A smiling man with swept-back red hair in a pea-green suit was running towards Mary with a large brown sack. 'Come here, Mary, it won't hurt!' he laughed. The girl screamed and ran out of the park via Glynn Street. The man with the sack caught up with Mary on this street and grabbed her by her pigtails. As the girl screamed and kicked at the would-be abductor, a man with pebble glasses left a car parked at the top of the street and ran to Mary's aid shouting, 'Oi! Leave her alone!'

The sack-man ran back to the park and the spectacled saviour picked up Mary, asking, 'Are you alright?'

Mary nodded as she sobbed and the man led her to

his car and said, 'Come on, let me take you home.'

'No, it's alright, I'm going to my auntie's,' said Mary, but the man pushed her into the car via the rear passenger door and closed it. He got in and said, 'Where does your auntie live?'

'Rathbone Road,' Mary told him. She felt something under her feet. It was a girl, around her age, rolled up in a carpet across the floor between the front and rear seats. She looked as if she was asleep – or dead.

'Mary, Mary quite contrary,' said the driver, and Mary realised the man at the wheel had something to do with the man who had tried to grab her in the park, for he had come out with that same nursery rhyme phrase. The car swung into Eastdale Road, and in a state of mounting terror, Mary tried to open the car door but it was locked. The driver said to the 10-year-old: 'You'll never see your parents again, Mary.'

The girl slyly rolled down the window and somehow climbed out of the car headfirst as the vehicle was in transit, and Mary fell into the road on Long Lane, spraining her wrist. She ran off and reached her auntie's home in tears. A neighbour of Aunt Marjorie named Val asked Mary if the car had been pale blue, and the child nodded. Val said, 'He's a ghost, and he's been going for years. Him and his brother tried to snatch kids but they were caught and both committed suicide, and then their ghosts were seen, always around Wavertree Park.'

'I've never heard such rot - and I suppose the car's a ghost too?' asked a doubtful Marjorie.

Val made the sign of the cross and nodded, saying, 'Before God, Marjorie, it's true.'

And Val *was* telling the truth; the solid-looking

ghosts of the child-abducting duo are still occasionally seen, prowling Wavertree in a silent sky blue Vauxhall Cresta. When I mentioned this bizarre and chilling case on local radio many years ago, a woman named Fiona telephoned the station and said that in 1966, she had taken four children, two of her own and two belonging to her neighbours, to the "Shrimp Club" in Wavertree Baths on Picton Road. The Shrimp Club was so-called because it was for very young swimmers, and it was organised by Ronald Bland, who had been running the club for twenty years. The children who attended were encouraged to dog paddle at first and then they would eventually progress enough in swimming techniques to join the proper swimming club. On the Sunday Fiona took the children to the baths, she had seen a boy, aged 10 in tears outside the baths. He said a man "with funny glasses on" had tried to drag him into a car (which he described as being blue). Fiona took the boy home after she had dropped the four children off at the baths, and on the way to the boy's home she had seen the pale blue car come slowly down the High Street in Wavertree. It turned around and cruised alongside Fiona and the boy, and then a police car came tearing down the High Street with its roof-light flashing and a bell sounding, and that blue car took off and turned the corner into Eastdale Road. As Fiona watched the car make its getaway, she could not believe her eyes; the car slowly faded away until it was no longer visible. The police car screeched around the corner and drove straight through the spot where the car had inexplicably melted into thin air.

I am occasionally asked if there are ghosts of

inanimate objects, and the answer is yes – there are phantom planes that have been seen in the skies over Liverpool and elsewhere and there have been many reports made to me of ghostly trains and cars travelling about in the dead of night. For decades, a ghostly Number 25 bus was seen travelling down Grove Street in Edge Hill all hours in the morning, long after the normal bus services had ceased. Witnesses always noticed that the bus was brilliantly lit up inside but there was never any sign of a driver or a passenger onboard the vehicle. The ghostly abductor in the blue car was dismissed as a mere yarn by many at first as people could not believe a ghost could get around in a car, but the ghosts of the child snatchers have been seen by people from all walks of life over the years, along with the spectral sky blue Vauxhall Cresta.

Another strange would-be abductor was at large in Liverpool, not too far from the scene mentioned in the last story, and this was a very weird character known as "Mr Babboo".

In April 1971, Liverpool City Council decided not to renovate the old wartime "pillbox" in Clarke Gardens, Allerton, because it would have cost £250. The pillbox – built in 1940 - a concrete structure with embrasures through which soldiers could fire at any advancing invading Germans in WW2 – still stands today, and in 1971 it acquired a sinister reputation as the home of a peculiar-looking individual nicknamed Mr Babboo by children. Babboo was an old man who had a bizarre, grotesque-looking face with a huge nose. He wore a ridiculously small bowler hat, a dirty old raincoat with a carnation in the lapel, and he walked with an odd bow-legged gait, rather like a monkey. He could also run at a phenomenal speed on all fours. Most people thought Babboo was an urban legend, a mere bogeymen, but one day in the summer of 1971, three girls – all aged 15 – named Melanie, Angela and Dawn – were walking with their boyfriends down Springwood Avenue when one of the boys – a lad named Martin - pointed at the concrete pillbox through the railings of Clarke Gardens and claimed a man named Mr Babboo who was "half-man half-monster" lived there. The girls said Martin was a liar, so he shouted the name of the alleged figure of fear – and a man came running out of the pillbox towards the teens. This man uttered unintelligible gibberish as he scaled the railings and then he raced after the kids until he caught up with the screaming girls and embraced all three of them. He bear-hugged them as they yelled for help, but they managed to escape. Babboo chased them almost two miles until he was caught by two policemen on their beat near Allerton Library. The girls claimed Babboo had tried to strangle them and as the constables were taking the weird molester to Rose Lane Police Station he broke free and ran off – but was knocked down by a van. He lay there, trying to say something, but blood spurted out of his mouth and the girls screamed at this. Just before he died, he pointed to one of the three girls and said something, but the blood in his lungs and throat made him sound as if he was gargling. Babboo's eyes then rolled up into his head and he died, still pointing at the hysterical girls.

Weeks later, Mr Babboo's solid-looking ghost stalked the three girls and their boyfriends in Calderstones Park. The kids ran off in terror, but then

Babboo started appearing in the bedrooms of the three girls in the middle of the night, singing old songs (such as *Roll Out the Barrel*) and asking some of his victims if they'd marry him. An old school janitor recalled how Babboo had been seen during the war, when Allerton Hall was used as an officers' billet, and even in those days the weird man had looked old. One of the girls was so terrified of Babboo's nightly visits she suffered a seizure and had to be hospitalised and sedated, and the hauntings went on for a year then stopped abruptly. Some said it was hysteria, whilst others swore he was a real ghost and some say Mr Babboo still haunts that pillbox in Allerton.

The unearthly abductor comes in all forms, even as a figure of authority or a symbol of trust, as in the following story.

On the night of Sunday 21 June, 1964, at around midnight, a pretty Huyton girl of seventeen named Heidi Glenn stormed out of her boyfriend Joe's flat on Clarence Street in Liverpool city centre after a row. Heidi had accused Joe of being very friendly towards her friend Maria. Joe denied liking Maria at first, but after Heidi had nagged him about the matter for a while, he snapped, and in a raised voice he told Heidi: 'I tell you what, I wish you were as witty and smartly-dressed as Maria! You're just a lazy ornament who smokes all my ciggies and you haven't got a kind word to say about anyone!'

Heidi had put on her shoes and her coat and had promised Joe she was leaving for good and her boyfriend had yelled: 'I'm not coming after you this time, Heidi, and if you go through that door, don't bother coming back, it'll be no great loss!'

Heidi then left the ground-floor flat, slamming the front door behind her. The 17-year-old rather unrealistically intended to walk all the way from Clarence Street to her home on Woolfall Crescent in Huyton – a distance of almost six miles and a walking time of nearly two hours – during the hours of darkness when anyone could mug or rape her, or bundle her into a car. The girl marched along, driven by her temper, and she got as far as the Irish Centre on Mount Pleasant when a white car pulled up and a priest got out. With a trace of Irish brogue in his voice he shouted to Heidi, 'Hey young lady! What are you doing walking the streets at this ungodly hour?'

Heidi halted and walked to the priest. She told him about the row with her boyfriend, and how he'd been flirting with her friend, and she became choked up and ready to cry when the priest – who told her he was Father Wren - said, 'Don't start upsetting yourself and crying over that silly boyfriend. Here, do you smoke?' He produced a packet of cigarettes and a lighter. He lit two cigarettes at once and offered one to Heidi.

'Thanks Father, that's really kind of you,' said Heidi, and she sensed there was something very benevolent about Father Wren. She no longer felt sad in his presence.

'Where do you live?' the priest asked the girl.

'Huyton,' said Heidi, 'but I don't really want to go home. My mum and dad really get me down. They don't like my boyfriend and they've been telling me I should move back in with them and get a steady job in Huyton. I've been living with Joe on Clarence Street for a month and I've been working in a shop in town.'

'Alright, so here's what I'll do,' said Father Wren,

and with a pensive expression he exhaled the cigarette smoke as a perfect halo before telling Heidi: 'I'll take you to Bowring Marsh Night Refuge; it's - '

'What's that,' interrupted Heidi.

Father Wren explained. 'It's a place near Bowing Park for young girls who are in trouble. You know, girls who have run away from home because they've had a falling out with their mother and father or fallen pregnant and so on. You'd have your own little room until you get yourself sorted out.'

'Does it cost anything?' Heidi asked, realising she had only six shillings to her name.

'No, not a penny, run by a charity,' said the priest, and he flicked the cigarette through the air into the road and said, 'come on, let's get a move on.'

Heidi walked with him to the car when a blonde woman who looked as if she was in her twenties came across the road from the direction of Hope Street. She had wild-looking eyes. She shouted to Heidi: 'No, love! Don't go with him!'

Her outburst startled Heidi and the priest.

'He's not a priest!' she yelled in a hysterical voice bordering on a scream. 'He'll take you to a dungeon and torture you and murder you!'

'What the Hell are you talking about, you demented woman?' Father Wren shouted to the unknown lady.

'He tried to kill me but I escaped!' the woman with the wild-looking eyes told Heidi. Heidi wondered if the woman was telling the truth, and Father Wren made a sudden grab at Heidi but the girl threw the cigarette he had given her in his face and evaded his clutches by running off down Mount Pleasant. She hammered on the door of a nearby hotel and screamed 'Help!' as the priest shouted something unintelligible to her. A young man answered the door of the hotel. He wore a white shirt and black waistcoat. 'What's the matter? You're waking the guests up!' he said, looking Heidi up and down in a condescending manner.

Heidi couldn't get her words out for a moment because she was so scared, but then she gasped: 'A man is trying to get me into his car and he's dressed up as a priest!'

'He's not calling himself Father Wren is he?' asked the hotel staff member as he narrowed his eyes.

'Yes!' said Heidi, 'Do you know him?'

The hotel worker went out into the street, spotted Father Wren further up Mount Pleasant getting into his car, and then he saw a stone lying in the gutter and he gritted his teeth and picked it up. As Wren screeched past in his car, the hotel worker hurled the stone at the vehicle and it glanced off the roof. The bogus priest got clean away. The man from the hotel told Heidi to wait with him in the reception area as he called the police. A detective turned up later that morning and interviewed Heidi and the hotel worker, and asked them to describe the model of the car and if they had noted the vehicle's registration. Father Wren was not traced and it turned out that the Bowring Marsh Night Refuge the impostor had mentioned to Heidi was fictitious. The woman who had warned Heidi was never traced nor seen again, and the mystery does not end there, for there were further abduction attempts made by a man in a white car, and also in a green van – and sometimes he went disguised as a priest and always operated near Mount Pleasant. The years went by and the weird abductor never seemed to age. Some think the last encounter with him was in 2007 when he asked two young women on the streets one night if they'd like a lift home. He assured them he was a priest but the girls sensed there was something creepy about him and ran off.

From Liverpool we cross the Mersey to Wirral next, to a quiet country lane, where another weird abductor is lurking...

Two very traumatic incidents took place that summer in 1974, and Judy and Pauline – who are now both aged 58 – remember these events as if they had happened only last week. It was the first week of an infernally hot August, 1974, and Judy had received a Budgie bicycle for her birthday. She was giving her best friend Pauline a "takey" down Barnston Road when the girls witnessed a collision between two cars which led to the driver of one vehicle – and her three young children – being hospitalised in Clatterbridge. On the following day on the same stretch of Barnston Road, another alarming occurrence took place. The time was half-past eight, the sun had set, and twilight was creeping across the sky. At the Milner Road junction of Barnston Road, Pauline asked if she could ride the Budgie bike the two miles to her home on Sparks Lane and bring the bicycle back in the morning, but Judy shook her head and said, 'No way Pauline, my mum would go spare – I've only just got it for me birthday.'

And so, Pauline got on the back of the bicycle, about to ride as a 'pinion passenger' when a red convertible sports car of some sort came down Barnston Road from the north. Although the sun had gone down, the driver of this impressive-looking car wore a pair of shades, and he halted the sleek vehicle alongside the Budgie bike. Judy noticed the car had a left-hand drive. In a well-spoken voice the driver asked: 'Am I going the right way to Landican Road?'

'No, it's up there – that way!' shouted Pauline, pointing northwards – the direction the car had come from.

'Oh, I must have gone past it,' muttered the driver, and he turned the car around and the vehicle crawled slowly alongside the bicycle. 'Could one of you possibly get in and show me the way?' he queried with a good-natured smile.

'Yes, I'm going that way, anyway,' said Pauline, struggling to get off the bike, but Judy turned to her and gave her a strong disapproving glance. 'Pauline,' said Judy under her breath, 'don't get in his car – he could be a sex maniac or a murderer.'

'I'm no murderer or a sex maniac,' laughed the stranger – he'd obviously overheard Judy's whispered warning to her friend. 'I'm actually a circuit judge, so I'm on the right side of the law - but you *are* right, young lady, you shouldn't really accept a lift from a stranger.'

Pauline longed to ride in a car that looked as if it could go pretty fast and she got into the vehicle and the man said, 'Thankyou. So, it's straight up this road?'

Pauline nodded, and the car started to slowly accelerate. And then the driver turned right to look at Pauline close up, and when she saw his eyes she recoiled in terror. Behind the dark polarised glass the man's eyes were jet black with luminous blue irises!

Before Pauline could even try and jump out of the car there was a burst of speed and the inertia pressed the girl back into her seat as the sports car peeled rubber. The vehicle was travelling at an uncontrollable speed towards a fork in the road with Barnston Road on one side and Storeton Lane on the other. Pauline screamed because she thought the car was going to crash, but somehow the driver managed to negotiate the sudden bend in the road and the vehicle screeched and swerved down Storeton Lane, the side of the car missing a low sandstone wall by a few inches. Storeton Lane was narrow, and hedgerows and trees flashed past as a green-brown blur as the driver threw back his head and screamed with laughter. He took both hands off the steering wheel and seized Pauline's left hand and pressed something into her palm. The girl screamed as she felt an agonizing pain in her palm. When she looked at her hand she saw she had a black circle with a symbol in it branded into her palm. The car screeched on down Storeton Lane and continued on into Station Road, passing the old brickfields, and then it suddenly decelerated and came to a halt, and the maniac at the wheel turned to Pauline, pointed to her painful hand and said, 'I put my mark on you, and now your soul is mine!'

The door on Pauline's side of the vehicle opened by itself and the man shoved the girl out of the car and it tore off as he screamed with laughter. Pauline walked miles in tears that evening till she saw a worried Judy pedalling towards her on her bike. She told Judy what had happened and said she thought the man had been the Devil. For seven years the mark on Pauline's hand remained - it could not be washed off no matter how hard it was scrubbed - and throughout that period she had many vivid nightmares about the sinister lunatic until one day the "mark" vanished from Pauline's palm. Unknown to Pauline, the demonic driver had been encountered before on Barnston Road and Chester High Road, with reports going back to the 1950s. I have even found a case from the 19th century where a girl is given a ride to her home in Wittering Lane, Heswall, by a chivalrous dandy on horseback who brands her hand so she will become his "slave in the life to come". A folklorist might say these are just recurring archetypal urban legends – a convenient catchall explanation for anything beyond the periphery of our limited knowledge – but I think these entities are real, and I sincerely hope you will never meet them on your travels – unlike Sharon – back in the 1950s...

It was a pleasant warm Sunday evening at 10pm on 1 June 1958, and a full moon was shining down on Tarleton Street, that side street which runs from Church Street, alongside Marks & Spencer to Williamson Square in Liverpool's city centre. An engaged couple named Sharon and David, both 21, were window shopping – something you could do before the era of roller shutters on shop fronts. At some point David realised Sharon was no longer standing beside him and he turned to see her standing with her back towards him. Then he saw what his fiancée was gazing at: a circular opening in mid-air, about six feet above the pavement, and within this hole in the air a very sinister red glowing face was smiling at Sharon. He had a long turned-up moustache and swept back black hair. The right hand of the apparition was beckoning the young lady with a curl of its forefinger. Sharon seemed hypnotised by the weird vision, and David had to shake her. 'Sharon!' he shouted, and his hands grasped her left upper arm and she shook her.

'He said he wants me!' she cried, and let out a scream, and the Mephistophelian face in the circle in mid-air gritted his teeth and shot a look of pure hatred at the couple.

Sharon and David ran off and David did not look back until he and his girlfriend reached Williamson Square. He saw the beckoning entity had vanished, but there was a reddish cloud still hanging in the air at the spot where it had looked through that circular opening.

I mentioned this incident on a local radio show and two listeners contacted me to say that they too had seen the same unearthly 'ghost'. A woman named Maureen said she and her late husband Harry had visited a restaurant called South Pacific on Tarleton Street on 18 July 1970; Maureen remembered the date because they'd gone out to celebrate her husband's birthday. Harry bumped into an old friend outside the restaurant after the meal and while he chatted to him, Maureen wandered off. It was a busy Saturday night and there were people walking by just a few yards away. Maureen glanced down a narrow alleyway known as Leigh Street, and there, floating in mid air, was a point of bright light which transfixed her. All time seemed to stop, and Maureen heard a Scottish voice whisper, 'What a very fine lady. Come to me, Maureen, come on lass.'

Maureen then saw an orange-reddish smiling face appear and he waved at her and blew kisses. Maureen then felt herself being shaken, and realised Harry had hold of her. 'It was as if I'd been roused from a dream,' Maureen told me, 'and I felt a strange numbness in my head.' The face had vanished and it transpired that Harry had not seen the apparition but he had been alarmed at finding his wife wandering halfway down the dark alleyway of Leigh Street in a daze.

The second call I received at the radio station concerning the hypnotic entity of Tarelton Street came from a woman named Judi. She told me how, on 8 June 1990 at 11pm, she and her sister – Sue – had encountered the exact same thing as Maureen: a smiling red face materialising in mid air on Tarleton Street – and then the sisters had fled in fright. On this occasion the entity said nothing but Judi said there was a horrible feeling of "evilness" emanating from the face, and she mentioned the circular opening the thing was looking through, describing it as "like a porthole". All of these incidents took place during a full moon, which might just be a coincidence, and I'm at a loss to explain the weird manifestations. I wonder what would have become of the females if they had somehow accompanied the red devilish man to his domain?

One of the strangest stories I've researched concerning supernatural abductions has to be the following one. In January 1961, Liverpool was hit by a 'flu wave. The city's Medical Officer of Health, Professor Semple was asked by the *Liverpool Echo* if it was an influenza epidemic and the professor became very cagey, as if he did not want to cause a panic but admitted the 'flu wave was not abating and warned people to use handkerchiefs when they sneezed and to wash their hands to keep the spread of the flu virus under control. One of the outcomes of the widespread flu outbreak was the cut in the city bus services as the crews fell ill, and the Liverpool Passenger Transport Department announced that over twenty buses were currently unmanned at the depot and the number was ready to increase because of the spread of the influenza. A 22-year-old Garston man named Doug – who had been training to be a bus driver for just a matter of weeks – was nominated as an emergency driver, put in charge of a 79 bus and he quickly memorised the route. It was a cold but sunny January afternoon as Doug drove the 79 up the High Street in Wavertree, away from the city centre with a bus packed with passengers when he saw a large grey metal sign in the road with the word "DIVERSION" on it and an arrow pointing to Prince Alfred Road, which was to Doug's right. He checked his mirror and swung the bus right, passing the Thatched House pub and then he shouted to the passengers, 'There's a diversion folks, so I'll be going up Fir Lane and onto Church Road to the next stop by the Picton Clock!'

Some of the passengers who'd got up from their seats, ready to get off at the usual stop, grumbled and sat down again.

The bus's engine spluttered and died as it passed Hunter's Lane. 'Oh come on, don't start!' Doug complained to the dashboard, but the engine seemed to be dead. The conductor, a man in his fifties named Cyril, announced to the passengers, 'Just a bit of engine trouble, probably with the cold weather. We'll be moving again in a mo!'

Doug looked ahead – and saw the road was clear, and the road was also devoid of traffic behind him as he glanced in the mirror. He tried to restart the engine but it didn't respond or make a sound.

Out of nowhere came nine weird figures dressed in black hooded robes, and they surrounded the vehicle. The passengers shot bemused and puzzled looks at them, and as the driver tried to restart the bus, one of these strangely-attired people somehow gained access to the vehicle. In his hood he wore a black mask with two eye-holes in it, and he shouted, 'Do not attempt to leave! You are all under my power! You cannot leave! You will not even be able to get up out of your seat!'

The conductor, Cyril, suddenly closed his eyes and sat on the one vacant seat on the bottom deck.

Outside, the robed intruder's eight hooded colleagues were standing close to the bus with their arms reaching upwards. People began to feel drowsy, as if some knockout gas had been released in the bus. A 16-year-old girl named Kathy hid under a seat at the back of the bus on the top deck and heard the hooded man saying, 'Sleep, sleep, go to sleep.'

Kathy heard the man come upstairs saying, 'You are all feeling very sleepy.' She waited until he went to the front seats on the top deck, and she ran down the stairs, where everyone had their eyes closed.

Kathy sneaked off the bus, fled up Hunters Lane and looked back to see two of the sinister figures in black running after her. Upon reaching Church Road North, Kathy saw a policeman near the Coffee House pub, but she was so scared she was unable to shout to him. She ran up to the officer of the law and after panting and wheezing, the frightened girl gave out a garbled version of what had happened. The policeman told Kathy to stay put, and he hurried to Prince Alfred Road. When the policeman reached the bus he saw no hooded figures in black robes, but he did see something very strange. The driver and passengers on the bus were all sitting in their seats, eyes wide open, but with blank stares, and at first they did not react to the constable as he asked them what was wrong. They appeared to be in a trance - which they eventually all snapped out of after a few minutes - and not one of the passengers – or the conductor or driver - could remember the creepy robed men for about ten minutes, and then the recollections came flooding back.

'Why were you going this way if you're doing the 79 route?' the policeman asked Doug the driver, and the latter recalled the diversion sign. 'The diversion sign by the Thatched House sent me this way,' said Doug, and he looked about, still feeling a bit sleepy.

'Don't move from here,' the policeman instructed Doug, and then he went to the High Street and he could find no diversion sign. He returned with a colleague and asked Doug if he'd been drinking. 'No, of course not,' replied Doug, and he felt insulted by the question.

'And the engine just conked out, did it?' the policeman asked, and his eyes swivelled to meet the eyes of his colleague.

Doug tried the engine again – and this time it started first time and continued thrumming. 'It was dead as a doornail before, honest officer!' Doug told the policeman.

Cyril the conductor told the policeman about the people in black robes and masks and how they had surrounded the bus. The sceptical-looking policeman told the driver and the conductor: 'Few years ago there was a case where a driver and the conductor were fined thirty quid for being drunk. The driver had his licence endorsed and he was disqualified from driving for a year. Driving a public service vehicle whilst under the influence of drink is a very serious offence, as you must know.'

'Hey - I'm not bleedin' drunk!' yelled Doug, 'And neither is he!' he indicated Cyril with his thumb. 'Smell my breath!' Doug forcefully exhaled into the policeman's face.

'Do that again and I'll wrap a truncheon round your head,' growled the policeman, 'blowing your manky germs into my face!'

'Officer, ask any of the passengers – they'll tell you what we've told you,' Cyril insisted, 'it was those weird fellahs all in black. I know it sounds far-fetched – '

'Look, just button it and get this thing moving,' said the policeman, slapping his hand on the green bodywork of the bus, 'and if I see you two again with your barmy stories, I'll – look, just get a move on!' The ruffled policeman then marched away with his colleague.

'Isn't it marvellous eh?' Doug asked Cyril, his face flushed with anger. 'I thought he'd go and try and find those barmpots in the black gear but instead he quizzes *us* and insinuates we're pissed! I might take him to court for defamation – making out we were bevvied!'

'Just put it down to experience, lad,' said Cyril. 'That's the thing with coppers, they don't believe anyone; that's the way they train them; they'd doubt Our Lord.'

The bus vibrated, its exhaust pipe coughing black

smoke, and it heaved its way along the road and turned into leafy Fir Lane, then swung left onto Church Road. It rejoined its usual route on Childwall Road. At the canteen, Doug and Cyril gave an account of what had happened on Prince Alfred Road to the other drivers and conductors, and there were the usually grins and sceptical bemused looks, but one of the drivers – a man in his forties named Norman – said something which intrigued Doug and Cyril. Norman said, 'A few years ago, 1958 I think it was, I was doing your route Doug, and it was about twenty to twelve at night – a Saturday night, it was. I had the usual drunks onboard giving me lip downstairs, you know – a typical night. Anyway, you know that bend in Childwall Valley Road where it passes Chelwood Avenue?'

'Yeah, I know it,' Doug replied, nodding gently.

'Well just there it happened,' continued Norman, 'there's like a field to the right. Anyway, there was a big full moon out this night and it lit everywhere up. As I'm slowing the bus as I get to this bend, these three figures in dead long garments – like black gowns – came walking out into the road, blocking the way, and they had hoods on, and I couldn't see their faces. Anyway, as they walked out and stood there the bus lights went out – all the lecky – all the lights on both decks went out, and the engine went. I didn't apply the brakes, but something pushed against the front of the bus – as if it had hit a see-through wall. I went forward with the inertia and nearly came out my seat. A drunk who had been standing up downstairs went flying, cracked his head as he went down. People screamed; they thought I'd crashed. Anyway, more of these people in the long black robes came out of the shadows of the trees to the field on the right, and I thought, what the hell is going on? This woman then walked to the front of the bus, and she was well-dressed and well-spoken – I'd say she was about fifty-something, and she looked out the window at one of these weird fellahs – and he was only about six feet away now, and she shouted, 'In the name of Jesus Christ stay away from this bus!'

The drunk was on the floor, 'effin and blindin' and she kept saying, 'In the name of Jesus Christ, stay away from this bus!'

'And what happened?' asked an intrigued Cyril.

Norman told him. 'The fellah who was in front of the bus just turned and walked away, and then the others followed him, and they went to the field on the right, and all the lights came back on - and the engine - but then it stalled. I felt like killing the drunk on the floor because he told the lady to shut up and started swearing at her, so I got out me seat and I picked him up, and this Teddy boy helped me – and we threw him off the bus. But those figures just seemed to vanish. It was one of the creepiest things I ever saw.'

'It's just been Satanists,' said a driver on another table at the canteen, 'and what's happened is that you just happened to have a bit of trouble with the electrics and your mind has joined the two things up.'

'Bollocks!' replied Norman, 'I know there are coincidences but this was no coincidence – the electrics failed - and the engine – when that fellah and the others stood in the path of the bus. Why would everything work again when they walked away?'

'Well what were they gonna do, Norman – steal the bus and go to a Sabbath?' asked another driver in a mocking manner.

'Well I hope you run into them, mate,' said Norman, giving his questioner the two-finger gesture, 'see how funny you are then, eh?'

I mentioned the Prince Alfred Road incident on the *Billy Butler Show* on BBC Radio Merseyside and received many telephone calls, emails and letters from people who had heard of the case and some who claimed to have been on the bus that wintry day in January 1961. Some claimed the nine robed figures were disciples of Satan who had intended to torch the bus with all of the passengers as a type of sacrifice to their master, whereas others believed the cultists had wanted to take virgins for some bloodcurdling ritual. To this day the strange incident remains a mystery, and the motives of those nine enigmatic people continue to baffle me, but it is possible that they might have intended to abduct one or more of the passengers, perhaps to be used as sacrificial victims in some arcane rite.

# SOME CREEPY ADMIRERS

There's a fine line between a romantic admirer and a stalker. In this era of social media, the infatuated admirer can look most people up – be they famous or everyday folk – but so can a stalker, and he or she can find out an awful lot about their prey from online sources. Most people nowadays have Facebook pages, Twitter and LinkedIn accounts, with pictures of themselves and their homes splashed all over Instagram, TikTok, Snapchat and so on. Even before the social media era, there were some unbalanced stalkers who made the flesh crawl, and there is a report of one of these types of weird harassers in the *Liverpool Echo* dated 28 December 1990. In the article, headlined, 'Woman Haunted by Thief who Dials Fear', it states that a 46-year-old Netherley woman is being taunted by the man who stole her purse from her handbag as she queued at a greengrocer's shop in Belle Vale Shopping Centre. The frightening telephone calls from the thief started on the very day her purse was stolen. Her purloined purse had contained all of the woman's personal details – as well as £325 in cash (which included the five weeks of DSS payments the woman had received for her disabilities: diabetes, thrombosis and severe arthritis). The victim of the theft – named Mrs X by the *Echo* to preserve her anonymity – said the thief mentioned her by name in his first call when he said, 'Hello X, merry Christmas.'

The lady – who lived alone - then received five more calls from the eerie creep who even told her: 'We have been standing right next to you in the precinct.'

'You've had my money, now leave me alone!' Mrs X sobbed and broke down. The sinister caller then hung up. The police investigated the frightening calls and British Telecom tried to trace the caller, but I can find no more about the case in the newspaper archives. The cowardly thief who taunted the disabled woman in Netherley is just one of many cases where the telephone was used to stalk a person, but it would seem that some supernatural entities have also utilised the telephone network to menace a victim, and the following story is a case in point.

On the polar afternoon of Tuesday 9 February 1971, a 15-year-old Gateacre girl named Sandra was returning from school when she heard footsteps behind her. She turned and saw *that* man again. He looked as if he was in his early twenties, and he was crossing an unusually deserted Station Road as he hurried towards her with a faint grin on his face. She'd seen him waiting outside her school yesterday afternoon, and he'd been standing in the queue behind her at the newsagents last Saturday. She'd first noticed him a fortnight ago when she was swimming in Woolton Baths with her best friend Lynn. He hadn't even been in the water, but had been watching Sandra from the balcony.

Sandra's house was only twenty yards away now, so the girl dared to glance back, peeping out from the hood of her coat, and she saw him briefly look at her before he overtook her. As he passed the schoolgirl, she heard him whistle the recent Dave Edmunds pop chart hit, *I Hear You Knocking*.

Upon reaching her home, Sandra knocked, but there was no answer, and then she remembered her mother telling her that she'd be home late from work today. Sandra's father wouldn't be home until five, either. The girl fumbled for the keys in her coat pocket as she watched that very suspect man walk on down Station Road. She opened the door, nudged the meowing cat aside with her foot and then she slammed the door shut. She went into the living room, peeped out from behind the net curtains and scanned the road. The full moon was hanging low in the sky, adding an eerie aspect to the empty street. The telephone in the hallway started to ring, startling the teenager. She hurried to it and picked up the receiver. 'Hello?' she said.

'San-drah!' a man's voice sang to her, 'San-drah - I love you!'

Sandra's heart palpitated. 'Who's that?'

'Listen Tosher, you're a bit of alright – have you got a fellah?' asked the stranger. Sandra thought the voice sounded young – perhaps belonging to someone under twenty-five, and he did not sound Liverpudlian – he sounded accentless and almost well-to-do, the girl thought.

'I said *who* are you – ' Sandra was saying when the unknown caller interrupted her.

'Oi!' he exclaimed with a chuckle in his voice, 'Don't get your knickers in a twist dear girl! You're no bigger than sixpence worth of chips, Sandra, so don't go talking to me like that love or you'll get my winklepicker up your backside!'

'Dad,' Sandra shouted, pretending her father was home, 'there's a strange man on the phone here, saying he'll kick me!'

'Your 'arlfellah's not home yet, love,' laughed the creepy caller, adding, 'you can't kid a kidder.'

'My dad is home and he's going to phone the police right now!' Sandra told the nuisance caller and slammed down the handset. She picked it up and started to dial 999, and a voice said, 'Sorry love, the police are off today. Phone back tomorrow.' It was that sinister cold caller, putting on a voice. 'I'll be round to yours in a mo,' he said, and hung up.

Sandra dropped the handset and left it dangling from the table as she rushed to the door and put the bolt on. She went into the kitchen to make sure the window's casement stay was secure, and then she went to the telephone and listened – there was no purring sound; she felt as if the weirdo had somehow blocked the line so she couldn't call for help. This was 1971 and there were no mobile phones Sandra could use to call the police. She drew the curtains and wondered if she should go next door and tell old Mrs Simpson. There was a noise outside. The cat ran into the hallway and looked at the door. Someone was trying to get in. Sandra froze. The front door was being shaken now. Then there was a loud ran-tan-tan on the brass doorknocker. 'Sandra!' came a familiar voice. It was the girl's father, George. Sandra unbolted the door and opened it. In came her father and mother. They'd both been let off from work earlier than expected.

'Why did you have the door bolted?' her annoyed

dad asked, taking off his overcoat.

Sandra didn't know where to start, but she said: 'Oh, Dad this weird man called me on the phone and said all sorts of horrible things and said he'd kick me up my backside and I – '

'Be one of your barmy friends at school,' George told his daughter, then turned to his wife and said, 'Anyway as I was saying, fourteen hundred people have objected to them closing Gateacre rail station...'

The parents didn't seem to care about Sandra's ordeal. In those days, stalkers were called pests, and when Sandra told her mum Janet about the man who seemed to be following her everywhere, she smiled and told her daughter: 'He's probably just in love with you, pet; it happens.'

Then someone started leaving things on the doorstep almost every morning. Little teddy bears, roses, a bracelet, and even a ring (which Sandra's uncle – an antiques expert – dated to the 1930s). Sandra told her best friend Lynn about the 'admirer' and Lynn said: 'Sandy, it mightn't be that man you keep seeing everywhere – it could be someone else. How does he know your telephone number? You said it's ex-directory. I think it might be the postman. He's out early and he could be leaving the things on your doorstep. Could even be the milkman.'

'It's not them, Lynn,' Sandra replied with a shake of her head, 'but that's a good point you made – how *does* he know my number?'

On the following Saturday, 'Sandra and Lynn were out riding on their bikes when they saw that young man Sandra had suspected of being the pesterer, and Lynn decided to go and ask him straight if he was the man plaguing her friend, much to Sandra's annoyance.

'Why the bloody hell would I want to bother her for?' The man replied, looking Sandra up and down. 'She's just a kid,' he said with a sneer, 'and a plain-faced one at that!'

As the accused man walked off in a huff, Sandra glared at Lynn, then rode off, close to tears. That Saturday evening Sandra had to mind the house as her parents went to the pub, and Lynn kept her company. At 9pm the telephone rang and Sandra answered it.

'Hello Tosher, it's yours truly,' said a creepily familiar voice - and it seemed to have an echo to it, as if the caller was in some large empty room. 'Now, m'dear, I think it's time we met. I'll be round in a mo.'

Again, when Sandra tried to dial 999 she couldn't get through, and Lynn said: 'Let's go and stay at my house.'

'Nah, he has said he'll call round before but he never turns up,' Sandra told her worried friend, 'it's as if he just likes scaring me. I'm that sick of all this, I wish he would call round so I could give him a bunch of fives!'

Through the window, Lynn saw someone walking along outside on the street. In the brief glimpse she had of the shadowy person, he looked tall and seemed to be heading for the front gate of Sandra's house. Seconds later the girls heard someone at the door sing Sandra's name.

'Oh Sand-rah! It's me-hee!' announced the eerie voice at the front door.

Sandra clung on to Lynn in fright as she stood in the doorway of the living room, gazing at the silhouette in the window of the front door. A tall slim man of about thirty came *through that door* as if it wasn't there and he walked a few feet into the hallway before he halted. He held a rose. He wore a blazer with deckchair stripes and light-coloured trousers. His shiny black hair was parted laser-straight in the middle, and he smiled at the terrified girls and said, 'So, we meet at last!'

Sandra and Lynn simultaneously screamed and both turned and ran into the living room. Sandra bolted to the window and opened it, and she climbed out into the garden as Lynn screamed, 'Get off!' because the ghost had touched her arm with its ice-cold fingers.

The girls scrambled over a thorny hedge and ran across Mrs Simpson's garden with the ghost following. The hysterical teenagers did not stop running till they reached the pub where Sandra's parents were drinking with friends. The girls were not believed but when Sandra's mum and dad came home they found a single rose on the hallway floor and a sweet smell hung in the air. There were no more anonymous calls after that night and no more gifts were found on the doorstep. The ring, bracelet and teddy bears the ghost had left also inexplicably vanished. The identity of the obsessive ghost that stalked Sandra remains unknown, but I wonder if he'll take a shine to someone else? There was a case four years prior to the last one where another ghost was obsessed with a young lady, but this time the stalker from the spirit world was something of an old flame of the girl it haunted...

One warm September evening in 1967, two young women – Juliet and Emma - both aged twenty, were sitting in the latter's bedroom, listening to records, sipping QC Ruby wine, and chatting about boys when Emma suddenly mentioned Peter. The very mention of the name induced a glacial coldness in the pit of

Juliet's stomach, and a nervous tic was visible in the left cheek of her face. Juliet's mouth opened slightly as if she was about to speak, but there was just a sharp intake of breath, and then a pause.

'I'm sorry, I shouldn't have mentioned him Jules,' said Emma, looking sheepish. Five years ago, when Juliet was fifteen, she had started going out with a man named Peter who was 21. From what Emma could recall, he was a welder and very slender with peculiar haunting baby blue eyes. He always waited at the school gates for Juliet in hail, rain or snow and would drive her to town in a Jag. Juliet had fallen head over heels in love with Peter, and he was absolutely besotted by her. She stopped going to town with friends at weekends because of him. He was very possessive and got into trouble a few times with the police for thumping lads who had merely talked to Juliet. Juliet's teachers and parents told the girl the relationship would have to end because she was legally under-age and it was only a matter of time before the violent Peter killed someone in a jealous rage. Emma remembered the stories of Juliet sleeping with Peter and even being pregnant that were constantly circulating the school grapevine. Peter seemed to have a hypnotic hold over Juliet and one day he told her they were going to elope in the middle of the night and go to Gretna Green to be married. Then he tragically died in a fire after dropping a lit cigarette on his blanket as he slept. Juliet seemed to have a nervous breakdown, and she started speaking about him in the present tense – as if he was still alive. But back to this day in September 1967.

'Peter is dead and buried,' Juliet said coldly, and

seconds after she uttered these words the window burst open and a cold wind blasted through the bedroom, startling the girls. As Juliet rushed to close the window she told Emma, 'You shouldn't have brought him up – talking about the dead stirs them up!'

'It was just the wind – that's all,' Emma replied, with fear in her large brown eyes, 'just the wind.'

The following day, Juliet drove her new car into town and parked on Bold Street. She and Emma went into a café to meet a boy they both liked named Eddie. When the girls and Eddie came out the café an hour later Juliet yelped as she saw a daisy under the windscreen wiper of her car. She told Emma and Eddie that Peter had put it there.

'He's dead though, isn't he?' remarked Eddie, and he took a sidelong puzzled glance at Emma, then looked back at Juliet. 'That *is* the Peter you're referring to, isn't it?'

'He's haunting me – he won't let go,' said Juliet, and she gingerly removed the daisy from under the windscreen wiper as if it was a dead spider, and threw it in the gutter.

Eddie found Juliet's strange behaviour creepy and he politely made an excuse to leave. Juliet told Emma that whilst picnicking with Peter years ago she had picked up a daisy and said, 'As long as these come up, I'll always love you.' Peter had pressed that daisy in a Bible, and he had tearfully told Juliet he'd cherish it till the day he died as a symbol of their everlasting love.

A week later the girls were coming out the same café when they saw a pallid-looking Peter standing there, holding a daisy. 'You're still mine,' he said, but Juliet screamed, 'You're dead! Leave me alone!'

Peter's ghost closed its eyes, bowed its head, and as tears fell from the closed eyes, the sad spectre faded away. Juliet was never visited by the heartbroken ghost again but I hear Peter's shade occasionally haunts young ladies who bare a strong resemblance to Juliet. When I mentioned this ghost on a local radio programme where I was a guest chatting about the supernatural, Emma – the lady mentioned in the story – telephoned the station and said she had been Juliet's best friend and she had indeed seen the ghost that day on Bold Street, and the memory of it had haunted her for years. Emma had no idea if Juliet was still alive or dead, for she had lost contact with her in the 1970s when Emma had moved to Canada for a few years.

Ghosts that haunt specific places are bad enough, but at least you can get away from them by simply leaving the haunted location; with a person-centred haunting it can be almost impossible to get away from an entity, and this type of ghost plagued a Wirral woman many years ago. It all started on perhaps the happiest day of her life – her wedding day – at a certain church in Bebington in 1968. The woman, 25-year-old Barbara Holt, stood beside her intended husband Lewis Dempster in a beautiful creamy white floral lace gown, covered in silvery pearls, and she wore an ivory Juliet cap upon her perfectly styled Titian-red hair. She was the very picture of elegance, and Barbara's parents surveyed their daughter from the front bench with a mixture of pride and sadness, whereas the bride's friends Moira and Patricia were washed out with jealousy; they both longed for a wedding such as this. The church was packed, and in the middle of the marriage ceremony, the vicar said to the bridegroom: 'Will you, Lewis Dempster, take Barbara Holt to be your wife?'

'I will,' said Lewis. He sounded a little tense and nervous.

The vicar continued to question the bridegroom: 'Will you love her, comfort her, honour and protect her, and, forsaking all others, be faithful to her as long as you both shall live?'

'I will,' said Lewis.

'You better! She's beautiful!' came a child's voice from somewhere in the packed pews. There were stifled chuckles, sharp intakes of breath, and the nettled vicar saw a boy – aged about seven or eight – standing about seven feet away to his left in the transept of the church. He wore black shorts, grey school pullover, and this little outspoken imp had a cherubic face and a head of golden hair. 'How dare you interrupt this marriage service,' gasped the vicar, and he turned to the congregation and asked, 'who does he belong to?'

People looked at one another and shrugged, and then the vicar noticed that the cheeky child had apparently left the church. After the service, at the wedding reception people mentioned the amusing interruption by that kid, but no one seemed to know whose boy he was. Barbara and Lewis honeymooned in Paris for just a week, and then they came home and settled down to their brand new married life at a house on Bebington's Acres Road. Lewis worked as a bus driver and Barbara got a job as a secretary and shorthand typist at an insurance company over in Liverpool. Six months into the job, the personnel manager – a 45-year-old man named Leo – started to make romantic overtures to Barbara, and at first she made it clear to Leo that she was a happily-married woman, but Leo persisted, and one evening in the car park as they were getting ready to go home he hugged her from behind and started to kiss her neck. She turned and kissed him back and she burned with guilt at first, but at some point Barbara was overwhelmed by Leo and she ended up going to his home – which happened to be in Woodhey Road - half a mile from her own home. And so began the affair. She told Lewis she was going out with her friends from work one evening and he believed her, but Barbara spent the night with Leo, and as they lay in bed at midnight, embracing one another with just the light of the moon streaming into the bedroom, they both heard a noise; it sounded like faint footsteps. A head popped up at the bottom of the bed, making the couple jump. It was a child, mostly in silhouette, but Barbara could make out his blond hair. 'I thought you loved Lewis!' said the boy, sounding upset, and for a moment Leo thought the child was some trespasser – but then the boy vanished into thin air. Barbara screamed and Leo clicked on the bedside lamp, then gingerly got out the bed and switched on the ceiling light. He looked about, thinking the boy might still be there, and then he went onto the landing and Barbara followed close behind in a terrified state. She suddenly recalled that blond boy who had interrupted the wedding service – and went cold; that's how he knew who Lewis was. She had to go home to her husband. Leo begged her to stay but Barbara went home, and Lewis asked her how the night had gone. Barbara said it had been a damp squib because it hadn't been the same without him. That night she clung to Lewis in bed, as she was scared the ghostly boy would appear again.

On the following morning back at work, Leo visited Barbara at her office and talked about the ghostly boy. She told Leo the affair was over and that she had been pressured into it by him in the first place. Leo left in a huff. When Barbara returned home around 6pm, Lewis said, 'You'll never guess who passed me on the street outside before, love – that boy who interrupted the wedding.'

Barbara shuddered when she heard this. That evening as she was looking for a dress in her room she caught a glimpse of the boy, hiding in the wardrobe and she stopped searching for the dress and fled from the room. He haunted her for weeks, and the last time Barbara saw him was on Town Lane one sunny afternoon as she passed the gates of Bebington Cemetery. He stood there for a moment, smiled, and then he waved. Why he chose to haunt Barbara remains a mystery, as is the ghost's identity.

# THE EXTRA

I've changed a few names in this story for legal reasons, but the story that was originally related to me by the girlfriend of the television extra in this account was researched thoroughly by me and I also interviewed and re-interviewed the extra on many occasions over a year and he never changed a word of his story. The backdrop to this incident is the Liverpool Playhouse Theatre – a place that is over 150 years old, has many ghosts, and has been the scene of some very strange goings on over the years. Without further ado here is the story I'm referring to.

He was on a high that night in July 1993. Mick Smith had been on millions of TV screens across the country as an extra on the topical Channel 4 soap *Brookside*. He'd replayed his four-seconds of fame over and over to his long-suffering girlfriend Lisa on the video recorder, and when she laughingly warned him he'd snap the tape or wear it out, he accused her of being jealous of his "breakthrough". 'I don't knock you and your dreams of winning *Stars In Their Eyes* do I?' Mick asked his girlfriend, sounding all choked up. 'And I don't laugh when your voice goes out of tune do I Lisa?'

Lisa left the room and went to get her coat. She

looked as if she was ready to cry. Mick ran after her and stopped her in the hallway. He took her coat off her and put it back on the hook. 'I'm sorry, Lisa, but you know how important my work is to me,' he said, 'and you know I'm right behind you with your singing ambition.'

'You said – ' Lisa's throat closed up with sorrow and she found it hard to continue talking. 'You said my voice goes out of tune,' and she started to silently cry. The tears came from her huge closed eyes.

'I was lying, Lisa,' backtracked Mick, hugging her hard, 'I only said it because I thought you were laughing at me because I kept playing back my scene on the video. I say horrible things when I'm hurt, but I didn't mean it!'

'Don't – don't say things like that,' she sobbed into his chest. 'I haven't got much confidence as it is after that other fellah.' She was referring to her previous boyfriend David, who physically abused her for years and had often mocked her attempts at karaoke.

Mick took Lisa out to see a musical. It was the opening night of *Only the Lonely* featuring Roy Orbison soundalike Larry Branson at the Liverpool Playhouse. All the way through the musical Mick said, 'I could do Orbison better than that,' and at one point he was almost thrown out the Playhouse by a burly theatregoer as he told an embarrassed Lisa how he should replace Joe McGann in the TV comedy *The Upper Hand*. When the couple left the theatre, Lisa growled, 'All you talked about was you, Mick. I couldn't hear a word of the play; people were giving us daggers! You ruined a good night out.'

'I started talking because it was a terrible play; dead

corny. The actors were wooden – they didn't even know how to move and how to throw their voices. Anyway, let's go the Everyman Bistro and mingle with proper actors.'

They walked through the warm July night to the basement bistro beneath the Everyman Theatre on Hope Street, where Mick stood at the bar telling bemused thespians and anyone who would listen that his stage name was Richard de Bourgeois and how he'd upstaged actors on *Brookside* and how the new BBC soap *Eldorado* had flopped because he had been turned down for a major role in it. He also talked about his idea for a detective series called *Striker* about a professional footballer who moonlights as a private eye and how he was ready to show his treatment to Jimmy Nail. Lisa had to kick him in the ankle to stop him from telling further fibs. He cornered an actor who had appeared in Alan Bleasedale's classic TV drama series *Boys from the Blackstuff* and advised him to move to Australia to get a regular part in *Neighbours*. The most cringeworthy moment for Lisa was when Mick spotted the TV and stage actor Drew Schofield among a group of other actors in the bar. Mick told Schofield he was the best John Lennon he'd ever seen on stage in the musical *Imagine*, but advised him to be a bit more nasal the next time he played the late Beatle. Lisa just wanted to walk out of the place that night because she was so embarrassed by Mick's inflated ego. Mick drank a bit too much that night, and came sobbing out the toilets at midnight. 'I'll never make it, I'm too old,' he said, and Lisa held him and said, 'Thirty is not old.'

'Do you think I'll ever make it, love? Be honest? Be

brutally honest,' he cried.

'No!' came an echoing reply from some joker in the toilets who had overheard Mick's question.

'You've been in Brookie haven't you? That's just the start, Mick,' a squiffy Lisa told him, and she led him out of the Bistro by the hand. They walked into a thick ectoplasmic fog that had rolled onto Hope Street, and now Mick was full of optimism again. The tipsy couple staggered about, stopping at a crowded takeaway for kebabs at one point to gab garbled nonsense. They continued to discuss their stellar aspirations when they came out the takeaway, with Mick going into Marlon Brando character mode every now and then. By the time the couple reached the bus gyratory on Queen's Square, the buses had stopped running and they realised it was ten past one in the morning. The couple crossed Williamson Square, and lingered in front of the Liverpool Playhouse.

'Your name will be up there on the front of that theatre one day, Mick,' said Lisa, looking at the classical stuccoed facade of the three-storey building. Lisa pinched a few inches of the air with her finger and thumb and slowly swept her hand through the fog-laden air, tracing out an imaginary banner. 'It'll say, Richard de Bourgeois – starring in – whatever the play's called.'

'*Death of a Salesman*,' announced Mick, 'that would be my dream come true, that. That, and marrying you Lisa.'

'Ah, you charmer.' Lisa sympathetically placed her hand on his head and rubbed his wispy hair. 'You'll do it, Mick. What's that play you wanna be in about, anyway?'

'Er, well, it's about a salesman, and he dies, like,' said Mick, struggling to recall what the play was about. He had a copy of the play he liked to carry around but he hadn't actually read any of it yet. He had gone into the Everyman Theatre with the play under his arm many times, picked up a few leaflets about forthcoming plays in the foyer before walking back out onto Hope Street, pretending he'd just left the rehearsals of some Willy Russell play.

'You'll end up in Hollywood and I'll be singing in Las Vegas,' Lisa told him, and she started to sway like a palm tree.

'You know who you reminded me of then, as you turned a certain way?' Mick asked, all gooey eyed. The ethyl alcohol was making him treacly sentimental.

'Who?' Lisa asked, 'Cher?'

'Nah! Cher's a brunette – you're a blonde – a bottle blonde like, but you suit it,' said Mick, insensitively. 'Anyway, you reminded me then of that Mariella Froth – frosh –' he stuttered as he tried to get the surname out. The alcohol in his brain wasn't helping.

'Mariella Frostrup?' said Lisa with a look of disgust.

'Yeah,' said Mick, and reading his girlfriend's repugnant expression, he smiled in an effort to reassure her the comparison was sound and said, 'Hey, she's one sexy lady. She's got this sort of hoarse, gravelly voice – '

'I look nothing like her!' Lisa fumed, 'And I've got a good voice, me!'

'I know you don't look or sound like her you blert; just *then* – just at a certain angle,' back-pedalled Mick. He walked a little nearer to the theatre and looked up – actually seeing that imaginary banner, advertising him in the Arthur Miller play – across the frontage – all in his mind's eye. 'I'd sell my bleedin' soul to make it, I would!' he told Lisa in a broken voice, and he sounded as if he really meant it.

They walked away, and turned left into Houghton Street, which seemed unusually thick with fog.

'Now is the winter of his discontent!' shouted Mick, misquoting Shakespeare. 'My kingdom for a horse!'

The stage door of the Liverpool Playhouse, a few feet to the left of the couple, suddenly opened, and faint rays of light raked the fog and caught the attention of Mick. He halted and turned to see a shadowy man framed in the doorway. This man cried out in what was obviously a theatrically-trained voice 'Ah, it is you! You were in Brookside were you not? You're just what we're looking for! Come in!'

'Don't go in,' said Lisa, eyeing the silhouette, but the man came out and he grabbed Mick's forearm and then he ushered the couple into the theatre. The stage door slammed behind Mick and Lisa and the man, who was dressed in a black polo-neck sweater, black straight trousers and shiny black slip-ons, led them through white-walled corridors until they were on the stage. There was a guillotine erected on the well-lit stage, and Mick was baffled by its presence.

'Mick, a certain talent scout has been following you around – ' said the man in black, pinching his chin between his finger and thumb as he eyed the extra with raised eyebrows.

'What?' Mick's surprised face turned first to the stranger and then to Lisa, who was looking very sceptical at the black-clad man. Through the fog of alcohol she could hear the bells of the warning buoys in her brain's suspicion centre.

The mysterious man started to pace up and down the stage in front of the guillotine as he said: 'I'll be honest with you Mick – you're a rough diamond – but you possess talent and charisma, and you need to be cut and polished if your talent is to sparkle. Acting is an extremely overcrowded business and you have to really shine to get noticed.'

'Excuse me, mate,' Lisa addressed the man, 'but *who* are you?'

'Lisa, don't be cheeky!' Mick whispered through clenched teeth.

The man stopped pacing and smiled at Lisa. 'I'm just a producer, love, and may I ask what *you* do?'

'I work in a shop,' Lisa replied, 'called What Everyone Wants on Lord Street – but I hope to be a singer in the near future, and I made a demo record last year. What's your name?'

'Michael Goodrich,' he replied, ' now, getting back to Mick here – '

'Why is the theatre open this time at night?' Lisa wanted to know.

Mick turned and glared at his girlfriend. 'Lisa! Let Mr Goodrich speak, please.'

Goodrich smiled at the couple and said, 'No, Mick, that's a very good question – why *are* we working so late? Well, let me answer that. I take it that you're pretty well-read regarding the classical dramatists?'

Mick nodded, 'Of course, I'm always reading them.'

Goodrich leaned against the guillotine. 'You must have heard of a very controversial writer called the Marquis de Sade?'

Mick returned a blank look. 'The name does ring a

bell somewhere at the back of my mind,' he lied.

'Well, let me refresh your memory, Mick,' said Goodrich, walking upstage towards him. 'The Marquis de Sade was a French nobleman – '

Mick smiled and nodded slowly – as if he now recalled who Goodrich was talking about.

'But!' cried Goodrich, 'He was also a writer of warped, erotic stories, some of them so shocking, he was incarcerated in the Bastille and even spent 32 years of his life in various lunatic asylums. He claimed to be the freest man in the world, unrestrained by religion, morality or even the law. He was the ultimate libertine. The word *sadist* is derived from his name, because he loved inflicting pain. He hired a poor poverty-stricken lady named Rose Keller on the pretence of wanting her to be his housekeeper, but he stripped her naked, tied her down with her four limbs tethered to the bedposts – and after he had whipped her, he rubbed some caustic irritant into her skin and also poured hot candle wax onto her. He was in the habit of hiring prostitutes and inflicting terrible harm to them for sexual kicks.'

'I think we should go, Mick,' said Lisa in a frightened voice, 'I don't like all this crap.' She looked at Goodrich, who seemed annoyed at being interrupted, adding, 'And *he* looks weird.'

'Lisa, let's just hear the man out,' said Mick, grabbing Lisa's arm as she tried to walk away.

Goodrich folded his arms and looked at the floor of the stage with his large hooded eyelids half closed in resignation. 'I suppose I *am* weird; I'm certainly not your ordinary run-of-the-mill producer, but anyway, to answer your original question: we are working late because the actor who was supposed to play the part of the executioner in a newly-discovered Marquis de Sade play has left the production because of artistic differences.'

'Oh,' Mick was surprised. 'Sounds like a big part, too.'

Goodrich nodded vigorously. 'It's a tremendous part. The play is called *La fin d'Élisabeth* - '

'The End of Elizabeth?' Lisa cut in, and again she made motions to leave the stage but Mick kept her there. 'Have you got worms, Lisa? Keep still!' Mick moaned.

'Very good Lisa – do you speak French?' Goodrich queried, thinning his eyes as he regarded Mick's pretty girlfriend.

'Just a little bit,' she replied, and turned to Mick and with great impatience she said, 'Mick this stinks to me. I have a really bad feeling about all this, now let's get the fu-'

'Mick!' interrupted Goodrich, 'You are welcome to leave, but they say when opportunity calls, don't knock it, and you'll probably never get another opportunity like this if you lived to be a hundred. There are actors out there who'd kill to get this role. It's even more important than the role of the Lord High Executioner in *The Mikado*. You chop off the heads of fifty women in this play with that guillotine, and you are in almost every scene, including the last one where you have to behead your lover Élisabeth. It is one of the most electrifying scenes in the history of the theatre – and you will be famous overnight for playing it for the first time on the English stage.'

'Wowza,' was Mick's underwhelming response.

Goodrich went to the edge of the stage and picked up a dog-eared manuscript. He struck it hard with the back of his hand. '*La fin d'Élisabeth*! The most romantic, horrific, thought-provoking play in the Western World! The audience will either faint from the beheadings in their seats or die of a broken heart when they get home, such is the power of de Sade! Top Hollywood directors will buy this for millions and the big stars of Beverly Hills will fight for these roles, especially the role of the executioner Chevalier Michael Forgeron!'

'Custy,' said an orgasmically impressed Mick, but he noticed Lisa's mouth was wide open. She seemed to be in shock.

'Michael Forgeron?' she muttered, 'That's Michael Smith in French - Mick's name! And my name's Elisabeth, but I call myself Lisa – oh my God!'

As soon as Lisa mentioned the word God, an awful groan filled the theatre, and the lights in the auditorium went up to reveal an audience of what seemed to be men and women in smart tuxedos and dresses – but they all had skulls for heads, and the jaws of those skulls were opening wide as they booed and shouted, 'Get off!' at what they were seeing on the stage. Mick knew the seating capacity of the theatre was 760 and he could not see one vacant seat in the dress circle, the stalls, or the upper circle. Lisa screamed and this time she succeeded in pulling Mick a few feet with her as she tried to get off the stage.

Goodrich ran to Lisa, dragged her from her boyfriend and he put her on the guillotine. Mick was a born coward where physical confrontations were concerned, and even though he was slightly drunk, he was that scared, his knees became weak as he tried to stop Goodrich. Surely, the producer was just demonstrating a scene from the play and he obviously wasn't going to kill Lisa? That guillotine was obviously just a harmless prop with a blade made of rubber - surely? Mick wanted to believe this, but he screamed, 'Stop that!' when he saw Goodrich put Lisa's head on the block of the guillotine, grab her long golden hair and throw it forwards out the way of the blade, then clamp the wooden frame called the lunette onto her neck.

'Mick! Stop him!' Lisa yelled, and she tried to pull her head out of the contraption and panicked when she realised she was trapped face-down in it.

'Make a clean slice of it and you'll go to Hollywood!' said Goodrich, and he pointed to the lever which would release the blade. 'Pull it!'

'You're insane!' Mick made a fist and got ready to punch the so-called producer, and the dead audience of 760 skeletons roared with laughter and clapped their bony hands.

'Mick! Think of all the famous stars who have passed through this theatre and made it big in Hollywood!' shouted Goodrich.

'Mick! Get me out of here!' screamed Lisa.

'Alec Guinness! Anthony Hopkins!' shouted Goodrich over the riotous audience. 'Richard Burton! Michael Redgrave! Robert Donat! And now you! You will go to Hollywood and be an overnight sensation! Richard de Bourgeois - star of the silver screen!'

'I can't – I love her! I'd rather be a nobody!' Mick Smith bawled back at the sinister tempter with tears in his eyes.

'Pull the lever!' Goodrich ordered him, and Mick felt as if some hypnotic force was being exerted by the devil standing before him, because he had a weird compulsion to pull the lever and released the blade to slice off Lisa's head.

'Jesus Christ – no!' roared Mick, and the audience booed. Mick threw himself down and he somehow managed to undo the lunette frame of the guillotine and he pulled Lisa's head out of it – but he heard a cheer go up from the audience of bony corpses – and realised with horror that the blade was falling with a grating sound. He dragged Lisa from the death machine and the blade took off almost a foot of his girlfriend's blonde hair as her head was pulled from the lethal spot.

'Spineless, gutless coward!' Goodrich growled, and the unearthly audience booed and swore at the couple as they exited the stage via the right wing of the stage. Mick fell over some prop and Lisa dragged him to his feet. They couldn't see anyone following them as they made it to the stage door. They opened the heavy slow door and ran through the fog. Lisa fell over on Clayton Square and two policemen approached out of the netherworld of the opaque fog.

'Been drinking has she?' queried one of the policemen, and as Mick picked her up, he said, 'Listen, there's a bleedin' maniac in the Playhouse, and he just tried to top my girlfriend with a guillotine!'

'I think you've been on more than the ale tonight, mate,' said the second copper.

'Officer, I *have* had a few slurps tonight but what happened to me and my girl in that theatre has sobered me up. Please go and investigate! I don't know how he got in the place but he's a psycho and he wanted me to guillotine Lisa!'

'Look, get home before I nick you,' said the first policeman, and then he was distracted as a call came through on the "babbling brooch" – the little two-way radio speaker mounted on his lapel.

Mick and Lisa realised no one would believe their story, and they walked as far as the Adelphi Hotel and got a taxi at the rank there. The couple stayed up all night going over what had happened, and whilst trying to explain and rationalise the incident, Lisa kept looking at her new short 'haircut' in the mirror. They looked at the weird mystery from every conceivable angle but they just went in circles. At 7:30am, the couple started falling asleep in one another's arms on the sofa, and Mick yawned and said, 'Something supernatural tested my love for you last night, love; something evil, and thank God I put you before my horrible craving for fame.'

And Lisa smiled as the two of them drifted off into the soothing world of sleep.

# THE GIRL WITH DEBBIE'S FACE

One of the most fascinating – and unnerving – entities in the world of the supernatural is the doppelgänger – a German loanword meaning "double walker" – and it refers to exact doubles of people that have been seen in mysterious circumstances over the centuries. A doppelgänger – also known as a fetch and a wraith – is not just an exact double of a person (although statistically, everyone must have a lookalike or two somewhere in the world) – it is a sinister paranormal entity which seems to deliberately *copy* its flesh and blood counterpart for some eerie, ulterior motive. We've already covered a doppelgänger case of this type in the chapter entitled *The Fetch* in this very book, but there are two others I feel I must mention. A case in point that comes to mind straight away is the doppelgänger of the late actor Jon Pertwee that was seen by scores of people on a train leaving Birkenhead Central for Liverpool at noon on Wednesday 18 March 1992. Many of those on the train were travelling over to Liverpool to see the real Jon Pertwee at WH Smith, where the former Doctor Who was signing copies of his video *The Pertwee Years*. People on the train asked the double for an autograph, thinking he

234

was the real actor, but the clone of Pertwee did not react nor speak. Stranger still, the living replica of the actor turned up at WH Smith and disrupted the signing at one point, and when the real Jon Pertwee set eyes on his dead ringer he told several of the people present that this living replica of himself had stalked him on and off for several years and it had a habit of vanishing whenever he or anyone else confronted it – and to prove a point, the actor got up from the table where he'd been signing copies of the video and approached his duplicate – and the entity gave a creepy smile – before literally vanishing into thin air. Some of those present who did not see the shocking vanishing act thought the whole thing was some publicity stunt, but I have interviewed many people who attended that signing and they all said Pertwee was haunted by some ghost of himself.

For reasons that will become obvious, I've changed the names in the following account of another doppelgänger – that of a young Wirral policewoman. WPC Deborah Courcy – aged 22 - and a male colleague were called out by residents on a certain housing estate in Birkenhead one night in April 1999 because a gang of youths had been throwing stones through windows and setting wheelie bins on fire. The main agitator among the gang was a 22year-old girl named Debbie, but whenever the police turned up she'd always go to ground in a flash and manage to make herself scarce. The police who had chased Debbie noted that the girl bore a striking resemblance to WPC Deborah Courcy, and during a disturbance one night on the Birkenhead estate, WPC Courcy finally collared the delinquent Debbie – and got the shock of her life. Debbie was an exact double of the policewoman. She wore a hooded coat when she was caught, but when Courcy told her to remove the hood, the WPC saw that Debbie even had the same shade of red hair as herself. 'What's your second name, Debbie,' asked WPC Courcy, and Debbie smiled and said, 'Courcy.'

The policewoman thought her double was just joking, but then she asked her where she lived, and the address Debbie came out with was the address of the house Deborah Courcy had been brought up in before she and her family had left three years ago. 'What's your National Insurance Number?' a policeman asked the 'second' Debbie, thinking he'd catch her out – but the number the carbon copy Debbie quoted was the policewoman's National Insurance Number. One of the residents on the estate – a Mrs McKay - told the WPC that Debbie had broken into her home a few days ago, trying to find money to finance her heroin habit, and then Mrs McKay noticed how much the accused resembled the policewoman and she asked the WPC, 'Are you related to her?'

The only difference between the two women was the slight tan the policewoman had, whereas Debbie the offender looked rather pale. 'We'll soon get to the bottom of this malarkey down at the station,' said WPC Courcy's colleague, and he turned and opened the door of his patrol car, ready to take the twin of his associate into custody – only to discover that she had vanished. WPC Courcy stood there with her mouth slightly open and a look of shock in her eyes. 'She disappeared,' said the policewoman. It was impossible for the other Debbie Courcy to have run off, as the police officers were standing in the middle of a wide open green space. Where then, had Debbie Courcy gone?

WPC Courcy drove to her old house, but an old widowed woman lived there, and knew of no one named Debbie. No trace of the other Deborah Courcy was found, and WPC Courcy was left with the impression that she had somehow met a version of herself who had chosen crime and drugs. 'There but for the grace of God go I,' she enigmatically remarked to her colleague with a faraway look. After that day Debbie never saw her doppelgänger again.

# GHOSTLY SHADOWS
# OF OLD CRIMES

Most crimes, by their very nature traumatise the victim, whether it's a burglary or the much more serious crimes of rape and murder, and I have noticed in my investigations into numerous ghosts over the years, that the victims of some crimes seem to generate a type of 'after image' or emotional print at the scene of the offence. This dark imprint left in the aftermath of some shocking or murderous act may remain at the location of a crime like an invisible but indelible stain for years. This chapter is concerned with these 'shadows of old crimes' and I will begin by relating a case in Wirral.

Because of the controversial nature of this story I have changed a few names to preserve confidentiality, but the rest is exactly as it was reported to me. On the sunny Wednesday afternoon of 24 April 1968, 25-year-old Claughton man Godfrey Davis shook hands with a middle-aged man named Monty on Birkenhead's Hoylake Road. Godfrey handed over £100 in crisp pound notes to Monty and got behind the wheel of the 1960 Ford Consul and drove off. It was a roomy, comfortable four-door forest-green-coloured car with great luggage space and a top speed of 80mph. Well worth the hundred quid he'd paid to Monty, Godfrey thought. He'd seen the car advertised in the post office window and needed a set of wheels because he'd started dating a girl over in West Kirby. Godfrey had only passed his test six months ago but he was a confident driver and he swung the Consul around the roundabout St James' Church was perched on and cruised up Sumner Road. He switched on the car radio and upon hearing *Lady Madonna* by The Beatles on Radio 1's *Parade of the Pops* show, Godfrey turned the volume up. As he crossed Bidston Avenue into Alderley Avenue, Godfrey suspected he was being followed by a police car. He wasn't speeding so he thought he might just be a little paranoiac, but upon reaching Park Road West he saw the headlights of the car that was shadowing him flash twice, so he pulled over by the park and rolled down his window.

'Your tax disc is out of date,' a vaguely familiar policeman told him. Godfrey smiled and said, 'Terry, it's me.'

PC Terry Spooner shot a startled look at Godfrey - then smiled. He recognised his old best friend from secondary school. The two men chatted about their careers – Terry's life in the police force and Godfrey's workaday existence as a joiner, and then Terry said, 'Get that tax disc sorted out, mate,' and went back to his car. Godfrey drove about fifty yards when a pretty young redhead walked out in front of him and flagged him down. At this point PC Spooner drove past and beeped his horn as he looked at the ginger-haired girl. Godfrey wound down the nearside window and the girl asked, 'Could you please give me a lift to Chester?'

'Chester?' laughed Godfrey, 'I'm only going as far as Claughton.'

The girl nodded, and she got into the car via the rear left door and sat behind Godfrey, which made him a little nervous. She wore a pale blue jacket with a daisy pattern and a matching short skirt, and she was well spoken. A sweet-smelling scent the girl wore filled the car. 'That's a lovely perfume you've got on,' remarked Godfrey, 'what's it called?'

'Diorama,' said the girl, and suddenly she looked as if she was on edge.

Godfrey drove off and tried to make conversation but the girl just sat there gazing straight ahead at the windscreen with wide eyes. She looked afraid of something – or someone. 'You live in Chester?' Godfrey enquired but there was no reply. The car negotiated the roundabout between Manor Hill and Ashville Road, and continued down Park Road West when something terrifying took place. The Ford Consul shook, and Godfrey turned to see a huge man with a nylon stocking over his head seated behind him. He held a flick-knife in his hand and as Godfrey looked on in shock, the armed stranger got on top of the screaming redhead – and started to undo his flies. He started to violently rape the young lady. Godfrey almost lost control of the car and sheared his tyres against the kerb as he pulled up on Park Road South. He yelled for the rapist to stop, then got out of the car and flagged down a lorry. Godfrey told the lorry driver about the assault and the driver jumped down from his vehicle and went with him to the Ford Consul.

It was empty.

'Is this your idea of a joke?' the lorry driver fumed, and headed back to his vehicle. Inside the Ford Consul, the scent of that perfume – Diorama – still hung in the air. Godfrey knew beyond a shadow of a doubt that he had not imagined the girl, but the fact that her perfume was still hanging in the air served to underline the redhead's existence, and, furthermore, when Godfrey bumped into his old friend PC Spooner, the policeman said he'd seen the red-headed girl standing in front of Godfrey's car on Park Road West when he had passed him in the patrol car. The hitch-hiker then, was not a figment of Godfrey's imagination, and Godfrey gradually realised he had given a lift to a ghost that day in April 1968. I mentioned the case on the Pete Price Phone-in on Radio City many years ago and was told by listeners that the girl had been raped one afternoon in April 1967 inside of a Ford Consul. She'd left home after an argument with her father and had tried to thumb a lift to her aunt's home in Chester. The girl's father blamed her for the assault, saying she had dressed too provocatively. The girl became depressed and died after taking an overdose of sleeping pills. The rapist is said to have died in a road crash months after the assault – and his car, a Ford Consul, was eventually sold via a man named Monty – to Godfrey Davis. The driver of the car during the assault is also said to have hanged himself after discovering he had a terminal illness. Godfrey felt the rape of the red-headed girl had somehow left a record of the appalling crime in the very fabric and framework of the car, and he soon sold it. I wouldn't be surprised if other owners of the car have also experienced a ghostly replay of the rape incident.

They say the murderer always returns to the scene of the crime – and sometimes this old adage is accurate, for it is known that some killers have revisited the place where they killed someone to relive the thrill and danger of their heinous act – especially if the body is still in the area, buried or hidden in woodland. I have no doubt that the ghosts of certain criminals also return to the scenes of their crimes – as in the following weird story.

In August 1976, a controversial article entitled, 'Dangers Lurk in a Party Game' appeared in the *Liverpool Echo*. In the article, the Reverend Chris Quine, Vicar of St Andrew's, Queen's Drive, Clubmoor, warned readers that parents were unwittingly leading their children into the dangers of black magic and witchcraft by messing about with Ouija boards. 'My advice to anyone having an Ouija board is to throw it on the bonfire,' said Reverend Quine, 'you may not think it is dangerous, but medical opinion supports the Church's stand.'

The Reverend was prompted to publicise his warnings about dabbling with the Occult because there had been an explosion of interest in the Tarot, Ouija board, séances, witchcraft and even Devil worship in recent years, and that very month in 1976 in Gateacre there was a supernatural incident thought to have been triggered by a Ouija board session. The scene of the terrifying haunting was a certain house on Rose Brow. I have changed the names of the people involved and will not reveal the house number where the weird incident took place as there's a family currently living at the address and I have no wish to alarm them. Two children – 13-year-old Oliver Stallybrass and his 9-year-old sister Dawn were left alone at the house between 8pm and midnight while their parents went to a friend's engagement party up in Aintree. Mr and Mrs Stallybrass believed their 13-year-old son was more than capable of minding the house, and they told him not to answer the door to any callers while they were at the party. A quarter of an hour after the Stallybrasses had left their home on Rose Brow in the care of their son, Oliver's best friend Ben Clarke called at the house. Finding nothing on the TV to interest the children, they decided to make an Ouija board with an upturned wine glass and 36 little squares of paper they had cut out from the blank side of an old wallpaper roll Dawn had been using to line her school exercise book. The squares were numbered 0 to 9 and featured the letters of the alphabet on the other 26 scraps of paper. These squares were arranged in a circle around the upturned wine glass and Oliver's young sister Dawn lit a candle and placed it on the table. The TV and the main light were switched off and by candlelight Ben asked, 'Is there anybody there?'

The children placed their index fingers on the upturned base of the glass and waited. The glass slid about, spelling out Y-E-S.

'Who are you?' asked Ben, a big smile on his face, whereas Oliver and Dawn looked nervous. The glass slowly slid about the table and Dawn named the letters touched by its rim: 'M-R-C-R-A-B-B' – she said, and Oliver gave a nervous chuckle before querying, 'Mister Crabb? Is that you pushing it Ben?'

Ben shook his head, then looked up at a point in mid-air, about six feet above the table, and asked, 'Where are you Mr Crabb?'

The reply was spelt out by the glass: 'O-U-T-S-I-D-E'.

There was a loud rat-tat-tat-tat-tat on the knocker which made the three children jump. Ben got up, intending to answer it, but Oliver said, 'No, don't open the door Ben! Dad told me I mustn't open the door while he and mum are out!'

'Oh don't be a scaredy-cat Ollie!' said Ben with a mischievous smile, and he went into the hallway. The flap of the letter-box was up and a pair of luminous eyes was looking in at the three kids. There was a sharp intake of breath from Dawn, and the two boys stopped dead in their tracks.

'Open this door before I break it down,' said a plummy sounding voice, 'I am absolutely ravenous and that girl looks very tasty.'

'Go away or I'll get my dad!' warned Oliver in an uneven voice fraught with fear.

'Your mother and father aren't there, are they?' said the stranger in his precisely modulated but creepy-sounding voice, 'I know, I know! Ha ha!'

'I'm phoning my dad now!' said Oliver, backing away from the glowing eyes of the evening caller as they watched him through the letter box. There was no telephone installed at the house and this was back in the days when there were no mobile phones in common use of course. The letter box flap fell, and then the children heard the weird stranger walk away. It sounded as if he had studs on his soles. When Oliver was certain the man had gone, he opened the front door a few inches and he and Ben peeped out. The caller was standing about forty yards away down Rose Brow, and he wore a top hat, a long black cape, and he seemed to be brandishing a dagger of some sort. His face looked as if it was painted red. He saw the children peeping out the doorway and ran towards them. Dawn screamed and Oliver slammed the door and bolted it. Dawn burst into tears and Ben suggested an escape from the house via the back door. 'We can get over the back garden fence and leg it!' he said, but then the children heard the sounds of the menacing man's studs tapping away as he walked off again. 'Let's go upstairs and see if he's gone,' said Ben, and he ran up the staircase, but when Oliver went to follow, Dawn held him back and said, 'Ollie, I'm scared, let's go next door and tell Mrs Jones!'

'Don't be scared Dawn,' said Oliver, 'he can't get in here and once he's gone we'll go next door.'

There was a scream upstairs, followed by a tumbling sound. Ben came running down the stairs holding his left forearm – which was dripping with blood. 'He bit me! He got in!' cried Ben, and he tripped on the third step from the bottom and fell as Dawn screamed. She saw the black boots and the end of the cape appear on the landing upstairs. Oliver slid the bolt off, opened the door, and the three children ran screaming for help down Rose Brow – and the top-hatted red-faced fiend chased after them, screaming with laughter with his cape billowing behind him. He waved the dagger as he gave chase, and Dawn felt her legs go weak with fear, but Oliver grabbed her hand and literally dragged her with him. He and Ben ran up Woolton Hill Road to the home of Ben's aunt, and thankfully the outdated-looking attacker disappeared into the gathering dusk. Ben's aunt could see the distinct impression of teeth in her nephew's arm, and the boy suffered nightmares for years. Mr Crabb was thought to have been a ghost who had been stirred up from beyond the grave by the

Ouija board. I discovered that a certain well-to-do gentleman who had lived in Gateacre in the 19th century had once asked the Captain of a vessel returning from China to Liverpool if he would procure for him a young lady – "but not for the usual pleasure" he had remarked, "but to eat." The gentleman said he had sampled human flesh at a banquet with a well-known earl at Shanghai and had found it delicious. 'The upper class palate had become so jaded,' the outrageous gentleman told the captain, 'so we sampled the tender meat of a young woman who was humanely finished off for the job.'

The captain struck the gentleman and threatened to have him arrested when they arrived at Liverpool, but someone in the upper echelons of high society stepped in to halt the proceedings and the cannibalistic nobleman was never charged. There were rumours that Crabb had gone on the prowl after dark in various areas of Liverpool and beyond in search for a source of tender meat – possibly the flesh of young people. There were many unsolved disappearances of children in Victorian times, such as the baffling West Ham disappearances in the 1880s (in which five girls, possibly more, vanished without a trace off the streets of West Ham), and when a child vanished in the poor areas of the country in those days, the disappearance was not always reported. I feel Mr Crabb had visited the house on Rose Brow in ghostly form that August night in 1976, perhaps to rekindle memories of his cannibalistic escapades. Some people in Gateacre have told me the red-faced Mr Crabb *still* occasionally goes on the prowl.

Some murderers are either so lucky – or so careful –

they not only get away with killing a victim – the victim is not always missed, and if he or she *is* missed, their absence is often put down to the person voluntarily vanishing for reasons best known to themselves. Sometimes though, the events of the past – murders included – can mysteriously replay themselves, and sometimes we term these ghostly repeats as hauntings. Just what replays the murders of long ago is anybody's guess; the mechanism could be what we vaguely term as a timeslip, or perhaps the victim is not at rest and the sheer emotion of their anger, crying out for justice, creates some re-enactment of their violent end. I strongly suspect that the sinister female ghost in the following story is returning from the hereafter in some vain attempt to get revenge on someone, but for what reason we can only speculate.

It all started on the Monday night of 12 June 1978. A Mossley-Hill-born chartered accountant named Peter Hadley Thomas, aged 52, and his 25-year-old girlfriend Zoe Richards, watched *The Hunting Party* - a gory western starring Oliver Reed on BBC1. The film ended at twenty past midnight, but halfway through the movie Peter thought he had heard someone walking heavily upstairs in the bedroom of his semi on Birkenhead's St Andrew's Road. He didn't want to alarm Zoe so he went upstairs under the pretence of going to the loo, but checked the three bedrooms and saw no one. All of the windows were secure, so Peter surmised the thumping walker had been his neighbour – an old man who was usually very quiet. After the western, the couple went up to bed and Zoe had no trouble dropping off as she'd been up since 7.30am (she was a nursery teacher) and she went out like a light after kissing Peter. He lay there for a while, and unable to sleep, he carefully switched on the bedside lamp so as not to wake Zoe, and read a newspaper and a magazine. He charily opened the drawer of the bedside unit, took out a small transistor radio and plugged an earphone into it. He listened to Peter Clayton, a DJ on Radio 2, then fell asleep just after one – until a stabbing pain in his heart startled him from his slumbers. As he sat up, thinking he was having a heart attack, he saw a silhouette – a solid black shadow of a girl – with a knife – back away from him. She had pulled the knife out of his chest and was now retreating from him. Peter heard the rustle of her clothes and he saw her make threatening stabbing gestures at him before she vanished. Peter felt his chest, expecting to find a wound but the skin was unbroken.

The pain in Peter's chest faded, but his heart pounded as he realised he had just encountered a ghost, and a very frightening one at that. He had lived here for a year and this was the first time anything supernatural had occurred in the house. He gently nudged Zoe awake and told her what had happened.

'You've had a nightmare, love,' she groaned, and persuaded him to settle down, but Peter insisted in sleeping with the bedside lamp on.

Peter talked of the shadow ghost over a rushed breakfast and again Zoe assured him it had all been a nightmare because he'd dozed off on his back. She said: 'My doctor told me you tend to have nightmares when you sleep on your back because it's harder to breathe when you lay on your back or something; I think he said the tongue slides backwards and can

248

block your throat and that causes the nightmare.'

'This was *not* a nightmare – it was an actual bloody ghost,' Peter insisted, but Zoe just smiled, leaned over him as he sat at the table and kissed his forehead. She then left for work.

That evening just after eleven, the ghost returned in a very dramatic way. Zoe went to bed first and Peter said he'd follow her soon, but twenty minutes later he heard his girlfriend scream. He ran up to see what the matter was and met a wide-eyed Zoe on the stairs. She said she had lain face down to sleep and had felt a 'punch' in her back, and when she opened her eyes she had seen a reflection in the dresser mirror of a woman – made of a solid black silhouette – leaning over the bed with a knife in her hand, about to strike again. Zoe asked Peter to check her back, and he just saw a red patch of skin between the shoulder blades. Zoe now believed her husband's account of the stabbing ghost. The couple got little sleep that night, and left the ceiling light on, but the ghost didn't make another appearance. Peter was up when the milkman called at 5:30am and he mentioned the ghost. With a knowing look the milkman said, 'I've heard stories and that; Mrs Jeffries – the lady who lives facing – knows quite a lot about it.'

Peter visited Mrs Jeffries on Sunday afternoon, and the old lady told him a terrifying story. Around 1930, a 50-year-old man named Thompson, who lived in the house now occupied by Peter's neighbour, was a notorious Peeping Tom, and one day he removed bricks in his loft wall, climbed into the loft next door, and set about creating a peep hole so he could look down into the bathroom next door. He saw the 18-

year-old girl next door leaning over the bath. She was dismembering the body of a man with a saw. The shock of this caused Thompson to have a stroke, and his wife found him paralysed and naked in the loft, still looking through the peephole. When Mr Thompson regained some of his speech, he told his wife what he had seen, and she later told the police what her husband had told her about the grisly dismemberment. The police searched the premises next door to the Thompsons, and they found no trace of a body, but the girl accused of cutting up the body was interviewed by detectives, and deemed insane. She was eventually sent to an asylum, where she died. Not long after this, her knife-wielding ghost – described as a shadow – came through the wall – sometimes even during the daytime – and it would always stab Thompson, who could hardly move or talk because of the stroke. The knife blade never left a mark, but the pain was excruciating and in the end, Thompson died of a heart attack. There were stories - just rumours - that the girl with the knife had been exacting revenge on a couple who had sexually abused her when she was in her early teens, and that she had killed and cut up one man who had raped her when she was about fourteen.

Peter Hadley Thomas and his girlfriend Zoe decided immediately to leave the house, and the couple went to live in a flat in Claughton. I hear the silhouetted apparition of the ghost with the knife still occasionally haunts the house on St Andrew's Road.

The older the house, the more history it has, but sometimes the history might be tinged with blood, and many of the houses of Rodney Street in Liverpool's city centre date back to 1784, so you can imagine the comings and goings of families and single people and all of their lives, loves, tragedies and triumphs that have been contained in the rooms of those grand old dwellings over the decades and centuries. It is no wonder that the street has so many ghosts – perhaps even the ghost of a *very* infamous killer.

At half-past three on the afternoon of Friday 30 September 1994, an 11-year-old girl named Suzanne rushed through the gates of her school in Walton. A mile away, her 13-year-old brother Jason was also rushing out of his school. For a moment Suzanne found herself running for the wrong bus. Her parents had recently moved from Walton to a house on Rodney Street in the city centre and so the girl had to say goodbye to her friend Michelle and wait for the next bus. Suzanne's dad Chas had been left a fortune by his late mother and he had put his redundancy pay to the sum to buy the house in town, and there had been rows between Chas and his wife Bonnie; she had wanted to move to the Lake District. Chas was now working again as a bus driver and Bonnie was a hairdresser. They wouldn't be home till well after six this evening.

Suzanne and Jason reached Rodney Street at the same time and Jason unlocked the door and disabled the alarm. They both wanted to watch *The Spooks of Bottle Bay* and *Knightmare* – their two favourite telly programmes, but a real spook put in a very dramatic appearance that afternoon. Before Jason could switch the telly on, he and his sister heard screams on the upper floor and the sound of running feet coming down the stairs. The children were so scared they hid in the cloakroom under the stairs and held the door shut. 'Murder!' screamed a female voice and then came the sound of a body tumbling down the stairs above the cloakroom. There were regular thuds above on the stairs, and then a very thin stream of blood came through the ceiling of the tiny cloakroom. It oozed and dripped onto Suzanne's new school shoes and she emitted a muffled yelp as she held her hand to her mouth. The kids heard slow footsteps which stopped at the door Jason was holding shut. The footsteps went away, returned, then moved away again, and the front door was heard to open. Jason and Suzanne heard the traffic outside, and wondered if they could run through the living room and out onto the street. They quickly made up their minds and made a dash for it, and as they passed the bottom of the stairs in the hallway they looked up – and saw a woman lying face down on the stairs with a huge bloodstain on the back of her blouse. That woman was dressed in an old-fashioned long dress, and she wore ankle boots and had her hair done up into a bun. The children went to the nearest telephone box – near St Luke's Church, just round the corner from their new home – and they called the police but when the law arrived they found no body or any trace of blood; not a single drop. The parents of the children arrived home and were startled to see the police and detectives in the house, and Jason's father was furious at him for leaving the door of the house wide open while he and his sister had gone to the telephone box to report an imaginary murder to the police. Every time the parents would come home they'd find Suzanne and Jason sitting on the step, afraid to go in, but they still thought the children were just over-imaginative in their new house.

Then the ghost was seen by the entire family one Sunday as they watched TV. It came into the lounge, ripped out the plug of the telly from its wall socket, and waved a long thin-bladed knife at them. The ghost was very slim, tall and handsome, with huge blue eyes and red hair. The apparition wore a black velvet suit with a white shirt, green waistcoat and a maroon tie. As Bonnie screamed, the ghost vanished. The house was subsequently blessed by a priest, but the ghost made a mockery of the blessing by walking into the house through the *closed front door* the same evening in a top hat – wearing blood-soaked gloves. Enough was enough, and the family moved out. I discovered the name of the man and found out that in 1889, he had suddenly returned to Liverpool after living in the Whitechapel area of London with a cousin for two years, but what he was doing down there, I do not know. Victorian Whitechapel is of course, associated with one of the most famous yet infamous murderers of all time – but no, surely it can't be *him*?

Not all shadowy re-enactment ghosts are attached to houses; some are tied-up with a variety of objects from things as small as a thimble to something as large as a car...

One Saturday morning in November 1971, 40-year-old Terry Burns was perusing Friday night's *Liverpool Echo* over coffee in the lounge of his house in Eaton Gardens, West Derby, when his gaze happened to fall onto an ad in the newspaper's used cars pages; it was just the vehicle he was looking for. The ad read, '1968 Austin Westminster 110 Saloon De Luxe; forest green; Automatic; power steering; M.O.T.; one solicitor owner from new; 34,000 miles; only £300.'

Terry's girlfriend Moira read the classified ad and said, 'Just 300 quid? He could get twice that much for it. Looks fishy.'

Terry took the paper from her, 'There's nothing fishy about it Moira, he's a solicitor – probably has a new car and he just wants a quick sale. I love Westminsters – reliable cars they are; first car I had.'

Terry went into the hallway and phoned the seller, who said he was welcome to look at the car right now if he wanted. Terry and Moira were given a lift to the seller's home on Blackburne Place by their friend Sid, who worked as a car mechanic. He looked under the bonnet and declared the car as 'perfect'. Terry handed over the cash, shook the solicitor's hand and then he and Moira got into the Austin Westminster. After filling the car up at a station, they cruised up to Southport for a day out. They visited the Southport Antiques Fair, where Terry bought Moira a Victorian rose gold turquoise ring. They had coffee and cakes at a Lord Street café, browsed a second-hand bookshop, then Terry and Moira got in the Westminster and were soon headed for home. Moira notice him first in the wing mirror; a man in a black suit and white shirt, running after the car in the middle of Crosby's Moor Lane, fifty yards away. 'Silly fool, he'll get knocked down running in the road,' said Terry, eyeing the running man in the rear view mirror. He accelerated and soon lost him. Two miles down the homeward route the couple saw the running figure again, and realised he'd have to be an athlete to still be on their tail. 'Shall I stop and see what he wants?' Terry asked, but Moira yelled, 'No! Get away from him!'

After the fifty-minute drive home, the couple

reached Eaton Gardens – and Terry gasped, 'I don't bloody believe it; it's him again,' as he looked in his mirror. Moira screamed for him to drive off and Terry peeled rubber.

'He's a ghost Terry, this car's haunted. I said there was something fishy!' Moira watched the figure shrink into the distance in the wing mirror.

'Maybe that ring I got you is haunted,' Terry said meekly, but Moira shook her head and said, 'Take this car back! It's haunted!'

Terry drove off, headed for Blackburne Place, and every now and then as he waited at the lights he would see the weird running figure appear in the distance. Terry managed to get his money back and the solicitor seemed to know something but he denied the vehicle was haunted. Years later, Terry heard that the solicitor had bought the car from a friend who had knocked down and killed a man who was about to be married. The furious ghost of the dead groom was later seen chasing the car and the angry ghost had even attacked the driver for taking his life.

And finally, there was an incident reported to me many years ago concerning what seems to have been a classic case of a supernatural re-enactment evoked, perhaps, by the ghosts themselves, possibly because they were angry at their young lives being cruelly cut short when they had so much to live for. To me, there seems to be a strange parallel between the recurrent dream or nightmare and the repetitive ghosts that go through the same routine whenever they come out the woodwork; perhaps, like the unconscious dreamer, the ghosts are not fully aware they are going through the same old motions – and emotions – they could be trying to come to terms with the unresolved issue of live being so suddenly snuffed out without any explanation. I suppose we are drifting into the psychology of ghosts now, so I'd better relate the following story before I go off at a tangent into psychoanalytical spookology...

Around 5:30pm one sunny day in April 1960 a truck driver named Jim Stafford was flagged down by two girls who looked as if they were in their early twenties. Jim had been driving along a minor road flanked by grassy embankments near Roby in his lorry when he had spotted the girls. One was a brunette with her hair piled up into a bun, and she wore a beige windcheater jacket and Capri pants, and the other girl had long blonde hair, and she wore a denim jacket, but Jim cannot recall if she wore a dress or jeans.

The blonde girl said, 'Thanks for stopping for us. Can you possibly give us a lift to Wavertree? As near to Earle Road as possible if you can.'

It just so happened that Jim Stafford was headed for a warehouse off Upper Parliament Street, and part of his route passed within 200 yards of the house on Earle Road that the girls wanted to get to. There was going to be a 21st birthday party held at the house from around 7:30pm and the girls were looking forward to attending it. Jim asked the female passengers how they'd ended up on the grassy embankment in Roby but received no reply. After Jim had dropped the girls off on Smithdown Road, which was near to their destination, he continued on his way to the warehouse when he noticed a tiny red leather purse on the front passenger seat. It had obviously belonged to one of the girls, and Jim opened it and saw that it contained a ten-shilling note and a light-brown manila wage packet with the name "Nancy" on it, along with a Huyton address. There was about seven pounds in the wage packet, and Jim put the purse in his pocket and decided he'd drive to the Huyton address on the wage packet and hand the purse in, as soon as he'd delivered his freight to the warehouse. Jim drove to the house in Huyton and knocked on the door. There was no answer so he tried to put the purse through the letterbox but then the door opened. A woman in her fifties asked him what he was doing, and Jim showed the lady the little red purse and said, 'That belongs to Nancy. She was one of the girls I gave a lift to earlier today.'

The woman opened the purse and seemed in shock as she took out the wage packet and the ten-shilling note. 'Nancy was my daughter,' said the woman, and Jim wondered why the lady had referred to the girl in the past tense, but then the woman said, 'but she died in a traffic accident three years ago.'

'Have I got the wrong address then?' Jim Stafford asked, feeling a bit confused. He looked at the number on the door.

'Yes, that's definitely her purse – we never found it,' the woman told him, and Jim saw tears fall from her eyes onto the wage packet. 'She was knocked down with her best friend, Elaine. It was up in Roby.'

'But – ' Jim tried to speak but he just couldn't get his words out.

'Come in,' the woman said, standing aside in the doorway, 'what's your name?'

'Jim,' said the lorry driver, 'Jim Stafford.' And he walked into the house.

'They said it was an accident, but I think the driver deliberately killed them,' the woman told Jim, wiping her tears with the back of her hand. 'He liked Nancy and Elaine but they didn't want to know him because he was a bad man. He used to hit his wife.'

Jim saw the large photograph of the girls he had given a lift to earlier that day. The monochrome picture was of Nancy and Elaine, and it was mounted in a huge silver frame over the mantelpiece in the living room. 'Yes, that's them. Jim said, his voice almost a whisper. He realised he had given a lift to two ghosts today.

'They were going to a party – ' said Nancy's heartbroken mother, but became too choked up to say more.

'Was it on Earle Road in Wavertree?' Jim asked in a grave voice.

'Yes! How on earth did you know?' the lady asked with a perplexed look in her pink tear-laden eyes.

'Nancy asked me to take her and her friend there,' was Jim's reply. He felt as if this was all some bad dream.

'Where did you pick them up?' asked Nancy's mum. She seemed to brace herself for the answer.

'In Roby,' Jim told her, and he offered the woman a cigarette but she just shook her head. 'It's a long road – just by Church Road I think.'

'That's where they laid their bodies out,' said Nancy's mother, 'on the grassy slope,' and she burst into tears and fell into an armchair. Jim tried to comfort her and he left forty minutes later, still stuck for words.

A fortnight passed, and it was an overcast but warm

afternoon as Jim Stafford found himself once again driving down that lonely lane in Roby where he had picked up two girls who had left this life.

And there they were again. Jim couldn't believe his eyes. The two girls were waving to him as they stood on the grass verge. This time he looked straight ahead, his hands gripped the wheel hard, and he kept driving.

# HOCUS THE CLOWN

The Pavilion Theatre, built in 1908, once stood on Lodge Lane, and legendary stars such as Marie Lloyd, George Formby, Arthur Askey, Ken Dodd, Robb Wilton and The Beatles appeared there. The theatre – like so many the world over – had its ghosts, and most of them were mere manifestations of cold spots and invisible mischief-makers who liked to move objects about and spirit away keys and even the odd pair of false teeth – but there was – and perhaps still is – a Pavilion ghost nicknamed Hocus the Clown. At first it was thought that the hilarious mime-artist extraordinaire Larry Jay – the "Silent Comedian" – was Hocus, but on some occasions the ghost was encountered in the streets around the Pavilion when Larry was onstage at the theatre, and it was also seen after his death in 1967. The clown had a heavily whitened face, red nose and dressed in a baggy white Pierrot clown outfit, and it always gave off an awful aroma of lavender mingled with the strong stench of body odour. The entity was often taken to be a solid person until it vanished and those who claimed they'd spoken to the ghost said that Hocus talked of saving the Pavilion and seemed in fear of it closing down. In 1954 the theatre's future hung in the balance when James Lovelace, the licensee of the "Pivvy" (as it was affectionately known) received a summons over an alleged unscripted sex-scene in a play called *The Respectable Prostitute*. The risqué scene involved nothing more than an actor sitting on the same bed as the leading lady. Hocus was seen prowling the theatre at this time, wringing his hands, crying tears of blood as he groaned, 'What shall become of me?' He was seen by the theatre fireman, the electrician Freddie Trinder (brother of comedian Tommy Trinder), Winnie the dressing room cleaner and an Australian singer named Florrie Forde.

In 1956, skiffle star Lonnie Donnegan appeared at the Pivvy, and noticed the awful sweet sickly smell backstage during a sound check. He went to look for the cause of the smell and returned white as a sheet. He never commented on what he had seen backstage. Incidentally, one of the people who went to see Lonnie at the Pavilion that night was a 14-year-old Paul McCartney.

Not long after Donnegan's uncanny encounter with something backstage at the Pavilion, rumours of the strange clown roaming the area around the theatre spread like wildfire across Liverpool and one Saturday afternoon the eerie clown attracted the attention of four Teddy boys who were always hanging around the Lodge Lane area. These Teds were a vicious gang, and all of them were under 21. They'd all been in trouble with the police before and one of them had come near to being imprisoned for his alleged part in the sickening murder of over fifty cats in the Brownlow Hill area two years before. *The Daily Herald* reported on the horrific crimes on 19 March 1954 with the headline: 'New Teddy Boy Horror Shames a City'. The article described how officers from the RSPCA investigating the disappearance of over 57 cats near the Bull Ring area off Brownlow Hill had been attacked with bricks and broken bottles thrown at them by Teddy Boys – and Teddy Girls. According to the newspaper, the sickened RSPCA officers found a number of feline corpses with ropes around their necks. The 'game' played by the Teds was to swing the cat around by the rope and then to let go and see how far the cat went. Most of the cats either died from strangulation or had their skulls smashed in if they hit a wall. A Mr Richard Clitherow, the district secretary of the RSPCA and one of the officers chased by the Teds, is quoted as saying: "Next time there will be more of us and we'll ask for police protection."

Of course, not all Teddy Boys were cruel cat-killers; they had the odd fight and on the whole they lived only for Rock and Roll, but the four Teddy Boys in this story were very wicked thrill-seekers who carried knives and chains. They were also involved at a surreal brawl at a skating rink on Myrtle Street where they actually skated about to the strains of the *Blue Danube Waltz* being played over the tannoy of the rink whilst slashing the faces of a rival gang and swinging chains in sync to the Straussian melody. One of these stylishly-dressed delinquents also managed to steal a US World War Two surplus flamethrower and planned to incinerate a rival gang at a certain Lime Street pub. Fortunately the Ted couldn't get hold of the special flamethrower fuel.

Anyway, these four Teds started taking the mickey out of Hocus as he walked along Lodge Lane in his outlandish-looking Pierrot costume and his white painted face.

The menacing quartet of Teddy Boys surrounded him. 'Why you dressed like that?' asked Tony - the snappily-attired leader of the gang - to which Hocus replied, 'And why are *you* dressed like that? You look silly!'

'How am *I* silly you stupid old codger?' asked Tony through gritted teeth. Already he was reaching into his inside coat pocket for the cosh.

'You're wearing a pink jacket and my, oh my! Those funny blue shoes!' laughed Hocus, adding, 'My boy, you look more like a clown than me!'

One of the Teds seized Hocus and held him in a headlock so the clown's face was pressed against his own, and already the Ted could smell the awful aroma coming from the eccentric man. Tony took out a cosh and swung it at the clown's head. Hocus vanished in an instant and the cosh aimed at his face smashed the nose of the Ted who had been restraining him.

'Arrgh! You've broken my nose, Tony! Oh God!' cried the Ted who had been holding the clown in a headlock seconds ago. Blood suddenly gushed down his injured nose and went all over his kipper tie and pink shirt.

Realising the oddly-dressed man was a ghost, the Teddy boys retreated to Smithdown Road, and they stood, confused in a row outside the Boundary Pub. The Ted who'd had his nose almost broken held his hands over his face and his eyes were narrow and watering from the pain. 'My looks are gone now you clumsy bastard!' he said to Tony.

'Oh shut up you big tart,' said Tony, 'you've just got a broken hooter; it'll heal. Where did he go?'

'Is he a ghost?' one of the gang asked Tony, who

never answered. He looked towards the spot outside the Pavilion where the clown had dematerialised in the proverbial twinkling of an eye.

'I think we should cut, pronto like,' said one of the Teddy Boys, 'I'm not scared of anyone but ghosts are something I don't want to cross, Tony!'

'Boo!' came a loud deep voice from behind the Teds which made them all jump and turn.

It was the clown, smiling paradoxically with a mouth that was painted with a downturned smile. One of the Teds swung a chain at Hocus, aiming for his eyes, but the figure of twisted fun vanished again and the end of the chain sparked against a wall instead.

The clown reappeared next to a docile member of the Ted gang named Charlie, an amateur boxer with huge fists. As the clown did a strange dance on the spot which resembled the Highland Fling, Charlie swung his fist into the abdomen of the sinister taunter, and everyone heard a crack. The clown stopped dancing and lifted the top half of its gown to reveal smashed-in ribs embedded in a mess of something that resembled sausage-like intestines, a yellowish goo and excrement. Hocus clenched his yellow teeth and seemed to be in agony, and he growled at Charlie, who ran off in terror down Smithdown Road. The clown then started grinning at the other Teds, and they ran off and soon overtook Charlie.

Many years after this weird incident, a woman named Sadie who had been a young girl living on Earle Road in the 1950s, telephoned me on air as I was a guest on the *Billy Butler Show*. Although Sadie did not see the clown, she recalled the scare regarding the ghost and how her father – who worked as a coalman

– had told her that he had seen the apparition chasing the Teddy Boys down Smithdown Road. Sadie's father initially thought the clown was just someone who had dressed up to pull off some barmy prank – but then he saw the figure vanish into thin air right in front of him. Sadie said every time the family's table talk conversation turned to the subject of the paranormal over the years, her father would always mention the ghost of the Pavilion clown. According to other witnesses, Hocus chased the Teddy Boys down Smithdown Road as far as Hartington Road, where he dematerialised into nothing.

It is said that Tony, the gang leader of the Teds, had terrible nightmares about the ghostly clown and ended up in a psychiatric hospital after claiming that the clown was appearing in the bedroom of his home on Nicander Road during the night. Tony later died in his sleep from 'natural causes' – but one naturally wonders if Hocus frightened the young man to such an extent in a nightmare that his heart failed. The history of Hocus is unknown, but I assume he once performed at the Pivvy, which is now a bingo club. Perhaps he's still roaming about...

# ALONE

They sat in La Cabala coffee bar on Bold Street that rainy neon-lit Friday night in August 1961 – a group of nine young Liverpool University students who wanted to right the wrongs of the world over sixpence cups of coffee, strong Russian tea and cigarettes. Harvey Hamilton sat ensconced in a corner seat with four friends on either side of him as he spoke of his lofty intentions to write a philosophical work entitled *The Individual Life of Man* and he rambled on about founding a religious group called the Solitarians that would shun society and spend weeks in the wilderness of Wales as hermits so society couldn't affect their minds.

'No man is an island, though,' said Harvey's girlfriend Julia, and she contended that humans could only thrive by interacting with one another – and she argued the point exceedingly well – so well in fact, her boyfriend Harvey seemed to take it as a personal attack on him and he roared at the girl, 'Well *this* human needs no one! I think for myself! Bloody sheep!' and he stormed out of the café and went to the Wood Street flat he shared with Julia and locked the door. Julia and her friends hammered on the door but Harvey cried, 'Go away! Stay away! I wish everyone would just leave me alone!'

Julia's friends gave up trying to coax Harvey out of

the flat, but Julia stayed put, and she opened the letterbox and tried to look in but the hallway was in pitch-black darkness. She said, 'Harvey, do you remember that day in June, just a few months ago, when we were all going to march from Paris to Moscow on our Ban the Bomb campaign? Ha! They stopped us and deported us from France. It was a disaster, but we were very close that day, and you told me you'd never leave me. Do you remember?'

Something smashed against the door and landed in the hallway with a metallic clang. It sounded like a saucepan.

'Piss off!' Harvey shouted, and it sounded as if it came from the bedroom.

'I wasn't attacking you before, Harvey,' Julia told him, 'I was just expressing my thoughts on your proposition, that's all. Are you sick of me or something? Is that what this is all about?'

'I'm sick of *everyone* at the moment! The whole human klan!' cried Harvey, his voice a little louder than before. 'I just need to be alone! I just need everyone to leave me alone!'

'Fair enough,' said Julia in a resigned voice, and she felt so sad, as if she was losing something precious and there was nothing she could do to about it. 'I'll be around tomorrow and see how you are.'

Harvey laid face downwards on the bed, his eyes squeezed tight as he felt the cold pillow press into his nose and cheeks. He wished he could just open his eyes and find himself on a desert island, far away from people and all of their irritating societal rituals and straitjacketed minds. Harvey fell asleep at some point after this longing to be on an island, and he awoke –

without even opening his eyes - from what seemed to have been a deep dreamless sleep on the Saturday morning. He yawned and suddenly remembered the row he'd had with everyone – and then he opened his eyes and saw the empty space beside him where Julia would have been. He closed his eyes again, replayed everything he'd said in his mind's ear, then swore under his breath and got out of the bed. He felt so down he didn't bother shaving or even combing his hair. He got dressed, put on his old coat, and went to have breakfast at a café. He wondered what apologetic crap he'd come out with when he met Julia and his friends. Outside, Harvey found the streets of Liverpool completely deserted and the eerie silence scared him. The café he usually went to was open – but there was no one serving behind the counter, and all of the nearby shops were also open – but devoid of a single soul. 'What the hell is going on?' Harvey whispered to himself. He walked to Ranelagh Street and saw a bus – but there were no passengers or driver onboard. Harvey heard a rustling sound behind him and turned, but it was just a crumpled sheet of discarded chip-wrapping paper being blown across the pavement by the wind. The wind was the only sound Harvey could hear, besides his own footfalls and excited breathing. There were no foghorns on the river, no aeroplanes droning overheard, no crying seagulls, and no incessant traffic hubbub – just a solid unearthly silence overlaid with the buffeting sound of the wind against his ears. Harvey drifted towards Church Street, on his way to explore the empty department stores when he suddenly heard distant howls of laughter, but the student could not trace the mirthful mocker. As weird as the unseen joker sounded, Harvey now knew he was not alone, but where had everyone gone? He dearly wanted to know. And then he saw a woman in a telephone box on Church Street! She looked tall and well-dressed – but who was she? Harvey ran to her – and saw that there was no living woman there; someone had put a shop window mannequin in the box. He found another female dummy on Bold Street, leaning against the wall of the Lyceum and in an effort to feel a little less lonely, he said to himself, 'Who is putting these dummies all round the place?' And he thought of the out-of-sight funster who seemed to be laughing at him.

Harvey entered a telephone call box and dialled 999, and he waited, and listened, his ear pressed against the earpiece – but there was no purring tone - the line was dead. He ran back to his home and turned on the radio and heard a constant white noise hiss – and then he again heard that invisible weird ridiculer laughing somewhere in the distance. The TV channels on Harvey's old set were a blizzard of static. Had Russia hit the country with some weapon that left no trace of a person? But why would he be spared? And who was that clown he kept hearing? There were so many unanswered questions. At one point in the dreadful stretch of solitude, a disturbing thought crossed Harvey's mind: had he died during the night and was this impossible situation just a dream in his disintegrating brain? Was he in fact now lying in some mortuary, about to undergo a post mortem examination? He dismissed the morbid thought by pinching his arm and feeling the pain; no, this was reality.

Night soon fell and the lamp posts remained unlit. By the light of the full moon Harvey entered Liverpool's Anglican Cathedral. He carried a torch and batteries he'd taken from a shop on Renshaw Street. He lit an entire rack of beeswax yellow votive candles in an effort to bring back the living, and then he got down on his knees at the High Altar and prayed for everyone to return. The ancient moon peeped through the lancet windows, its unparalleled light energising stained glass representations of Moses, Adam and Eve, Noah, Solomon and the prophets, and in that one moment, as the religious figures became beings of pure light of every wavelength of the rainbow, Harvey became so moved and sad. The multicoloured lunar lantern show resonated with something spiritual deep down in the great Marianas Trench of his psyche. He was kneeling there before the High Altar of the cathedral with splotches of polychromatic light dappling the tiled floor, and now, he felt like the Biblical Adam before the creation of Eve; there was just himself and that someone else up there – was this actually God he was sensing? He was like an urban dweller who had gone into the country to see the stars for the first time without the light pollution of his city's lamp posts. With humanity removed, the presence of something else had been accentuated. 'Are you there?' he whispered, looking up at the moon, moving almost imperceptibly across the kaleidoscopic icons of the Bible. 'I believe in you now,' he added.

*Ha ha ha ha!*

The laughter from that elusive someone (just *who* was it?) echoed somewhere in the cavernous cathedral, reminding him there *was* someone else on this lonely

270

earth.

'I believe!' Harvey shouted, for he now suspected that the laughter was from someone very old – most probably the Devil.

*Ha ha ha – oooh! Ha ha ha!*

The laughter was louder, nearer.

'*Go outside and embrace the first one you see,*' said a serene inner voice. It was like the phantom voices Harvey had heard in the wee small hours when he studied too long, when the ticking clock lost its rhythm and he was ready to drop from mental fatigue. The voice had a calming, dreamlike quality to it, and yet he felt as if something spiritual had just issued a command to him, and as a man who was now grasping straws – reaching out for any help to release him from the biggest open air solitary confinement cell ever, a world without people, he was eager to obey the whispered decree. And so, with roaring laughter reverberating back and forth between the Woolton-sandstone walled vaults of the nave, Harvey Hamilton walked out of the cathedral, and there stood a young man, about to enter the grand house of worship. He looked startled as he saw Harvey gazing at him wide-eyed, as if he thought he recognised him.

'What's your name?' Harvey asked, and his voice was wrought with emotion.

'Why?' the youth replied, then said, 'John Jeudwine.'

Harvey embraced him and the youth became reflexively rigid, and meekly hugged him back.

A foghorn sounded on the river, but in the ears of Harvey it could have been the horn of the Archangel Gabriel, announcing the return of the human race.

John Jeudwine regarded Harvey as a drunk and

impatiently wrestled from his hold and rushed into the cathedral, and then others came out of the fog, and they passed an awestruck Harvey who was now in tears. He wandered, like Gershom in Exodus, feeling like a stranger in a strange land, for the world and the living people all around Harvey now seemed unaccountably more real. He felt as if he'd spent his life watching cartoons featuring caricatures of people and had now seen the first movie featuring real people – and it was some time before this heightened sense of reality faded away. He went to La Cabala coffee bar on Bold Street and there was Julia, talking to three friends. She didn't even ask him where he had been. He wanted to tell her about the last twenty-four hours living on some far side of the moon without any company, but he was too upset to speak, so he threw his arms around the girl and hugged her, and to him she was a treasure above diamonds and gold.

'What's wrong, Harvey?' she whispered close to his ear as her friends looked on in bemusement.

'You were right,' he answered in a choked-up voice, no man is an island.'

# PEOPLE CAN CHANGE

The idea of a human turning into a ravening wolf-like demon has been with us for centuries, and I have interviewed so many level-headed people over the years who have sworn that they have witnessed a person change into an animal or some supernatural being before their eyes. In most legends the world over it is considered a curse when someone must be periodically turned into a werewolf, and often the curse is due to the victim being bitten by a werewolf, but I have a case in my files in which a man underwent a regular transformation into a beast of fang and claw through a powerful form of Black Magic, mingled with the equally potent workings of Hoodoo. Growing up on the cusp of Toxteth in Edge Hill, I often heard stories concerning the dark legend of Yolande, a young black man – originally from Jamaica – who settled in Trinidad for a while to learn a potent form of Nigerian magic from a Bokur – a Hoodoo sorcerer – so he could find a beautiful woman named Leonora – the daughter of a Liverpudlian sugar plantation owner in Jamaica he had admired from afar. The Bokur carried out an arcane divination ritual and told Yolande that Leonora had returned to Liverpool after falling out with her father. The Bokur told Yolande that love was a dangerous emotion that roused the animal in man, and advised him to stay and study Hoodoo rather than chase an object of lust. There was some disagreement between the Bokur and Yolande which ended with the sorcerer laying the following ghastly curse on his client: 'Whenever the fires of love burn in your heart you will become as low as the blood-hungry beast! Will be done! Will be done!'

Not long afterwards, whenever Yolande yearned with a burning heart for Leonora he would undergo an agonising change into what seemed to be a wolf, and he would tear his clothes off and find himself hungry for flesh and thirsty for blood. These 'episodes' could happen by night *and* day, and Yolande would find himself covered in hair and able to run on all fours. He was also possessed with incredible strength after the change. He turned to meditation to suppress his emotional trigger, but remaining fixated with Leonora, Yolande moved to Liverpool in 1960 and settled in Toxteth. One day as he walked down Church Street, Yolande set eyes on his beloved Leonora, and he seized her by the wrist and tried to take her to a jeweller to buy her an engagement ring but the lady screamed for help. In broad daylight the emotionally-torn Yolande underwent his eerie metamorphosis and tore off his clothes as Leonora ran off into the crowds. The horrified jeweller closed his shop and called the police. In minutes, a police car arrived, and before a crowd of astonished and scared onlookers, two policemen wrestled with the madman, and they naturally thought he was wearing some Halloween mask – till they were thrown against their vehicle as if they were rag dolls. Yolande raced off, to what fate I know not, but I recall lying in bed as a child, sometimes hearing howls in the night, and passing locals would whisper about the 'Trinidad Werewolf'.

There is an intriguing report in the *Newcastle Journal* of 11 February, 1991 with the headline: 'Police in 'Werewolf Appeal'. The article states that a weird rumour had been rife in the Cumbrian market town of Brampton (which lies about 9 miles east of Carlisle) about a real-life werewolf being at large. A man, who showed no signs of personal injury, then appeared in Brampton covered in blood – and he told the authorities that he was a werewolf, but then he refused to divulge any more about the strange claims to the police. The article stated that the police believed an injured person was possibly lying undiscovered somewhere in the countryside surrounding Brampton but their searches were hampered by severe wintry weather. The police eventually checked on every man, woman and child in Brampton – six thousand individuals in all – and none were unaccounted for. The blood covering the man who allegedly said he was a werewolf was, according to the newspaper reports, tested and found to be human and not belonging to an animal – so whose blood was it? No corpse was ever found and the strange matter was never resolved, and closer to home, here on Merseyside there have been similar alleged cases of people undergoing a kind of rapid metamorphosis to become something very beastly. A case in point is the strange tale of the three Nigerians who lived together in a single room at a house on Falkner Square, Toxteth, a very desirable place to live today, for its white painted town houses, built between 1830 and 1835 in the Regency era, lie at the heart of the beautiful Georgian Quarter and they line an elegantly tranquil well-kept park, but back in 1970 this fashionable square was a noisy place with rowdy students and some of the landlords who were letting out the houses there (many of which were badly-maintained "hard-to-lets") were a rather unscrupulous lot. One landlord – who we shall call Mr Canning (not his real name), let a single furnished room on the second floor of a property in the square to three Nigerians who had recently come to live in the UK. Mr Canning gradually started to increase their rent, and when a cooker in their flat became faulty, Canning took weeks to address the problem and brought in a 'cowboy' – a dishonest and unqualified man named Arthur – who attempted to fix the cooker but only made it worse and also caused a gas leak. Then one of the Nigerians came down with a bronchial condition and his doctor asked him if the flat he was living in had a damp problem. The patient said it had, and that there was a black fungal growth around the windows that could not be washed away, even with bleach and disinfectant. The patient was sent for tests at the Liverpool Infirmary and a type of Aspergillosis – a serious lung condition caused by the Aspergillus mold – was diagnosed. The three Nigerians confronted Canning when he came to the house one day to show two young female art students a flat, and the trio also warned the potential tenants about the damp, the fungus, and the couldn't-care-less attitude of the landlord. One of the students then told Canning, 'I think we'd better look elsewhere,' and she and her friend left.

Canning stormed into the flat of the three black men and told them he was evicting them. One of the men questioned the legality of the proposed eviction. Canning resorted to using the N-word as he exploded in anger, and after insulting the men he shouted: 'If this place isn't empty by three in the afternoon tomorrow, I'll bring a few people over and they will throw you through that window! Got that? Get packing!'

Later that day, at around 5pm, Canning was walking through Falkner Square after he'd collected £400 in rent from a few of the flats he owned in the area, and he was headed for his home on nearby Sandon Street, when he saw three huge tail-less dark brown dogs running towards him. They were as large as Great Danes but resembled Alsatians. Fearing he was about to be attacked by the hounds, Canning froze, thinking he'd have a better chance of not being bitten or savaged if he made no sudden moves. One of the huge dogs stopped in front of him, and in a weird growling voice it actually spoke. 'Give me your money!' the unearthly beast said, and its eyes were red and Canning trembled at the sight of the animal's long sharp teeth. Again the dog issued the same guttural request, and Canning slowly reached into his inside jacket pocket, took out his wallet – and the dog seized it in its jaws with a snap and ran off. Canning stood there in shock, unable to take in what had just happened as he watched the dogs run off towards Grove Street. In seconds the three strange oversize canines had turned the corner and vanished. Canning knew he could not report the 'theft' to the police; how on earth could he tell them that the dog who had snatched his wallet had actually issued a *spoken* threat? He wouldn't have believed something like that himself had he not experienced it firsthand. Canning had a heart condition, and the unearthly traumatic experience left him with chest pains, a shortness of breath and dizziness. He gripped the green railings surrounding the gardens and steadied himself for a moment. A dog appeared and sniffed the landlord's right ankle and he let out a cry of horror, but it was just a poodle being walked by an old lady who had come over to Canning to see if he was alright.

'Those dogs were huge,' said the old woman, 'did they bite you?'

'Oh, so you saw them,' said Canning, relieved that the woman had witnessed the uncanny incident, for he was starting to think he'd hallucinated the whole thing. 'No, they didn't bite me, but one of the things snatched my wallet!'

'Oh dear,' said the elderly lady, putting her hand to her mouth, 'perhaps they were trained to do that; how odd. You'll have to go to the police before someone else gets attacked by those dogs.'

Canning wanted to tell the woman that the dog that had snatched his wallet had talked but decided to say nothing. He took a deep breath and hurried to his home to take his heart tablets. At 6:30pm the landlord called at the flat the three Nigerians had occupied and found it empty. On the floor in the centre of the room he saw his wallet. He Picked it up and found that the £400 it had contained was missing. He wondered if the old lady's suggestion about the dogs being trained to rob could be true, but how on earth could anyone train a dog to speak? It wasn't possible. Canning dismissed the notion, and he went home and decided to tell his wife what had happened.

'You must think I was born yesterday;' she said after she had heard his bizarre account, 'what a tale you've spun there! You blew that money on the horses! Talking dogs!'

'I know it sounds barmy but it's true!' Canning roared back, 'Look, if I had spent that money on betting I could have just said I'd lost the money or it had been stolen! Why would I come up with a far-fetched story about a talking dog?'

'I don't know!' his wife yelled back at him, 'Have you been drinking or smoking that whacky baccy from that Jamaican friend you've been hanging round with?'

'I am telling you the truth!' Canning shouted, then his hands clutched his chest. The next thing he knew he was on his knees. He woke up in hospital with his tearful wife holding his hand. He'd had a mild heart attack.

Three months later, Canning was in a club in Toxteth one night when one of the evicted Nigerians came in. Canning went over to look at him, and wanted to ask him why he had found his empty wallet in the flat he and his two friends had left that day, but the Nigerian suddenly turned around and noticed Canning gazing at him. The Nigerian flashed a broad smile at his former landlord, and then, in a growling voice, he said, 'Give me your money.'

Canning went cold because that voice sounded exactly like the same guttural voice that dog had somehow possessed.

The Nigerian's eyes seemed to now have a red tint, and he turned away from Canning and left the club.

That night on his way home from the club, Canning had the unsettling feeling that someone – or something – was following him, and as soon as he got indoors he bolted the door and went up to the bedroom where his wife was sleeping. He told her about the encounter with one of his Nigerian tenants and how he had put on the very same voice that demonic dog had spoken in. His wife was a bit groggy, as she'd taken a sleeping pill earlier, and she said, 'Well, just get to bed, dear; remember what the doctor told you about the effects of these late nights on your heart.'

Seconds after Mrs Canning said these words, she and her husband heard a strange harmony of howls outside on Sandon Street. Mr Canning switched off the bedside lamp and crept over to the window. He gently pulled the curtain aside a few inches and looked out onto the moonlit street.

At first he thought he saw the black silhouette of a man with the red glowing tip of a cigarette that he was dragging on, but as the landlord squinted at the amorphous black object down below, he saw it resolve into the silhouette of a huge dog that was sitting on the pavement. The red glowing point was one of the hound's eyes, and when it looked up at him, the other incandescent crimson eye became visible. Already, Canning felt a dull pain in his chest and he gasped. His wife noticed his sudden intake of breath.

'You alright, dear?' she asked from the bed.

'Yes. Come and have a look at this – quickly!' There was a slight harshness to Canning's whispered words.

A yawning Mrs Canning dragged herself from the bed and went to stand next to her husband. She saw the giant dog sitting on the pavement on the other side of the road, and she and her husband then saw the arrival of two other dogs. They sat in a row, their glowing eyes making it obvious that they were watching the window the couple was gazing from.

'Do you believe me now?' Canning asked his wife.

'Go downstairs and call the police!' she said, her eyes bulging with terror as she looked at the menacing shadowy dogs, then she remembered the way her husband has been gasping, and she said, 'On second thoughts, *I'll* go down and call them!'

'Don't bother,' said Canning, 'there's nothing the police can do about three stray dogs this time of night. I wish I still had my old Army revolver – ' Canning was saying when one of the dogs came running across the road towards the house.

'Oh!' Mrs Canning drew back from the window and clutched at her husband's arm.

'It's alright dear, they can't get in,' said Canning, and he leaned forward and watched as the canine goliath stopped below the window and sat down. It looked up at him and opened its mouth. 'Give me money!' it said, and this time the words were much clearer than the last time he had heard the thing utter its demand.

Mrs Canning screamed, but her husband hugged her and said, 'It's alright, dear, it can't get you!'

The dog below suddenly lowered itself almost to the pavement and with his belly brushing against the ground it crept behind a car, and the couple wondered what it was doing. Then they saw a man come staggering down the street. He was singing *Ah! Sweet Mystery of Life* in a dismal attempt at the singing style of the late American tenor Mario Lanza. The two other dogs across the road suddenly charged at the man, and he turned, tried to flee, but fell over, cracking his head on the pavement. He lay there with a spreading pool of blood under his head, and one of the dogs lapped at this blood.

'*Now* we're calling the police!' decided Canning, and he and his wife rushed downstairs and he dialled 999, then told the operator what had just happened, but of course, he did not mention the vocal ability of one of the strange dogs. An ambulance and a police car arrived in Sandon Street ten minutes later, and by then the three dogs were nowhere to be seen. The drunk was unconscious but alive, and the police called at Canning's house and quizzed him about 'the three big dogs' he had mentioned to the police operator, but he said he had no idea who the hounds belonged to. After that night, the Cannings never saw those three canine behemoths or the three Nigerians ever again.

# KELLY AND EDWARD

The most sensational materialisations of the violent
"Renshaw Street Ghost" (as it was called in the local
press) were from 2006 to 2010, when the ghost started
to prowl Central Hall – then the home of the displaced
Quiggins folk from School Lane – who reunited en
masse to create a spectacular emporium of alternative
stores known as Grand Central, and the reportedly
nasty Victorian ghost walked amongst the motley
clientele – mostly Goths, emos, hippies, skaters, punks,
rockabilly's and other people of the unfolding
subculture scene. The ghost was always described as a
tall, caped top-hatted man with bushy white sideburns
and piercing icy blue eyes who strutted through solid
walls and struck out indiscriminately with his walking
cane. In 1922 the spectral ruffian appeared out of the
blue one evening and terrorised a Mr Parry, who ran a
bookshop on Renshaw Street, and then, after a few
weeks of nerve-jangling goings on at the shop, the
ghost went away for a few years. In the 1980s the same
figure in a topper with his distinctive piercing blue
eyes, silvery-white sideburns and swinging cane was
seen with a contorted flame-lit face on the very same
premises where Parry had been haunted – but by then,

Parry had passed into the hereafter himself and the bookshop had been extensively remodelled to become a Kwik Fit garage. Around this time, the ghost was allegedly seen in the cellar of a nearby pub on Renshaw Street (and I detailed his antics in the *Merseymart*, as well as in one of my *Haunted Liverpool* books, and then the cloaked bellicose phantom moved into Grand Central around 2006. In the October of that year, a very pretty 19-year-old girl named Kelly went into Grand Central with her best friend, 18-year-old Avril. Kelly was in a mood because her trainee hairdresser sister Fliss had made a royal mess of dying and styling her hair. The Venetian red streaks looked bright orange and the Phthalo blue ones looked purple – and the crocheted dreadlocks were too tight and hurting her scalp. On top of that, this was the day she was supposed to be actually physically meeting up with Murray, a man she had only met in the sterile insubstantial cyberspace of a chat-room. He was into vampires and Jack the Ripper and said he'd turn up in full Victorian garb. That wasn't the end of Kelly's angst; in addition to the ultimate bad hair day, Avril was supposed to lend her a pair of Converse trainers – but she'd clean forgotten to bring them. Kelly went to a vintage footwear shop at the hyperbazaar and as she sat down, trying the different shoes on and trying to calm herself down by singing The Kooks' song *She Moves in Her Own Way* - Murray appeared, wearing a top hat, a long black frock coat, straight black trousers and highly-polished glasslike shoes. He sported a full, well-kept black beard – but the Murray Kelly had seen on a webcam had a wispy ginger goatee beard. 'Hi,' Kelly said, looking up from her seat, and Avril returned from browsing in a graphic novel store and asked the man, 'You Murray?'

The retro-clothed six-foot-tall man ignored her and in a rich, sonorous voice, he said to Kelly: 'You have been mine before – but how long ago I cannot tell! That pale visage, those cherry lips and those green eyes that sparkle like Sirius shall be mine again.'

'Yer what?' was a puzzled Kelly's reply, and the man stooped and picked her up and held her in his arms. The girl behind the counter of the shoe shop stopped poking her thumbs into her mobile and watched the proceedings as she chewed her gum.

'Okay Murray, this is beyond cringey and super-uncool,' sighed a barefooted Kelly, and she tried to get out of his arms, but then she started to feel strangely lethargic and weak. Grand Central started to fade away and Avril shrieked, 'Oh fuck!' as she gazed at Kelly in the arms of the over-affectionate man because her friend was now semi-transparent.

'You shall be my wife in the world beyond this hell on earth!' the man of mystery announced, and Kelly was overcome with the concentrated scent of lavender. A bright halo of multicoloured light shone around the would-be abductor and Kelly – and Avril could not believe her eyes. A tunnel of blue phosphorescent light opened up behind the top-hatted gent. There was a flash of red light to the right of Avril, and she saw another outdated (and older-looking) figure in a top hat and cape appear. He had prominent white sideburns which contrasted against a reddish skin. This had to be the Renshaw Street Ghost. This mature apparition roared 'Edward! Release her you damned fool!' And he struck the head of the ghost holding

Kelly with a cane. Avril saw the topper crumple from the impact of the cane smashing down upon it and "Edward" grimaced before he and the other ghost vanished. At this point, Kelly saw the Grand Central return abruptly all around her and now, unsupported by Edward, she fell to the floor. The impact winded her because she landed on her back. She lay there in shock, then smiled and told Avril, 'Forget Murray - Edward's my type of guy!'

Avril kept saying, 'Oh my God,' over and over and she helped Kelly up. Minutes later, Kelly saw Murray enter Grand Central. He was about 5 feet 3 inches tall, and he wore a trilby and a long black coat. Kelly ran off and hid from him behind a clothes rack and she made a fist at a giggling Avril, who pretended she was going to go and tell Murray where her friend was hiding. The girls later went upstairs to the café in Grand Central and drank coffee after coffee as they discussed what had happened. A young man on a nearby table overheard the girls talking and said that the ghost in the top hat with the cane had been seen all over Grand Central, from the basement shops up to the rooms in the higher reaches of the building. No one knew whose ghost he was. Kelly had the feeling that the ghost that had struck Edward – and possibly prevented him from taking her to God knows where – had been his father. Kelly wondered what Edward's ghost had meant when he said, 'You have been mine before.' Had she known him in some previous life, perhaps? Kelly never saw Edward again, and yet she went to Grand Central almost every day in the hope that she would meet him, and when she told Avril she would go off with the ghost the next time he tried to take her, her friend told her in a sad voice, 'Oh don't, Kel – I'd miss you.' Alas, the diverse hive of Grand Central with its stalls and stores that catered for every shopper of the alternative is sadly no more, and the place is now the scene of some other development, and curiously, the ghosts have also apparently left – or perhaps they have gone into a period of hibernation until they come back out of the woodwork with a vengeance; time will tell.

# MORE TALES OF THE UNDEAD

I've written a lot about local and national cases of vampires over the years, and even published a book solely on the subject called *Vampires of Great Britain* to show, using little-known historical and contemporary cases, that the vampire is not only found in Eastern Europe, but in Britain too, and that these parasitic beings can, and do, turn up in the most mundane everyday places. They can also walk by day, but most choose not to – not because they are allergic to ultraviolet rays or the 'pure sacred' light of the sun, but because they are cunning creatures of stealth who use the cover of darkness to attack their prey and to carry out reconnaissance with a low chance of being seen. The moon is *not* the sun of the vampire; the tactical advantages of attacks during darkness (when the victim might be tired or asleep and hence off-guard) are also used by the armies of the world and are known as night combat.

And the vampire can strike in the middle of a busy urban setting just as easily as an attack at a secluded spot in the country. I recall a case years ago where a petite and very beautiful 20-year-old blonde girl named Emma Lee Hall-Lambert went out with her friends in Liverpool city centre one night. Emma Lee went from pub to pub and had a bit too much to drink. She somehow became separated from her friends and after staggering out of McDonald's on Lord Street around midnight, she ended up blacking out in the badly-lit doorway of a closed store. A 19-year-old friend of the girl named Josh happened to be walking up Lord Street that night, and he saw Emma Lee lying in the doorway, and there was a man with long red hair who looked as if he was in his thirties, and he was kneeling on the floor by the unconscious girl and appeared to be sucking her big toe. He'd even removed the girl's platform shoe to indulge in the toe-sucking. Josh lunged at the man and asked him what he thought he was doing, and the stranger turned to him and said he had a foot fetish and smiled. He then quickly got up, and Josh threw a punch, but quick as a flash, the red-headed man's hand flew up and intercepted the fist. Josh felt as if he had punched a brick because the stranger's hand felt as hard as stone. The red-headed man then ran from the doorway at a phenomenal speed and vanished into the night. Josh described the speedy departure as looking like something out the old silent films where the people seem to move faster because of the slower film frame rate. The man did not even make a sound as he flew off, and Josh thought he moved too fast for a human being. The teen lifted Emma Lee to her feet and she opened her eyes and seemed puzzled to see him. She had not seen Josh since the night of her 18th birthday. Josh helped her put her shoe back on and he invited her to his flat and assured her he was not after sex – he merely wanted to be her friend. He'd just split with his girlfriend and felt lonely. Emma Lee got in a taxi with him and when she got to Josh's flat, she saw that the insole of her platform shoe was squelching with blood. It transpired that the girl had a tiny hole in her big toe that would not stop bleeding. Josh put a plaster on the hole but the blood still came through and then he bandaged the big toe and eventually, around 4am the blood started to clot and the bleeding stopped. Josh then told Emma Lee about the man with the long red hair who had been sucking her toe as she was out cold, and he also told Emma Lee how he'd tried to confront the man but he had run off at a phenomenal speed. Emma Lee started to recall things; she said that she had been followed by a man with long red hair all night. He seemed to be in every pub she went to and she vaguely recalled him walking behind her on Mathew Street. 'If he bit my toe, maybe I should get a tetanus jab,' said Emma Lee.

'Nah, you'll be alright,' Josh tried to assure her, as he was feeling tired at almost five in the morning, but Emma Lee was renowned for being a hypochondriac and she told Josh she didn't want to die of lockjaw if she had tetany. He therefore had to telephone for a private cab to take him and the girl to the A&E of the Royal Teaching Hospital, where a nurse said the wound on Emma Lee's toe looked as if it was a puncture mark of the type made by an animal's fang, and the nurse asked the girl if she had a cat. Emma Lee said she had but it would never bite her. She didn't mention the red-headed man who seemed to have inflicted the strange bite. Emma Lee insisted on getting a tetanus jab and eventually the nurse gave her a shot. Emma Lee and Josh started going out together as the girl thought it was lovely how he'd been concerned about her. About a month later, the couple went to town one Wednesday night for a meal at Bella Italia, and then they decided to go and have a drink at a pub at the Albert Dock where a relative of Josh's worked. Around eleven, Josh went to call for a cab but Emma Lee told her boyfriend she felt her dress "which used to be dead floaty on me" was now a bit tight – in other words she thought she'd put on a bit of weight – so she said she'd rather walk a bit of a distance from the Albert Dock – for exercise - before they jumped in a cab. Josh shook his head but took her hand and the couple walked off, intending to get a hackney cab at the rank on Hanover Street. 'Hey, look at this picture of me here;' Emma Lee held the screen of her phone up to Josh, and then she said, 'am I fatter now than I am there?'

Josh smirked and looked at the picture of his beloved girl on her phone and said, 'You just look the exact same, Em – don't start going all anorexic.'

The young couple then laughed and talked about the night they'd had and their minds were as far away as the dark subject of the supernatural as they could be, when something very strange occurred. As Emma Lee and Josh, were walking along Lord Street, they noticed the thoroughfare was a bit quiet, although it was the mid-week. The couple passed a secluded alleyway called Dorans Lane – which runs from Lord Street to Harrington Street. There is a canopy over the entrance to this lane with a sign proclaiming it as a way to the boutique shopping centre Cavern Walks. About three quarters of a way down this alleyway, Josh caught a glimpse of that red-headed man – the one who had siphoned off the blood from his girlfriend via her toe – and he was at it again. The girl was a brunette, and looked as if she was only eighteen, and this time she was face down and apparently out cold – and that sinister individual was again sucking at her big toe.

'Emma! Look! I don't believe it,' said Josh, stopping and pulling Emma Lee back by her hand.

'What?' the girl asked, and then she followed the line of Josh's gaze and she saw the two figures on Dorans Lane. 'Oh God – it's *him*.'

Josh tried to let go of Emma Lee's hand but she tightened her grip and held onto his arm with her other hand too. 'Josh, don't! Call the police instead!' she cried, trying to prevent her boyfriend from tackling the weirdo.

'By the time the bizzies get here she'll be dead!' Josh replied and yanked his hand away from his girl.

'Josh, if you love me you won't go!' Emma cried, and her stomach went into freefall in panic.

'Just stay there, I'll be alright!' Josh told her, and then something incredible happened – Josh and Emma Lee turned their attention back to the bizarre blood-sucker – to find him gone. In literally a couple of seconds he had run off. Josh and Emma Lee ran to the girl's aid, and Josh shouted to his girlfriend, 'Where did he go?' and then he ran around the corner and saw the attacker was not on Harrington Street – but then he heard a voice. 'Hey lad, are you looking for *him*?' said an elderly drunken man who was leaning against a steel roller shutter. He was pointing upwards. Josh looked up, and there, peeping over the top landing of a black cast-iron fire escape was the red-headed assailant. He jumped from that fire escape onto the roof of the four-storey building like Spring-Heeled Jack. Josh and the old man on Harrington Street then watched the figure above leap from the roof. He sailed through the air, crossing a 12 foot gap between buildings, and landed on the roof of the British Home Store. His observers on the ground then lost sight of him.

The drunk looked at Josh, shook his head, and said, 'What drugs do to people, eh?'

Josh ran back to Emma Lee and the girl on the floor. The victim was sitting up and holding the hand of Josh's girlfriend, and she was in tears. 'She said he grabbed her on Lord Street and must have dragged her down here,' said Emma Lee, adding, 'Her name's Beth – she's only seventeen.'

Josh looked at Beth's right big toe; it had the same red spot he'd seen before and there was a small amount of blood on the ground and her sandal was lying close by.

'We should call the police,' Emma Lee suggested.

'That fellah who did this,' said Josh looking at his girlfriend, and then he wondered how to phrase the remainder of the sentence without sounding like a nut. 'Well, he escaped by getting onto a roof, and he jumped from the roof of this place on the right here, and landed on the top of the British Home Store, honest. If I tell the police that, they'll think we're all on acid.'

'Can you help me up?' Beth asked Emma Lee, as she put on her sandal, but Josh helped her to her feet and as the young girl walked along, she said her toe was 'stinging'.

Josh telephoned a cab and took the girl to A&E – and the same nurse who had treated Emma looked at the girl's toe very suspiciously. Perhaps she thought the girls were injecting something via their toes. She put a dressing on Beth's toe and the young lady seemed scared when Josh told her how the same thing had happened to Emma Lee just a month back when she'd been attacked by the red-headed man. Beth half-joking made a remark that made Josh think; she said, 'He's not a vampire is he?'

Josh looked at Beth and said, 'You know what? My Nan used to say "There's many a true work said in a joke" – and you might have hit the nail on the head.'

'How do you mean?' Emma Lee asked, intrigued and a little bit unnerved.

'Em, you should have seen the way he jumped from the top of that fire escape,' said Josh, recalling the creepy agility of the attacker, 'and remember how fast he got away from you when I first tackled him? Athletes who have trained for years can't move that fast.'

'Oh my God, if he *is* a vampire wouldn't we become vampires too because he bit us?' asked a worried Beth.

Emma Lee, the perfect hypochondriac, gulped and then looked at Josh and her eyes were asking the same question Beth had posed.

'Well, hopefully not,' Josh said, and then he tried to back-pedal. 'I mean, let's not let our imagination run away with us like, and er, there are those people – what do they call them? Traceurs! Yes, they do that sport thing, Parkour – they run across buildings and jump from roof to roof. They break the law and trespass sometimes because it's just like a challenge – that's what that fellah might be.'

'But why is he going round sucking people's toes?' Beth asked, 'And how does he knock people out? He touched my shoulder and then I was gone.'

'I think she might be right, Josh,' said Emma Lee, 'I'm going to start wearing a crucifix.'

'That's a good idea,' said Beth, 'I will too.'

And the girls did; they bought crucifixes from a jeweller and slept with Bibles in their bedrooms. Emma Lee and Beth became good friends, brought together in a most peculiar manner. Josh had the feeling that the red-headed man, whatever he is, might be living in the vicinity of Lord Street, because the two attacks had taken place off that thoroughfare, but so far, he has not been seen by the trio and they hope they never set eyes on him again.

Going back half a century, we come to another case of a possible urban vampire. On the Sunday evening of 10 May 1959, temperatures across the North West suddenly rose to 70 degrees, and a rare phenomenon known as "vapour lock" took place; petrol in the fuel delivery systems of cars changed from liquid to gas and the vehicles stalled. Hundreds of cars – including many in Liverpool – came to a halt on the roads. David Avery's Ford Anglia conked out on Huyton's Stanley Road, and when he and his friend Alan Holt – both aged 18 – tried to bump-start the vehicle, they noticed a wild party in full swing at a nearby terraced house. The lads could hear Jerry Lee Lewis singing *Great Balls of Fire* on a record player at the house and the lads could see the shadows of people jiving away on the blinds. Two girls came out onto the doorstep of the house, smoking cigarettes as they held bottles of Coke in their hands. They giggled as they glanced at David and Alan, and David gave up trying to start the car and went to chat to the teenage girls. David learned that the party was being thrown by a popular girl named Sylvia, and her parties always went on till the milkman arrived, the girls explained.

'Are her parents away or something?' David asked

the girls, but one of them shook her head and explained that Sylvia owned the house and she was an orphan.

David fetched Alan from the immobile car and they went into the house and joined the wild party. Sylvia looked as if she was aged about nineteen and was very beautiful with shoulder length black hair. She was dancing barefoot in a tight white dress and all the young men encircled her, seemingly mesmerized by her beauty and sex appeal. David and Alan fell for her immediately. There was an endless supply of bottled beer and food, and by 3am, David realised his friend was missing. He asked some of the guests if they'd seen his friend and one of them told him a lad of Alan's description was upstairs with Sylvia – in her bedroom. David was going to knock at the bedroom door and see if his mate really had 'copped off' with the hostess of the party but he decided to drink and dance with the many girls present instead.

At 3.15am two policemen called at the house because neighbours were complaining about the racket, and there was a scream upstairs – a male scream. Alan Holt appeared at the top of the stairs in his underpants, clutching his neck. Blood was pouring from between his fingers. David and the policemen rushed to the teen's aid, and he told them Sylvia had bitten his neck and left wrist. The police went into the bedroom of the hostess – and saw her throw open the window before fearlessly jumping clean out of it. She landed in the street and ran off through a hailstorm at an incredible speed towards St Michael's Church. Years later I interviewed one of the policemen who chased Sylvia, and he told me how she jumped clean over an 8-foot wall in the church cemetery to escape, and how he found what looked like contact lenses and blood near a grave. The landlord Sylvia had rented the house from recalled her "strange eyes" (so perhaps she had worn contact lenses to make her eyes seem normal), but whoever – and whatever – she was remains a mystery, for she was never seen again. Alan Holt had nightmares about the way she had bitten him that night. He said she had playfully nibbled his neck earlier in the evening as he lay in bed with her, and at one point Alan said, 'I've always wanted a girl like you Sylvia,' to which Sylvia had replied, 'How romantically Byronic.' He was sure she had said "Byronic" and not "ironic" because she had then told him: 'You remind me of Byron.'

She might have simply meant that Alan's romantic remark about always wanting someone like her reminded her of Byron's poetry, but Alan thought something in her eyes was much older than her young teenaged body, and he wondered if perhaps she had actually met Lord Byron – who had died in 1824. Was she a vampire? No one seemed to know who she was or where she came from. She was well-spoken and did not have a local accent. It really is difficult to say whether Sylvia was a vampiress or not, but she did bite Alan's neck and she survived a jump from an upper floor window - and a policeman witnessed her clear an eight-foot-tall cemetery wall.

It's a basic fact of nature's food chain that higher life forms eat lower ones. The human race have walked on the moon and unravelled their own genetic code but a majority of them still eat the flesh of 'lower' animals – and likewise the vampire (mentioned by every religion on earth) is said to live off the blood of the human. Vampires are mentioned many times in the Bible, most graphically in Proverbs 30:14: "There are those whose teeth are swords, whose fangs are knives" and the Bible categorically forbids the drinking of blood, "for the blood is the life". In October 1888, at the height of the Jack the Ripper scare, 40-year-old Louisa Johnson, a Roby widow who was staying at the North Western Hotel on Lime Street, sensed there was something very eerie about a tall foreign-speaking man who had recently booked into the hotel. He wore a velvet mask, supposedly because he was said to be disfigured, and was alleged to be a wine expert, but when one of the cases being transported to his room (on the top floor) opened by accident, the porter said he had seen bottles of what looked like blood come tumbling out of the case. Mrs Johnson told the hotel manager that the foreign guest could possibly be the Ripper, but was assured that "Mr Zigismund" was a respected Hungarian vintner on business in the city and that the bottles had probably contained a rich red burgundy. That evening, Louisa Johnson caught a fleeting glimpse of Zigismund in the corner of her room. She screamed and he vanished. Louisa ran into the corridor and met an American guest named William Powell who calmed her down for a moment, but then she became highly nervous again and rattled off a garbled version of what she had just witnessed and she also told the American about the porter's story of the bottles of blood. Powell said something odd which frightened the widow. 'Well ma'am, if it was blood in the bottles, and if you did see him appear and vanish in your room, is this Hungarian fellow a vampire?'

Seeing how afraid Louisa was, he made light of his comment and reassured her there were no such things as vampires, but that night, Louisa hardly slept, although she did not experience anything supernatural.

The next morning, Powell called at Louisa's room and told her he had purchased a silver crucifix which she should wear – just in case Zigismund was a bloodsucker.

'But Mr Powell, I thought you said there are no such things – ' a worried Louisa said in a trembling voice, but the American took her hand and placed the silver crucifix in her palm.

Powell smiled and nodded. 'I know what I said, but this is just a precaution, that's all ma'am – and I hope you won't be offended by the gesture.' That evening - 31 October - the city was visited by a thick fog, and at midnight the screams of a prostitute named Lizzie Stewart echoed along Lime Street. She told police constables Barr and Byrne a man in a cloak had swooped down on her from one of the windows of the North Western Hotel and had tried to grab her. The policemen looked at one another with grinning faces, then PC Barr said to Lizzie, 'I do believe someone's as drunk as the moon in a puddle.'

Lizzie's eyes seemed to flash with anger and she replied, 'No, no drink has passed my lips! As true as we're all standing here, he jumped out of that top window and floated down – and that's before mighty God, constable!'

'And Billy's uncle here is a monkey,' laughed PC Byrne, nodding to his colleague.

'And if Jim's aunt had been a man, she'd have been

his uncle,' joked PC Barr.

'Ooh!' Lizzie huffed, and then she made a grunting sound of disapproval before turning her backs on the police and marching off into the fog.

Later that night, the two sceptical policemen – and many others - encountered the sinister cloaked man – who was said to have had "the face of a devil". The weird figure was allegedly encountered outside the North Western Hotel and when he was confronted by baton-wielding policemen, he bounded off into the fog like Spring-Heeled Jack; in fact some swore he *was* the "Leaping Terror" who, as most readers of my books will know, was a bizarre-looking entity – a type of cross between Batman and the Joker – who visited Liverpool on many occasions. Mr Zigismund vanished from his room that same night and was never heard from again.

From the Halloween of 1888 we travel forward in time to the Liverpool of 1955, to another alleged case of vampirism.

Many years ago in the 1950s, an eerie rumour circulated Liverpool; a real-life vampire was at large in the city. In my own experiences over the years, it would seem that there is often a grain of truth in rumours, and this was certainly the case with this one. I mentioned a very abbreviated form of the story I am about to relate on the *Billy Butler Show* one afternoon on BBC Radio Merseyside, and through listener feedback I eventually traced the woman at the centre of the sinister gossip. Her name was Carolyn, and she supplied with a lot of the details concerning this strange account. One sultry August evening in 1955, as the sun dipped into Liverpool Bay, 18-year-old Dingle waitress Carolyn Grace cut a stunning figure in her black stilettos and a flared carmine dress as she left her workplace - a café on Stanley Street. She had a pale but beautiful face, and her hair was done up in a fashionable beehive. She was pursued by a Teddy Boy pestering her for a date, and although she told the Ted she was not interested, he kept walking in front of Carolyn, asking her, 'Why, aren't I good enough for you, eh?' and then he started to hurl some very nasty insults at her, and this went on until he reached Dale Street. Miss Grace heard a loud bang, and something struck the side of her face, just under her left eye, and whatever it was it stung her. The startled waitress turned left to see the Ted falling to the floor with blood on his lips. A man was standing six feet away and he looked as if he was in his early twenties. He still had his left arm extended and his fist clenched, and Carolyn realised he had just punched the Ted. She then saw one of the Teddy's boy's front teeth on the pavement; that had been the mysterious object that had struck the side of her face.

The Ted hit the floor with a thump and knocked his forehead hard against the pavement. Although he was unconscious, the Ted's eyes were open.

'Was there *any* need for that?' Carolyn asked the violent stranger. He was a very handsome but exceedingly pallid. Even his hands looked as white as milk. He had coal-black hair, dark penetrating eyes, and was dressed in a long black trench coat.

'I'm sorry, but I can't stomach degenerates like that who talk to women in that tone,' he said, and he looked about, then turned up his collar and fixed his strange staring eyes upon Carolyn's frightened blue eyes.

'I could have dealt with him myself,' she said, then shot a disgusted look at the tooth on the floor and hurried away across the road before the lights changed.

'Carolyn, isn't it?' the man said to the back of her head, and he was very close behind her now. 'I've seen you round the town a few times.'

'How did you know my name,' she said, without turning around. She was scared to turn around as she reasoned that if he'd been following her, he obviously had some fixation – and was so obsessed he had almost killed that Teddy Boy. She wondered what he'd do to her if she rejected his advances.

'Carolyn! Please wait! I would never harm you so stop thinking that!' he cried, and several passersby heard him say this and they slowed down and looked at him as he grabbed the arm of the waitress.

'Get off me or I'll call a policeman!' she yelled.

'Carolyn, please just hear me out; please Carolyn!' he insisted, and she thought he sounded hurt, almost as if he was going to cry in the way he had addressed her. She halted and turned to face him, and now, at closer quarters she thought he looked vaguely familiar. She felt as if she had perhaps noticed him around the city before, but she couldn't recall just where. Carolyn had a sharp sense of intuition and she just felt that although there was something uncanny about this man, he was also very sad.

'I give you my word I will not harm a hair on your head,' he said, 'I'd rather kill myself than do that. Please, let me give you a lift home. My car is over there and I need to tell you something.'

She looked into his eyes and she felt strangely calm

all of a sudden. She wondered if some kind of hypnotic power was at work, influencing her, but for *some* reason, a reason unknown even to her, she accepted his offer of a lift. He drove her homewards in what seems to have been an old 1939 Bentley, and whilst driving through the dusky streets of Liverpool, he made a startling claim.

In a calm voice, as he read the road beyond the windscreen, the man said: 'Dearest Carolyn, you may find this hard to believe, but I cannot lie to you, and if we should become friends, or hopefully more than that, I cannot hide this thing deep down that could ruin a relationship if I don't bring it out into the open. I am what you would call a vampire.'

Carolyn froze with fear, because she believed him; her sharp intuition sensed he was telling the truth. She could almost detect the black aura around him. Straight away she thought about throwing the door of the car open and running away, but he suddenly said to her: 'Please don't think about that – you might be run down by car or a bus.'

'You can read my mind,' she said in a resigned tone, and her lips twitched with nerves.

'Carolyn, I was bayoneted in the first lot – World War One – and I was left to die – and I did die. I'll show you the bayonet wounds if you don't believe me.'

'I believe you,' Carolyn answered, and her voice was barely a whisper. She felt so afraid. She recalled the offer of a lift home from a regular at the café where she worked, and how, if she had only taken it, she wouldn't have ended up in this terrifying situation.

'I was dead in the mud with all of my friends – and enemies – around me, all dead. And then I opened my eyes and saw blinding sunlight. I thought I'd entered the Kingdom of Heaven. A young French woman all in black was standing over me. She said 'Je suis la résurrection et la vie!' ['I am the resurrection and the life!']. I didn't understand French then, and she told me in broken English that she was a vampire, and that she had brought me back to life so she would have company. She said she had chosen me for everlasting life because I looked like her brother. He'd been put on the guillotine over a century before. Anyway, she had bitten my neck and infused her blood with mine making me immortal – but at a price, though. I have to now continually feed off the blood of the living to survive.'

'Please let me go,' Carolyn said, and she had her hand on the handle of the car door.

He started to cry. 'Carolyn, you are the exact double of Catherine, a girl I was engaged to back in 1913, but she died and I can't bring her back. Please, if you were mine, I'd make you immortal too if you so desired and we'd be together forever.'

'Why didn't you marry the woman who brought you back?' Carolyn asked, her hand gripping the handle – it felt stiff as she tried to turn it.

'She was a lesbian. She had someone – ' the vampire was telling her as Carolyn suddenly forced the door open and threw herself into the road. She screamed as she rolled along the cobbled surface of Princes Avenue and a car screeched behind the Bentley and hit it, and then Carolyn got up, and she looked at her grazed palms and she ran off and hid behind the front wall of a house in one of the streets off the avenue. She expected him to come peeping over the wall, but he didn't. Carolyn rushed home in a terrible state as skies darkened, and when she finally reached her house, she burst into tears. Her mother and father said the man she had met had just been either some prankster or someone "away with the mixer" – a slang term in that day and age for a person who had mental health problems. Carolyn said she was sure he *was* indeed some sort of real-life vampire and she was so afraid of meeting him again, she gave up her job at the café, which caused quite an argument between the girl and her parents because she gave them five pounds' keep each week and now she'd have nothing whatsoever to contribute. A fortnight elapsed, and then, in the dead of night, Carolyn Grace awoke – and there was the vampire, standing at the side of her bed. He did not say a word, but his face looked so sad. Carolyn had been in the habit of sleeping with her bedside lamp on since the last encounter, and by its light she could see him clearly standing there – this was no dream. She ducked under the blankets and screamed, and as her father opened the bedroom door and rushed in to see what the matter was, Carolyn came up from under the covers saw that the man who she believed to be a vampire had vanished, and he was never seen by her again.

Next in this sanguine chapter of the mysterious undead, we come to the strange case of the Vampiress of Cavendish Road...

There are a dozen Victorian mansions lining Cavendish Road on the verdant fringes of Birkenhead Park, all of them built in the early 1850s. In 1858 something sinister took place at one of the mansion houses on Birkenhead's Cavendish Road which generated a wave of gossip in the neighbourhood and beyond. What is whispered in one ear is often heard a hundred miles away thanks to the grapevine of the rumourmonger, and in the autumn of 1858 some very strange rumours concerning one of the palatial residences on Cavendish Road are known to have circulated as far as London, where the weird story concerning a vampire was discussed in hushed tones within the panelled rooms of many a gentleman's club. The rumour had it that the wealthy Gallienne family of Cavendish Road had been visited by an actual real-life vampire one night, and the fiend had bitten a sleeping daughter of Charles Gallienne before making its escape from the mansion. The daughter, Pandora Gallienne, aged nineteen, had since been transformed into a vampiress, and despite several exorcisms by Jesuits, the girl continued to hunger for blood. Charles Gallienne, unable to have his daughter ritually killed by having a stake driven through her heart, had entombed Pandora alive in a specially-constructed vault in the cellar of the mansion, and the afflicted young lady had also been bound in chains with crosses cemented into the door of the tomb. Miss Gallienne had been suspiciously absent at her church for over a month, and her father had maintained that his beloved daughter was gravely ill with consumption. Months went by and Charles Gallienne claimed his darling daughter had died from her accursed illness – but people on Cavendish Road had heard a girl's screams emanating from the Gallienne house in the dead of night. Over a century passed and in the 1960s the mansion once owned by Charles Gallienne was purchased by a draughtsman named Arthur Moss, and he hired a gang of workmen to renovate the house in October 1962. There was a lot of water in the cellar, so much so that the iron lintels down there were badly rusted, as were the water pipes. When Jim Griffiths, the boss of the workmen inspected the waterlogged cellar, he noticed that an archway in the cellar wall had been bricked up and there was a huge rusted cross mounted on the bricks of this filled-in archway. The cross fell off the wall when Jim gently pulled at it. Water dripping from a leaky gutter had seeped through the floor in the backyard and into the cellar, so the gutter was mended and then the workmen set about installing vents and an extraction fan in the cellar – but then some strange things began to happen. Davy O'Sullivan, an Irish plasterer, said he had heard a woman singing *Star of County Down* – an old Irish folk song – in the cellar. 'And why would a ghost be singing that song?' asked a bemused Jim Griffiths, and he accused O'Sullivan of drinking on the job. A few days later, however, Davy O'Sullivan, Jim Griffiths and a plumber named Harry Lewis were in the cellar when they distinctly heard a woman's eerie-sounding voice singing, and the plumber said, 'That's an old ballad my grandmother used to sing. It's called *The Unquiet Grave.*'

'You're wrong it's an Irish song called *Star of County Down*,' O'Sullivan insisted, and the plumber shook his head and said, 'No, *The Unquiet Grave* has the same melody as that song, but it's much older.'

All of a sudden the cellar wall appeared to dissolve into swirling vapour and standing three feet beyond the disintegrating walls stood a beautiful smiling young lady in an old-fashioned white dress, bound in chains. O'Sullivan fled from the cellar but Griffiths and Lewis remained rooted to the spot, hypnotised by the luminous green eyes of the weird woman. She broke the chains leading from the walls and floor to a metal collar and she lunged at the plumber Lewis, but a single chain attached to a band around her waist prevented her from reaching him, and she hissed as her face underwent a demonic transformation. The owner of the house, Arthur Moss, alerted to the terrifying incident by O'Sullivan, entered the cellar and exclaimed, 'Jesus Christ!'

The female entity shrunk back at these words and spat blood at Moss, and the two mesmerised men suddenly snapped out of the spell exerted by the fiend and recoiled in horror, stumbling backwards. Moss instinctively picked up the rusted cross that had been attached to the wall and bravely thrust it at the ghastly-looking entity as Griffiths and Lewis ran out of the cellar. In an instant the wall of the tomb reappeared and Moss had the cross reattached to that wall. Priests were brought in to bless the cellar but the sounds of a demented woman singing and shrieking were heard night after night so Moss sold the residence. I researched the history of the 'vampiric woman' and discovered why she sings that song, *The Unquiet Grave*; it's a song about a woman who loved her husband so much, she brought him back after he died, and upon kissing him she in turn became a corpse – only in Pandora's case, her lover was allegedly a vampire, but he abandoned her after she became one of the undead.

I know a doctor who once laughed at the concept of vampires. He could not believe there were beings that could live far beyond the Biblically allotted lifespan of threescore years and ten and live off the blood of others for centuries. The doctor was a man of science, an adherent of the rational and not the fanciful and the superstitious, but one evening at his club when drink had loosened the tongue of the doctor, he told me of a very strange incident. One evening in the late 1970s when he was a trainee doctor he had been driving back from the Scarisbrick house of his girlfriend (later to become his wife). She was sitting next to him on the pleasant moonlit evening, and somewhere along the line, the doctor took a wrong turning and ended up travelling down a very narrow and winding country road called Acres Lane, not far from Lydiate. There were no Sat-nav computers in cars in the 1970s, and so the doctor's girlfriend consulted a trusty little old A-Z road atlas to find out just how to get home to Liverpool. As the car curved around a bend in Acres Lane, the doctor saw something in the road ahead, and he quickly braked.

A rather large, corpulent man lay in the middle of the road in a strange unnatural position – a position the doctor would see years later when he stopped to treat a man who had been knocked down by a taxi. The man in the road had obviously been knocked down by a vehicle, and he lay in pools of blood. Kneeling around the man were three girls – all aged about ten or twelve perhaps – and they all wore knee-length white nighties. Two of the minors were calmly lapping up the pools of blood around the inert figure like a cat lapping up milk from a dish. One of the girls looked as if she was kissing the road victim but she was engrossed in sucking blood out of his mouth. One of the children stopped lapping up the blood from the puddle for a moment and she looked up at the car. As she did this her eyes reflected back the headlamps of the doctor's vehicle in such a way, the girl seemed to have luminous eyes. The whole grotesque scene was so shocking, the doctor's girlfriend cried, 'Get out of here!'

The doctor beeped the car horn, but there was no reaction from the three girls, so he put the car into reverse and the wheels squealed as the vehicle rocketed backwards up Carr Lane – and those three bloodthirsty girls suddenly ran sideways like startled foxes across farmland. The doctor then stopped reversing and tried to go forward but stalled the car, and his girlfriend screamed, 'Get out of here! Oh my God, what were they?'

The vehicle screeched off down Carr Lane and the couple talked about the strange sight until they reached Maghull, where the doctor found a telephone box and anonymously reported the apparent hit and run incident to the police. He thought it wise to say nothing about those three little 'vampires' he and his girlfriend had seen enjoying the blood of the man. The doctor scanned the *Liverpool Echo* every day from then on but he never saw any reports about a hit and run on Carr Lane, although not every road accident is reported in the newspapers.

Still, the doctor could not accept the existence of vampires; he thought that perhaps the three girls might have been suffering from 'clinical vampirism' – also known as Renfield's syndrome – where a person develops a craving for human blood – but it's rare enough in one person, never mind three. 'That is true,' the doctor said, 'but to accept the existence of vampires would mean rewriting the text books of medicine'. I reminded him about all those textbooks that had to be rewritten when the theories of Copernicus, Einstein and Planck were published, and he clumsily changed the subject.

# JOHN'S GHOST

I've changed a few names to protect the guilty in this strange story of the supernatural. It was Saturday 23 November 1985. Lindsay, a 15-year-old girl who lived on Fazakerley's Montrovia Crescent, got up at 9am, watched the children's TV show *Saturday Superstore* on BBC1 as she dozily munched her toast in her pyjamas. The girl then washed her hair, dryed it, put on her make-up and got ready to go to town with her best friend Kayleigh (also aged 15), who lived just around the corner on Hawksmoor Road. Around 10:30am the girls boarded the bus into town for their usual Saturday morning mooch around the clothes shops and St John's Precinct and then it would be a Wimpey burger and a milkshake, then back home again. Today, Lindsay had been told by her Uncle Ray to call in at Penny Lane Records on Bold Street to buy a single (for £1.50) by L.A.M. – Liverpool Against Militant – called *Militant Out*. Lindsay bought the record and then the girls left the store. Kayleigh noticed something across the other side of Bold Street near the Halifax bank. 'Hey, what's that?' She pointed to a gaggle of people standing around a young bearded man who was sitting cross-legged on a carpet in the middle of a pedestrianized Bold Street with someone well over six feet in height standing next to him – and this someone was covered with a white sheet that stretched from his head to the pavement. The girls went to see what was going on and Lindsay asked two lads who the fellah was under the sheet. 'John's ghost,' said one of the lads with a lopsided smirk, adding, 'supposed to be a real spirit that can talk to people who've died, like. That divvy sittin' down is John. He's nuts.'

'What did you say your ghost's name was?' an old woman asked John, who replied, 'Frankalmoigne,' and he spelt out the odd name. 'Ask him about anyone you've lost, love.'

'Hey Frank,' the woman addressed the figure in the shroud, and there were ripples of laughter from the crowd, 'can you talk to my husband Billy Hudson?'

There was a pause, then a deep voice replied from the sheeted man: 'Billy died at the Northern Hospital in 1976, and you held his hand, Maggie...'

Old Maggie said, 'Oh, he knows my name!' She stumbled, unsteady on her feet and a young lady gripped her hand and said, 'You alright Nan?'

'Billy wants you to go to the allotment to get some fresh air, Maggie,' said the ghost. 'And Billy loved the roses you put on his grave on his birthday last month.'

Old Maggie got out a handkerchief and dabbed her eyes with it, and in a broken voice she said to some of the sympathetic women in the crowd, 'I don't know whether it's a gimmick, but I *did* put roses on Billy's grave last month. Oh, I have so many questions for my Billy.'

But Maggie couldn't get a word in edgeways because other people in the crowd bombarded Frankalmoigne the ghost with requests for people they'd lost.

'Frank – whatever you call yourself,' said one woman who looked as if she was in her twenties, 'I lost my little boy when he was five, can you...' she said but started to cry. A few women hugged her and held her hand and one of them said, 'Ah, it's alright love, take your time.' Tears rolled down the lady's eyes as she fought to make the request again. 'His name was Bobby and he was...he was knocked down.'

'Bobby was adopted by your grandmother Elsie on the other side,' said the ghost in the pure white shroud, 'and because he died just before his sixth birthday, your grandmother and grandfather spoiled him rotten. He's being taken care of, and he knows you'll be joining him one day, so don't be sad, Bobby is in very good hands!'

The woman said to the ghost, 'Oh thank you! Thank you!' and she opened her purse and tried to offer John a five pound note but he rejected it with his palm and a shake of his head. 'You keep that love,' said John, 'your lovely smile was payment enough.'

Quite a crowd soon gathered, and money was continually offered to John, but he consistently refused it and uttered variations of his reply to one father who had lost his daughter in a car crash: 'My payment is giving you comfort.'

Lindsay was a quiet girl but she had to ask about her late Nan, and she went red as she asked Frankalmoigne: 'Excuse me, but can you tell me if my Nan is alright? He name was Jean Jones and she died a few years ago.'

'She had just come back from Spain hadn't she?' Frankalmoigne replied, and all the faces in the crowd turned to the blushing face of Lindsay, who nodded, and found herself with an immense lump of sorrow in her throat. 'Yes, that's right,' Lindsay answered, and her friend Kayleigh put her arm round her shoulder.

'Your Nan is looking over you all the time Linz,' said the ghost, and straight away, Lindsay recalled how her Nan had always addressed her as "Linz". The ghost continued: 'You used to watch *Worzel Gummidge* and *The Incredible Hulk* with your Nan on a Saturday didn't you? And she always gave you big slices of sandwich cake and you both drank cream soda. Your Nan is over there with your Auntie Pat, and whenever your ears start burning, it just means they're talking about you Linz.'

Lindsay silently sobbed and nodded, and on her behalf, Kayleigh said to whoever was behind that white sheet: 'Thanks!'

The two girls slowly made their way through the gathering crowd and Kayleigh sat her friend down on a bench and asked, 'You okay Linz? Was what he said right?'

Lindsay nodded and wiped her tears away with the sleeve of her coat. 'Everything was spot on; we did watch the Hulk and Worzel Gummidge and me Auntie Pat died from complications after she'd had heart surgery or something.'

'That's amazing,' said Kayleigh, and she looked back at the crowd. 'Do you think it's all a trick though?'

'I don't Kay,' said Lindsay, 'he never takes any money, does he?'

'Maybe I should ask him about my dad,' Kayleigh pondered. Her father had died from cancer five years ago when Kayleigh was just ten years old. She still missed him so much.

'Yeah, go on, Kay,' Kayleigh urged her, 'might take a bit of time getting to see the ghost though, look at how big the crowd is now.'

The girl got up off the bench and tried to slowly worm their way to the inner circle of people waiting to consult Frankalmoigne, but then a priest turned up –

and he was accompanied by a policeman. 'Get away from here you charlatan!' the holy man yelled at John, who ignored him.

Then the police man looked down at John, who was still seated on the carpet, and he said in a firm voice: 'Come on sir, you and your ghost will have to move along! You are causing a public disturbance.'

'Hey, hang on a mo, I want to talk to him,' said an irritated stocky man in his fifties who was standing close to John, 'he's not doing any harm, is he?'

'He is conning these people,' the priest told the man, 'letting them believe that idiot under that white sheet is a ghost, and he's taking money from them.'

'Isn't that what your lot do in the Church, father?' an old man asked the priest, 'You promise us everlasting life and you pass the plate round.'

'You sound as if something's possessed you,' the priest replied to the elderly man, 'coming out with blasphemous stuff like that.'

'Hey, Father Bunloaf!' shouted a small ginger-haired woman, 'This lad here hasn't taken a shilling off anyone – he's refused money being offered to him left, right and centre!'

'Well that's where you're wrong you see, madam,' the priest retorted to the woman, 'a man came into my church today and told me all about him taking money off people.'

'Well he's a damn liar,' said a woman in the crowd, 'because I've been stood here watching him and he hasn't taken a penny off anyone!'

'Look, listen everyone!' the policeman addressed the crowd seeking the dead, 'I don't care if this fellah has taken money or not – he's causing a breach of the peace and he's got to go.'

'How can he be causin' a breach of the peace if he isn't threatening to harm anyone?' asked a tall gangly man standing close to the figure covered in the white sheet. 'The law says that you can only have a breach of the peace – '

'Don't tell me my job sunshine!' the irritated copper told the man and then he turned to John and said, 'So, come on lad, off you pop!'

'He's genuine, Stephen!' the ghost said to the policeman – and the constable looked very distracted all of a sudden – because he recognised the velvet voice coming from the "ghost" as that of his late mother. 'Leave him son, he's helping these people,' said the female voice.

'Son?' John asked his ghost – and then he looked up at the stunned policeman and queried: 'Is that your mother coming through?'

'Yes, I am his mother,' said the ghost, and the policeman saw the faint flutter in the mouth of the covered figure as it spoke. 'Stephen, it really is me. I'm over here with Shep.'

Shep was the name of the policeman's border collie. It had been knocked down and killed on West Derby Road when he was eleven. This message left the policeman speechless, and he stared at the enshrouded figure in awe.

'Ventriloquism!' yelled the priest, and he turned to the policeman and said, 'And a man of your station believing all of this, constable. Move this confidence trickster and his confederate on! Go on!'

The ghost said, 'Shall I tell the policeman your dark secret, father? They could put you away for years for the things you did; those disgusting, despicable things!'

The crowd turned its eyes upon the priest and saw the blood drain from his face, leaving it white. 'All lies,' he said, 'all lies told by the devil!' The priest then lunged forward and grabbed at the sheet and yanked it off to reveal – nothing. There were screams – and yelps of surprise – because no trickster was standing under that shroud; there was nothing there but empty space. John got to his feet, folded the carpet and the sheet and left with many believers following him. He was seen on a few other thoroughfares, and they say people from various churches harassed him, sceptics from the university constantly accused him of being a fraud, and certain well-known local mediums also tried to discredit him, all to no avail. Around 1986 John and his ghost left the city, leaving behind a legend that has snowballed as the story is exaggerated with each telling – but as far as I know, what I have related is the factual version of this strange story. Just what Frankalmoigne the ghost was remains a mystery, and how the entity knew details about the most private lives of certain people is also an insoluble mystery – but whatever the ghost was and however it got its information – the Church and the so-called mediums did not like it one bit.

# THE HALLOWEEN MAN

In April 1971, a Mr Alfred Marshall of Eleanor Road, Bidston was mending fencing that encircled a private wood when he noticed a hole in the ground. It was not a rabbit hole, but a clearly defined circular and apparently extremely deep hole – the type of hole that had been seen before in rural places where WW2 German bombs had impacted into terra firma without going off – leaving the local authorities a "UXB" – an unexploded bomb - to contend with. The "Bidston Hole" as the local press called the mysterious aperture – was duly investigated by Sergeant Major Norman Humphrys – one of the country's top bomb experts. He travelled up from Felixstowe with specialist electronic equipment and he dug more than 12 feet down but his hypersensitive metal detector remained silent, and the residents of Eleanor Road breathed a sigh of relief when Sergeant Humphrys declared that the hole seemed to be an ancient one that had been uncovered by the recent heavy April showers which had eroded the limestone lining of the shaft. What the purpose of the shaft was, he could not say. A curious 13-year-old boy named Patrick later shone a torch down the shaft and saw something resembling a ball. Using a fishing line and a hook he eventually reeled the thing up with great difficulty as it was heavy. The hook had caught a diamond-shaped opening in what turned out to be a stone sphere, which was as big as a lawn bowl and it was caked in mud. Patrick took it home and washed the globe, which seemed to be made from granite. The globe had a lid which, when prised off, contained a dark red resin. There were two diamond-shaped eyes cut into the stone, a triangular hole for a nose, and a zig-zagged mouth. There were thirteen longitudinal grooves running from the crown of the weird stone 'head' to its base, and Patrick's dad said the thing looked like a stone Halloween pumpkin. This was 1971 when Halloween was still known as Duck Apple Night in England, and Patrick had never seen a carved pumpkin. The only pumpkins he'd heard about were the ones in the Cinderella tale. Patrick's personality seemed to change after he found that "stone pumpkin", and one evening his mother found him in his bedroom squeezing blood out of a self-inflicted gash he'd made in his palm with a penknife blade, and he was draining the blood into the receptacle of the stone head. Patrick swore at his mother and told her to leave his room. He later apologised to her, but he then started to come home from the local library with books on the Occult and witchcraft. He informed his mother that the thing he'd found was an ancient "Celtic head" talisman; these heads – made from sandstone, limestone and granite – are found all over the British Isles and date back thousands of years to an obscure Celtic cult which has weird deities at its centre such as the Lord of the Dead, Muck Olla, Lubin (origin of the children's skipping rhyme *Here We Go Loopty Loo* - originally *Here We Dance Lubin Light*) and other forgotten pagan gods.

Patrick started to hang around Bidston Hill after dark – an intensely haunted place with an immense supernatural history dating back to the Druids - and one night Patrick's father followed his son – and saw him meet a weird tall figure on the hill. At one point during the surveillance, Patrick's dad saw the silhouetted figure raise its arms vertically and slowly sink into what looked like a pot hole as Patrick waved at the entity. The frightened father confronted his son and asked him what the thing was he'd been talking to and Patrick started speaking gibberish – but it later transpired that he was speaking in some ancient form of Gaelic. Patrick told friends that the "Halloween Man" was now his best friend, and he sometimes referred to him as the "Samhain Man" – (Samhain is the original Gaelic name of the Halloween festival). When October 31st arrived, Patrick became very excited and painted spiral symbols on his face with blue ink from his fountain pen and he rushed to Bidston Hill as twilight was falling. Three local girls – all aged thirteen - had a crush on Patrick, and knowing he was into witchcraft, they dressed as witches in home-made outfits made of black cardboard hats and dark curtains for capes. They carried broomsticks up to the hill – and they joked to Patrick about putting spells on him to make him kiss them, but the boy was more excited at the prospect of the pending rendezvous with his ghostly friend, and he kept saying to his three admirers, 'The Halloween Man's coming!'

The girl's followed Patrick to a spot on the slopes of the hill. By the light of a waxing gibbous moon, the giggling girls stood there watching Patrick spout his supposed Gaelic 'incantations' – but then something very eerie took place which wiped the smiles off the faces of the girls. A man dressed all in black who wore some sort of ghastly mask rose steadily out of the ground from a hole. He carried a huge axe, and he walked towards Patrick, speaking in a raspy voice. The girls screamed but Patrick told them: 'Don't be scared, he's good. He's the Halloween man. He's a good spirit from the Lord of the Dead; he protects people with that axe.'

The girls ran home and told their parents about the axeman and then a gang of older teens who had heard the strange rumour from one of the girls arrived on the hill, and they threatened Patrick – now known as the local oddball. Then they saw the approach of the tall figure in black brandishing the axe, and his face, with its black eyes shaped like the diamonds on a playing card, and that jagged mouth – and the gang drew back, wondering if it was just someone who had dressed up to scare them for Duck Apple Night. The mob threw stones at the figure and ran, and the stranger's hurled axe went sailing through the night air. It narrowly missed the head of one of the gang members and embedded itself with a loud bang in a tree trunk.

Some of the gang members returned out of curiosity to see who the 'headcase' was who was throwing axes at people, and one young man fired an air rifle loaded with .22 pellets at the so-called Halloween Man – but he didn't even flinch.

Patrick returned to his home in such an exalted state – laughing hysterically with the strange spiral marks on his face – his father thought he'd taken drugs and grounded him in his room for a few days. Neighbours of the troubled boy claimed that they had seen a tall figure in a mask standing at the gate of Patrick's house in the wee small hours, gazing up at the child's window. One neighbour noticed that this unknown man was carrying an axe.

Patrick's father confiscated the stone head on Guy Fawkes Night and travelled to Liverpool to see his cousin Martin, a student at Liverpool University who was studying archaeology. He showed him the stone head his son had found, and Martin – who was usually a very level-headed man, examined the carved granite globe and said, 'Chuck it – they're supposed to be very unlucky. It looks as if it might belong to the early Iron Age, definitely Celtic. The Celts were into some strange occult practices; they even scared the Romans. I know two people who owned one of these heads and they were both injured in really bad car crashes.'

'That thing has sent my son loopy,' said Patrick's dad. He took the advice of Martin and when he drove home, he tossed the stone head out the window of his car near Halewood and it landed in a ditch. Patrick's son slowly returned to normal, and the Halloween Man – whatever it was – was seen no more on Bidston Hill – but that is not the end of the matter.

The mysterious graven image of the pumpkin-faced deity seems to have been rediscovered in October 1977, when a 14-year-old Halewood girl named Debbie showed the strange granite head to her mum. By now the artefact had lost its lid. Debbie had been using hollowed-out melons bearing carved faces and containing candles as her pumpkins, and she was looking forward to Duck Apple Night. The girl seemed mesmerised by the stone "pumpkin" and her brother caught her wiping blood from her pricked finger on the object one night. He asked his sister what she was doing and Debbie said, 'I don't know; I just felt that I *had* to put my blood on it.'

Not long after this, there were reports of a ghostly man with an axe who had attacked a car on the M62 one night. His face looked exactly like the features of a carved pumpkin, and Debbie said she had sent the ghost to try and kill a man who had said something horrible about her father. Debbie's friends said they saw the "Halloween Man" appear in the girl's bedroom one evening during a séance, and they started to scream but Debbie told them not to be frightened because he would protect them. A girl named Carla who was present when the Halloween Man materialised that night was interviewed by me on a radio show about the supernatural. She told me how there seemed to be nothing behind the mask of the entity – just blackness. The apparition looked solid and three-dimensional, but after standing there motionless for about a minute, it became smoky and then vanished. Debbie spoke to the solid-looking ghost in a strange language she claimed was ancient Gaelic, and one night when the figure appeared in a wood off Finch Lane, the entity put its arms around Debbie and hugged her. She then walked off with him into the moonlit fields and she told her friends not to follow. When Debbie's friends saw her on the following day, her eyes looked strangely distant and sunken, and she said to them: 'I must be the only person who is looking forward to death because I'll be with all the spirits in their world.'

The girl's behaviour became stranger and her parents contacted a priest, suspecting that some form of possession was taking place. The priest came to collect the stone head and he took it to his study, but the next day he discovered the object was missing. He drove to Debbie's house in the evening, intending to tell the girl's parents what had happened, but as he was driving down a poorly-lit Gerrards Lane, a figure jumped out in front of the car and the priest swerved to avoid him and went into a field. The priest reversed his vehicle as he wound down his window, ready to give the insane jaywalker a piece of his mind when he heard a bang which he initially thought was a gun being discharged. There was a second bang and this time the car rocked, and the priest realised it was being attacked. He got out of the vehicle and saw a tall man in dark clothes wearing a weird mask, and he was striking the back of the car with an axe. The priest ran to a row of houses about fifty yards away and hammered on the door of one of these residences. He told the man who answered to call the police and pointed to the berserk masked figure in the field smashing the car up. The police arrived in minutes but there was no trace of the insane attacker or his axe. The priest's car was a complete write-off. The bodywork was destroyed and all of the windows were gone.

When Debbie's mother heard about the attack on the priest's car, she told him she thought the "evil spirit" connected to the accursed Celtic artefact was to blame for the attack, and when she went up to Debbie's room, the girl was sitting on her bed with the stone head in her hands. Debbie's mother snatched the stone from her daughter, and as Debbie screamed for her to come back, the priest stood in the doorway of the living room and prevented Debbie from chasing her mother. Debbie's mum then drove a mile through torrential rain and hurled the haunted stone head out the window of the car. It landed in a field near Yew Tree Farm. Debbie's daughter returned to normal within days, and the Halloween Man was seen no more, but I wonder who has the stone pumpkin now?

There is an article in the *Liverpool Echo* for 17 March 1978 which says that a museum assistant named Gill Chitty will be giving basic archaeology lessons to motorway builders making excavations for the M58 between Aintree and Skelmersdale so they can recognise ancient pottery and other relics. When the M62 was being built in our neck of the woods in the 1970s, there were many archaeological finds, and also some strange hauntings that seem to have been triggered by the unearthing of ancient relics. The Bowring Park Charioteer – the vivid ghost of a woman with long flowing red hair who rides in a horse-drawn chariot from somewhere near Tarbock Green and northern parts of Halewood – became very active when the M62 was being built. Some thought she might be the ghost of a long-forgotten Boadicea-like queen of a tribe fighting Roman occupation, as some Roman artifacts were unearthed during the excavations when the phantom charioteer was seen. A number of Celtic heads have also been found in this area, and perhaps with a lot of people on Merseyside (especially Liverpool) being of Celtic descent, the heads – and the psychic, emotional energy they contain – provoke more of a supernatural reaction than those found in places where the people are mostly of Anglo-Saxon descent.

# DON'T BRING LULU

Violent ghosts are a rarity, and when they do become
physical we tend to stereotype them with the label
"poltergeist" – but Lulu is one of those rare
apparitions who can draw blood, claw faces and leave
people with bruises. Lulu is her nickname, and why
this is so is not known; the reason has evaporated in
the mists of time; I only recently discovered her real
name was Lily, but first let me tell you the type of girl
she was – and if the many accounts of her ghost are to
be believed, *still* is. She was born in 1906 to a well-to-
do Liverpool family, and at the age of 22, in the midst
of the Roaring Twenties, she went wild and became a
flapper – she wore excessive make-up, had a bobbed
hairstyle, listened to jazz, loved doing the Charleston
and the Black Bottom dance, lived on champagne and
cigarettes, dabbled with cocaine now and then, and she
flouted the social and sexual norms, having a new
boyfriend almost every week, and sometimes she had
two or more 'on the go' at the same time. Once Lulu
left a beau, she never took him back, and one of her
lovers begged her to have him back five times, then
committed suicide by driving his car into the Leeds
and Liverpool Canal at Gathurst, Wigan, and when she
heard about his death, Lulu threw back her head and
cruelly laughed. As a dare, Lulu once ran into a South
Liverpool church during a high society wedding
wearing nothing but a mask and jumped into the arms

of the shell-shocked reverend. The young lady also had a penchant for trying to steal husbands; she constantly wanted them, and then she became fixated with one married man in particular. One night in December 1925, by the rusty light of a waning moon, the "Moonlight Masquerade" – a free public event heavily advertised in the *Liverpool Echo* – was in progress. Thousands of young men and women skated on the frozen lake of Sefton Park – and believe it or not, there was a full orchestra on the ice that night. Lulu was amongst the skating revellers, and she had her eyes firmly focused on a dashing young married man – an architect named Eric Williams – who was skating with his wife, Mary. Lulu followed him, and when he stopped to talk to some friends the lively flapper stood inside a circle of industrial strength halite salt crystals she'd slyly sprinkled down. These crystals quickly thawed the ice and Lulu let out a perfect scream as the disk of ice she was standing on plunged into the icy waters – and Eric, always the dashing hero, jumped through the hole and rescued her. Lulu had counted on his derring-do, and she suspected he had a thing for her but was forced to remain loyal because his wife was the daughter of one of the richest men in England, and a man who sent many contracts to the architect. Lulu clung on to Eric, and as he tried to lay her on her back in an effort to pump the water out of her lungs, she sat up and began to kiss him – but Eric's outraged wife separated them and a young man carried Lulu out of the park and drove her home. She then started to stalk Eric; wherever he went, he'd find Lulu there. He went to a dance ball at the swish Embassy Rooms (later the Irish Centre on Mount Pleasant) that had been put on for a duchess, and Lulu turned up dressed very provocatively. Upon this evening, when Lulu made her entrance, most of the women did not cast condescending looks on the flapper, because there was some aura of comedic lovability about the girl that made her hard to dislike. Eric tried his utmost but he could not take his eyes off the beguiling Lulu and his wife, noticing his constant glances at the girl, rowed with him in front of all of all the couple's friends, as well as the duchess.

The fast-thinking conductor of the Hometowners Orchestra decided to quickly drown out the row before it soured the rapturous mood of the Embassy Rooms, and using his cryptic code of tic-tac, he gave the signal to his musicians and suddenly the orchestra struck up the novelty hit *Don't Bring Lulu* and Eric smiled and shook his head as he realised who the song was being played for. His wife Mary stormed out of the dance hall and someone took hold of Eric by his wrist and said, 'Go on, old boy, you know you want to,' and he steered him to Lulu. The whole room did the Black Bottom dance, and Eric and Lulu grinned inanely at one another as they did the dance as a couple, and each of them moved as if they were marionettes operated by the same puppet master. They danced side-to-side and back to back; they swayed in a two-step motion and lifted their feet simultaneously as if they were pulling their shoes out of deep mud, and the coordination and synchronisation of the couple was faultless. They double stamped in perfect time to the music and combined a swing to the stamp and strutted forward at the same time. Every dancer on the floor cheered the Hometowners Orchestra after the dance, and Eric and Lulu laughed and panted, and then, as the life of the party went on all around them, the couple gazed into each other's eyes, and their smiles settled into expressions of seriousness. 'Don't you know what you mean to me by now?' Lulu earnestly asked Eric, and he averted his gaze from her eyes because they were so beautiful and intense. He took out a slim silver cigarette case, clicked it open and offered it to Lulu, but she shook her head once and kept her gaze fixed on his face.

'What *do* I mean to you, then?' Eric asked, placing the cigarette between his lips at the corner of his mouth.

'Oh you know the old story, Eric,' she replied, 'they call it love.'

'Love,' Eric lit up, puffed on the cigarette, thinned his eyes, and looking up at the bright scintillating chandeliers he said, 'a temporary insanity – that's what love is – cured only by marriage or death.'

'You're married,' Lulu reminded him, 'so, are you saying it has cured you of your love for *her*?'

Eric's friend Ralph came over to him and Lulu with the waiter, who carried two Martinis on a silver tray. The waiter smiled at Eric and the handsome architect took the glasses and gave one of them to Lulu.

'Where's Mary?' Ralph asked Eric, then his small eyes darted over to Lulu.

'Home I imagine,' Eric told him with a shrug of his square stocky shoulders.

'Oh, I *see* old chap,' Ray replied with a knowing look, and then he nodded and smiled and winked at Lulu and walked away.

The Hometowners Orchestra played a "slowy": *It*

*Had to be You*, and as soon as Eric heard the opening bars, he dropped the cigarette to the floor, calmly stepped on it, and then he put down his Martini and took the glass out of Lulu's hand and placed it next to his on a shelf. His right hand took her left hand and clasped it softly, and his left arm curled around her waist. They danced, and they felt as if they were the only two people in the universe. The Embassy Rooms, with their flowery garland decorations, baby blue and white Regency period décor and rose-pink prismatic crystal chandeliers, were fading from view to two people who only had eyes for one another. With the exception of the orchestra and its leader, every man in the room and three of their girls danced with Lulu that night, and Lord knows how many hearts secretly ached as Eric took to the crowded dance floor with the Belle of the Ball for the traditional last waltz. The music sounded ethereal and dreamlike that night in the ears of Eric, and he later told his best friend Ralph that if the high-spirited atmosphere of that magical night could have been bottled, it would have easily outsold every drug and drink known to the human race. Eric let something slip as he was caught up in the heady effervescence of that whirling waltz. Just as the clock struck midnight he said something, and his eyes said it too, and it threw Lulu in such a way she missed a step as she danced. 'Did you just say you loved me?' she asked, and her eyes twinkled as a tear was born.

He looked away towards that two-faced Janus of a clock which slowed in times of mundane boredom and whirred like a dervish on stellar occasions such as this.

'Eric!' she squeezed his hand and stopped the dance.

He lunged forward and quickly kissed Lulu on the

lips, and then he tried to pull away, but she held his head and pressed her lips upon his until he mumbled something and pushed her back.

After the dance ball, the couple left by separate exits so as not to arouse suspicion, but then they both headed for their rendezvous – the Adelphi Hotel, and that was the night Eric and Lulu – booked into the hotel as Mr and Mrs Jones - embarked on their affair. They embraced at an open window in their hotel room with the lights out, and together they looked out at the eternal sentinel stars twinkling in the sky. 'Compared to those stars, are lives are but a moment,' said Eric, and then his eyes turned from the starry heavens to see Lulu gazing up at him with her large eyes half closed.

'You have a real dopy smile Mrs Jones,' said Eric, and he grinned and kissed her, and then he took her to the bed and they made love, and Lulu said, 'I wonder if this is what Eve felt like when Adam first made love to her.'

'Oh Lulu, please don't bring religion into this; I feel guilty enough already;' said Eric, 'leave all that to the Archbishop of Canterbury.'

Her fingers felt his lips bend into a smile in the darkness after he had said those words. And later that morning, as the stars above crept incessantly across the sky on the tides of time and space, the two lovers from different lives – two people who should have been brought together a long time ago – held on to one another, cherishing each passing second, for they knew that in the morning they would have to go their separate ways into a world that would seem more grey and cold than ever before.

'We should go on a cruise in the spring next year,'

said Eric, gazing at the ceiling with Lulu's face snuggled into his chest, 'perhaps on a zeppelin. The Graf Zeppelin Cruises are starting soon, and what a way it would be for us to get away – just you and I drifting over land and sea.'

'A zeppelin?' Lulu turned and raised her head and he could see her eyes open wide with excitement, even in the low light of the bedroom. 'That would be the cat's pyjamas!'

Eric stroked her head. 'Yes, they can fly from Paris to Moscow, and we could even visit Africa; Lulu among the Zulus – nah, they'd probably kidnap you.'

'You'd have to fight them to the death to rescue me,' said Lulu, and she kissed his chest.

'No, I'd pay them to keep you,' joked Eric.

The affair went on for three months – and then he dropped the bombshell. They met at Reece's Café on Castle Street one lunchtime, and straight away, Lulu felt that something was wrong. Eric looked at her differently – the fire was literally gone from his eyes.

'Eric, what's wrong?' Lulu asked, her voice uncharacteristically low.

Eric raised his eyebrows and looked at the pink gingham tablecloth. 'Lulu, I have something to say to you and I know it will hurt you, and well, it will hurt me too.'

The girl's heart palpitated and a numbness manifested itself in her stomach. She knew what he was going to say and she wanted it all to just be some cruel dream she could awaken from.

'Lulu, Mary is ill, and I have decided I have to look after her. I can't be with you and her at the same time, and this is probably the most heart-wrenching decision

I have ever made in my life – but – '

'It's over,' Lulu whispered, and tears covered her eyes and her long eyelashes, and for some cruel reason her memory took her back to that night in the Embassy Rooms when she had heard him say those words she had always longed to hear.

'We will always be friends,' Eric said, looking up from the table. His eyes were red and they glistened.

'But,' Lulu began, but became a little choked up, 'but you said you loved me.'

'I did, and I always will,' Eric replied, and yet he withdrew his hand from her clasping fingers. 'You must try and see things from my point of view; I have a sick wife and she knows of our affair – she's not blind, Lulu. If I was to continue seeing you with her in that condition, I think it could be fatal to her and – '

'You don't have to explain,' Lulu told him, and she picked up the paper napkin and dabbed her eyes. 'It's over,' she said, 'our beautiful love has died.'

'Don't – ' Eric closed his eyes and slowly inhaled, and she saw a spasm in his throat. 'I think we should – ' he started as Lulu got up and hurried out of the café. 'Lulu!' he shouted after her, 'Come back!'

The diners watched him as he knocked over his chair and rushed out of the café. When he got onto Castle Street, he thought he saw her, and ran to her and grabbed her forearm, but it was a girl dressed in the same coloured cloche and similar attire to Lulu. Eric apologised to the startled lady and ran through the milling crowds, but Lulu was nowhere to be seen.

Three days later, there was a heavy knocking on the door of Eric's palatial mansion in Grassendale. The butler, Franklin, answered and – he found a woman lying outside in two widening pools of blood. There were also splashes of blood on the rest of the portico and pillars of the mansion's entrance. Lying next to the girl was a razor, and upon seeing this, Franklin guessed that the unknown woman had cut her wrists. He ran inside the house and told a young servant named Stephen to go and fetch Dr Randall, the physician who tended to Mrs Williams. Franklin then went into the drawing room and told Eric Williams about the woman outside. When Eric saw it was Lulu, he began to sob and cried to Franklin, 'Call Dr Randall!'

'I already have sir,' Franklin replied.

Eric tried in vain to stem the bleeding by squeezing his hands around the slashed wrists of his former lover, and he looked at her eyes, which were partially open, and he said, 'Oh Lulu, why did you do this? Why?' as tears covered his face.

Randall arrived soon afterwards in his car and he established that the girl was still alive, but her heartbeat was faint and irregular. He bandaged the cuts on Lulu's wrists and he and Eric put her on the back seat of the car, and then the physician drove pell-mell to Garston Hospital where surgeons stitched up the cuts, and they gave Lulu a blood transfusion, even though her chances of survival looked very narrow. Lulu eventually recovered, and the first person she asked for upon regaining consciousness was Eric, but he only visited her once – in the presence of his brother-in-law – and so he did not even touch the girl. He promised to visit again but he never did and Lulu was discharged from hospital four days later.

Lulu began to write letters to Eric in which she begged him to take her back, but he never replied, and then one summer's day that year, Lulu booked into a hotel on Church Street and cut her own throat. Her well-to-do family hushed up the suicide and Eric was plagued with guilt regarding the girl's death for the rest of his days. He spoke of seeing Lulu's ghost, but most of his friends put it down to a mental condition caused by the trauma of her suicide and that ghastly attempt at self-destruction on his very doorstep. Eric never gain frequented the Embassy Rooms on Mount Pleasant, much to the annoyance of his wife, for the place held that special memory of Lulu.

The Church Street hotel Lulu chose to end her life in is now a well-known department store, and her ghost has been seen on the premises many times over the years. Lulu has also been encountered on Church Street, and in 1990 a mouthy bouncer bumped into her one night. Assuming she was someone who'd been to a fancy dress ball because she wore a 1920s outfit, the doorman flippantly said, 'What's that you've got on? You look stupid, love.'

The solid-looking carnate ghost of Lulu almost took off the tip of his nose with a razor before vanishing to echoes of laughter. On another occasion in 2010, a couple in their twenties returning from a night club were passing along Church Street at three in the morning when the boyfriend started arguing with his girlfriend about something she had supposedly said about him to a friend, when he slapped her hard across the face. A woman in an old fashioned cloche hat approached from the direction of the Schuh footwear store. She wore what looked like a sequined cocktail dress, a long pearl necklace, and she wore a white choker – possibly a bandage – that looked *blood-soaked*.

'Hello,' she said.

Her eyes were huge but had dark circles around them, and the boyfriend turned to his girl and said, 'Who's this?' because he imagined she knew her.

The strangely-attired lady rushed at him and clawed his face, and when he tried to punch at her, she slashed the back of his hand with either a knife – or a razor. The young man's girlfriend screamed, and then the attacker was suddenly nowhere to be seen. Realising he'd been attacked by a ghost – and a ghost that had left him with a deeply cut hand and a clawed face, the young man and his girl went to the Royal Teaching Hospital. I am currently researching a case where Lulu's ghost seems to have wandered down from her usual haunting ground on Church Street to Mathew Street, where she allegedly smashed a bottle in the face of a man who had been hitting his wife outside of the Flanagan's Apple pub in 1991.

If you happen to see Lulu one night when you're in town, don't insult her – just do a u-turn...

# SOMETHING AT THE
# FOOT OF THE BED

How many times have you got into your cosy bed, closed your eyes, and being in need of a good night's sleep, entered the Land of Nod almost immediately – only to be startled out of your slumbers minutes later by a terrifying nightmare? It's an occurrence that seems to make a mockery of modern psychology because if nightmares are generated by our own minds (as psychologists claim) then why would the brain want to wake itself up from a sleep it so badly needs? Perhaps, as the occultists believe, our nightmares are caused by some mischievous spirit that infiltrates the sleeping mind to show a disturbing little horror film specifically designed to scare us and wake us up. The bedroom is supposed to be that sanctuary of rest where we spend a third of our life sleeping, and sleep is the best medicine of all. But there have been many stories reported to me over the years where the peace of the bedroom has been shattered by things from the world of the supernatural, and here are just a few of these types of stories.

It was 6.30pm on 9 October 1940, and over at Oxford Street Maternity Hospital, the newborn John Winston Lennon was no doubt bellowing out his first vocal creation to mother Julia and the midwife. Above in the gathering autumn twilight, a half-moon hung over a city at war, and it was being pensively watched by a lonely little 7-year-old girl named Sandra, who was feeling down with the flu. She closed the blackout curtains and returned to bed because she was feeling shivery. All she'd had today was chicken soup and a few goes of the lollipop she was hiding from her two sisters and three brothers. She sat up in the bed, feeling ever so sorry for herself with a protruding bottom lip, when something odd happened. Through a half-inch gap in the curtain a moonbeam shone on that old radio her dad was always saying he'd fix – and it began to crackle. Sandra's eyes bulged as she saw a little man in a tuxedo come out from behind the radio, and a spotlight followed him. He announced: 'My name is Giles Cross and I am the compère of the Moonlight Radio Show!'

He introduced two ladies in red dresses with black skulls printed upon them, saying, 'Give a warm welcome to the Strychnine Sisters!' and the duet launched into a harmonious catchy song about giving a boy "a kick up the hooter" which made Sandra laugh. A magician then came out the back of the radio and took off his own head and juggled it with two others, which scared the child at first, but she smiled when Giles introduced "Denny the Dancing Dog". The weird shadowy figures of three top-hatted tap-dancing men called the Singing Silhouettes unnerved Sandra a little, but the little girl was mesmerised by the "Crying Wallflower" – a lanky lady in a tight-fitting green costume and a round face framed by yellow petals who played the guitar and sang a melancholy song about a lonely butterfly who discovers she's a moth.

The show went on till Sandra started dozing off to a soothing lullaby sung by the compère Giles. He sang: 'This was the Moonlight Radio Show, we hope we put a smile on your face, but now you have to go to bed little child, I'm afraid it's getting late. So until we meet again, goodbye my little friend. Goodnight Sandra. Sandra, give Teddy a hug, and you'll be snug as a bug in rug.'

And Sandra felt herself drift off into a strange dream where she was running with teddy bears in a wood.

When Sandra awoke in the morning she told her dad about the Moonlight Radio Show but he said that old radio in her room had not worked since 1929. Every now and then, always on a moonlit night, the little performers would come out the radio, and on one occasion Sandra's best friend Jenny also saw them, and Giles knew Jenny's full name and even knew her dog's name too. On the occasion when jenny stayed over at Sandra's home, another strange little ghostly figure also came out of the radio, and she was a pretty ballerina dressed in a pale silvery blue outfit with a white tutu. Her dancing was hypnotic, and she danced with Giles the compère who referred to her as 'my darling wife, Anastasia'.

The fact that Jenny witnessed these pint-sized paranormal performers as well as Sandra indicates that they were not the products of Sandra's imagination, and on one occasion, Sandra's mother, Martha, was standing outside her daughter's bedroom when she heard the Crying Wallflower character singing as she played her guitar. Upon entering Sandra's bedroom the music stopped and Sandra said the Crying Wallflower had vanished because adults weren't suppose to see the show.

After the war, the radio was thrown out, and lay in the alleyway behind the house, awaiting collection by the dustbin men. Two boys who dismantled the 'wireless' found old faded and dusty photographs in the rusty innards of the radio set featuring the Crying Wallflower, Anastasia the Little Ballerina, the Strychnine Sisters and other long-dead variety performers...

From wartime Liverpool we jump now into the 1970s and hop across the river to Wirral to look into a very eerie case of a supernatural bedroom invader.

I've noted that there are certain areas of urban Wirral where there is a high incidence of hauntings and there are certain roads that stand out because they seem to have quite a few ghosts. One of these ghost-ridden roads is Prenton's Arkle Road, which is a crescent made up of mainly semidetached dwellings with St James' Church as its cynosure. Of the seventy-two dwellings on this road, a dozen of them seem to have been the scene of paranormal goings-on, ranging from poltergeist activity and time-slippages to a bizarre-looking entity resembling a vortex of white smoke and a white-haired skeletal ghoul that crawls along on all fours in the wee small hours. This latter being was encountered one Saturday night on 16 September 1978 when a 14-year-old girl named Denise invited two friends over for a sleepover at her new home on Arkle Road. Her family had moved there a month ago from Speke. The girl's mother was in hospital recovering from an operation and so Denise's father Ken had let his daughter bring two friends over instead of just one. The girls sleeping over were Kate and Cressy (short for Cressida) and like Denise, they were also aged fourteen and both attended the same school as their host.

Denise and Cressy slept at the top of the double bed

in the so-called guest bedroom and Kate slept at the bottom (top and tail style), and they talked about boys and other girls and around midnight Denise heard the sudden swell of the theme music of the TV chat show *Parkinson* as the programme ended. The girl's father had opened the living room door and was going to put out the cat – Rosy - before retiring. As soon as Ken went to bed, Denise sneaked outside and let the cat back in and brought her up to the bedroom. She also went to the kitchen and brought up three packets of Bovril-flavoured crisps, chocolate digestive biscuits and a bottle of Alpine dandelion and burdock. The full moon was out that night and was peeping into the darkened bedroom as Cressy told Denise that she had fallen in love with a boy named Charlie who had sat next to her on a bus. The mention of the boy's name prompted Kate to start singing, 'Charlie had a pigeon, a pigeon, a pigeon, Charlie had a pigeon, a pigeon he had. It flew in the morning, it flew in the night, and when it came back it was covered in shite! Oh, Charlie had a pigeon -'

'Kate! You're going to kick my dad off!' Denise warned her friend and playfully pressed her bare foot in her friend's face.

'Your feet pong!' Kate giggled and then she deliberately crunched her Bovril crisps as Cressy continued to talk about her unrequited love. Eventually the girls settled down and by half-past-one they were all asleep.

Rosy the cat woke Kate around 2.40am by placing its cold wet nose against the girl's cheek. It was then when Kate heard a strange howling noise. It sounded like the wind somewhere down in the hallway but it was making a groaning sound and seemed to be saying 'Charlie'. It really spooked Kate and she told Denise – who said it was just the wind making the noise, before falling asleep again. Kate couldn't even wake Cressy as she was so deeply asleep. Rosy the cat looked at the door and tilted her head sideways; she could also hear the weird sound. 'What is it, Rosy?' a nervous Kate asked the feline – and then the bedroom door clicked. Kate peeped over the top of the bed's footboard and watched the door slowly and steadily open. She hoped it was the wind or Denise's dad messing about. In came a bizarre and frightening figure of what seemed to be a naked old woman on all fours. Her hair was white and hung in scruffy, greasy-looking strands, and her body was covered with sores and the skin looked leathery – like snakeskin, Kate thought. As the entity reached the centre of a rug, Rosy hissed at the unearthly figure before leaping off the bed and running out of the bedroom. The head of the bedroom intruder swung to face Kate, and just before the girl ducked behind the footboard she saw the scary glowing orange eyes of the entity. Kate began to say the Lord's Prayer in her mind as she lay there tensed up under the blankets.

'Charlie, where are you?' said a gravelly voice, and Kate thought it was coming from under the bed. She was right. She felt thumps beneath the mattress, and then a scuffling sound which went towards the door. The bedroom door closed, and Kate jumped with fright. She waited until she had to come up gasping for air, and she looked into the moonlit room to see that the door had indeed been closed – but then she saw a strange grey shape in a corner of the ceiling, and as her eyes adjusted to the low lighting, she received quite a shock. It was that creepy, emaciated woman; she had somehow defied gravity and was peering over her bony knees with those bright orange eyes as her feet rested on the wall. Kate screamed and ran out the bedroom. Denise and Cressy woke to the scream and they saw the entity as well. All three girls ran out onto the moon-silvered Arkle Road, and minutes later Denise's father appeared in the doorway of the front door and he shouted to the three hysterical girls, 'What the hell are you lot playing at?'

'Dad, there's an old witch in my bedroom!' shrieked Denise, and she kicked off the two other girls who began to cry.

Ken went up to his daughter's room and saw nobody. He could not get his daughter and her friends to go back into the house and Denise went to stay with Kate in her home.

An old neighbour who later heard of the weird incident in Denise's bedroom tantalizingly said, 'She's been looking for Charlie, God rest his soul,' but she would not say who Charlie was and refused to divulge what else she knew about the history of the house. Almost every week, the sound of a wind rushing through the hallway of the house and an echoing voice crying, 'Charlie' in the small hours of the morning was heard, and in the end Denise's parents sold the house.

In the world of the supernatural there are a group of strange but intriguing entities known as the Shadow People. As their name implies, these are beings made up of pure silhouette, and in recent years, sightings of them have been on the increase; they have been seen in every county in the British Isles, and Merseyside in particular seems to be a hot spot for the manifestation of these creepy beings. In 1996, a very sceptical friend named Rob took up my £100 challenge to stay overnight in a well known local cemetery where some baffling lights had been seen drifting among the gravestones after dark. Professing to be a man who was not afraid of ghosts – because he didn't believe in them – Rob visited the cemetery with sandwiches, camera, torch and a thermos flask of coffee in his satchel. It was early autumn and around 4pm dusk began to fall but it still wasn't too dark to see. Rob was startled by a fox and he tripped and fell into a six-foot hole which I presume had been dug by gravediggers for some early internment on the following morning. Rob lay there on his back, fuming in the mud as he looked up at the mouth of the grave – when something bizarre took place which turned him into a believer.

A solid black silhouette of a head and shoulders scrolled into view, peeping at him in the grave, and then a second eerie shadow form did the same on the other side of the grave's mouth. These creepy entities seemed to be hovering because they slid towards one another almost to their waists, and when they presented their faces to each other, Rob could see their profiles. He got the impression one was asking the other, 'What's he doing down there?'

Then the shadow figures turned sideways – and Rob could see they were thin as cardboard when viewed side-on. He swore at them with nerves and they both flitted away from the grave. Rob somehow clawed his way up out of the grave and he ran non-stop to the cemetery wall, which he scaled in seconds.

One afternoon in late September 1975, a few pupils and a couple of teachers are said to have seen around nine weird silhouettes of children performing a peculiar dance in the playground of New Heys Comprehensive in Garston. Some of these "shadow children" seemed to be wearing top hats and some looked barefooted. One silhouette of a girl was leaping high into the air and kicking her legs up as she spun about. The unearthly spectacle went on for about a minute and then all of the figures seemed to merge into an amorphous mass which faded away.

In August 2014 at a house in Knotty Ash, a woman in her forties named Carol went to bed one night at around 11.45pm. Her husband Larry was downstairs watching the TV with his friend Jay from next door. Carol had been up since seven in the morning, looking after her cat Maxine, who had just given birth to six kittens, so she was, to use her own colloquial description, 'totally knackered' by the time her head hit the pillow. She closed her eyes, and felt herself drifting off when she suddenly heard a faint voice call out: 'Carol.'

Carol opened her eyes and looked straight ahead, towards the drawn blinds of the windows and the thin lines of orange light bleeding through them from the sodium street lamp outside. She then closed her eyes again and thought she had been hearing things with being so tired. Carol's ears often played tricks on her when she was overtired; sometimes she heard whole sentences of words spoken by a voice that sounded just like her own voice, or she heard echoing bangs which often startled her – but once again she heard her name being called.

*'Carol.'*

It sounded as if it was coming from the foot of her bed. She wondered if it might be her husband Larry, even though it did not sound like his voice, so she lifted her head off the pillow a few inches and turned to look towards the foot of the bed.

Silhouetted starkly against the white wardrobe was a bizarre figure, male in shape, and it was wearing some type of hat which reminded Carol of the hats medieval jesters wore, only the three horns sticking out from this hat were huge – about 2 feet in length. Carol tried to scream but suddenly discovered to her horror she couldn't move. The paralysis did not affect her breathing and the woman could move her right hand slightly, but otherwise she was not able to get up and run from the room or even shout.

'St Bartholomew brings the cold dew, ha ha!' said the creepy solid black shadow, and then it slowly moved around the bed and approached a frozen Carol from her right side, but she couldn't turn her head right, so she was now perceiving the sinister intruder with her peripheral out-the-corner-of-her-eye vision. The thing gave off a sweet sickly smell, and it came close to Carol, who could now hear her heart pounding, and said, 'You are Jane Fool, and your other half is laughing behind your back.'

The figure then seemed to vanish, and all went quiet; so quiet that Carol could hear the TV downstairs – but then the voice of the chilling 'jester' was then heard on the left side of the bed, and he made another random remark. 'A jester has just ended his life, and you know him. Bye Carol.'

Carol suddenly regained the power to move her

body, and she threw off the blankets and ran out of the bedroom. She ran down the stairs and burst into the living room and there was Larry and his friend Jay watching porn on a cable channel. Larry fumbled with the remote, trying to change the channel, but he switched the TV off in panic.

'Larry!' cried Carol, 'I've just been visited by a horrible ghost!'

'What?' asked Carol's red-faced husband.

She described the terrifying figure and recalled the weird things he had said. 'He said I'm Jane Fool and you're laughing behind my back!'

'Oh, you've had a nightmare, love,' Larry assured her and he stood up and hugged her.

'No, Larry, that was not a nightmare,' Carol told him, shaking in his arms, 'he was real and he somehow paralysed me.'

'I've had dreams like that, Carol,' said her neighbour Jay, getting up off the sofa, 'woke up and couldn't move an inch.'

'No Jay, this was real, not a dream, and he had this horrible sweet aroma,' said Carol, 'and he said some random things about a jester ending his life and something about St Bartholomew's Day.'

'The best thing to do is have a few gin and tonics Carol, and then get into bed and read for a bit,' suggested Jay, 'and take Larry up with you – no ghost will go near him with his aftershave.'

'I'm serious Jay,' Carol persisted, 'look at my hand.' She held her hand out and it was shaking.

'Well, I'd better be hitting the flock myself folks,' said Jay, and he said goodnight to Larry and Carol and left.

The couple went up to bed and Larry could smell a faint sweet scent in the bedroom but chose not to mention it in case it scared Carol. She had taken Jay's advice and had a a drink – a glass of wine – and now she sat up in bed reading a Mills and Boon book.

'Is it okay if I leave my bedside lamp on?' Carol asked, and Larry kissed her and then said, 'Yeah; listen Carol, you were overtired before. You were up at the crack of dawn looking after the cat and her babies.'

Carol smiled as she thought about Maxine and her little furry brood. Jay's daughter Lottie was now looking after the cat and kittens and Carol asked, 'How's Lottie coping with them?'

'Jay said she won't leave them alone; she's doting on them by the minute,' said Larry, and he got in the bed and turned so he was facing away from his wife.

'Larry, were you watching porn before on the telly?' Carol suddenly asked.

'I *knew* you were going to ask me that,' replied Larry. 'Jay was messing about and he put that channel on.'

There was a little pause then Carol came back with: 'Oh, I just wondered that's all.'

'As if I'd watch porn in my own house – *if* I was into all that rubbish,' said Larry, 'anyway, try and get some sleep soon love, and put that nightmare out your mind.'

Carol eventually dozed off and when she awoke, Larry was standing at the foot of the bed with a tray, and upon it was a full English breakfast and a glass of fresh orange juice. He hadn't treated Carol to breakfast in bed for years, and it was a pleasant surprise.

'No nightmares of any jesters?' Larry asked with a smirk.

'No, I had a really good kip,' Carol told him, and got stuck into the breakfast.

Later that day, Carol saw the death of American actor and comedian Robin Williams on the news. She had always like Williams, especially his role in *Mrs Doubtfire* - but then sometimes later, she thought about that comment by that apparition which had appeared in her room last night. She played back its unnerving voice in her head when it had said: 'A jester has just ended his life, and you know him. Bye Carol.'

Was it just a coincidence? Robin Williams was, in a sense, a modern-day jester who was reputed to have been manically funny offscreen in his real life. But if that thing had somehow known Williams had died – apparently through committing suicide – why did it tell her? Carol pondered on this, and then she recalled that the entity had also said: 'St Bartholomew brings the cold dew, ha ha!'

She knew of no one called Bartholomew, and as far as Carol knew, there were no churches of that name near her. What did it mean? She Googled "St Bartholomew's Day" and the search engine told her his feast day fell on 24 August. Was something going to happen that day? She looked at the calendar on the wall and saw that date was twelve days away.

When that day came, Carol's sister, who had just turned fifty, died of a stroke in her bath. Carol was devastated by the death, and forgot about that jester's remark about that fateful date at first. On Christmas Eve of that year, Carol was still up at midnight, wrapping all the gifts for her relatives and friends, and she never asked Larry to help because he was hopeless at wrapping up presents. Just after midnight, with all the gifts neatly wrapped and with all the ornate seasonal tags filled in, Carol poured herself a well-earned glass of wine and slumped onto the sofa. She then noticed something black behind the Christmas tree in the corner, and the tree's fairy lights went out one by one. It was that menacing jet black form in the guise of a jester again, and as it stepped out from behind the tree, Carol screamed and threw the glass of wine at it, and it vanished immediately. Carol heard a thump upstairs as her husband jumped out the bed in response to her scream, and then she heard the heavy footfalls on the stairs and she knew before he even came through the door of the living room that he'd say this latest visitation was all in her mind. She was right. She told him what had happened and he saw the wine stains on the wall by the tree and some had gone on his wrapped gift. 'Carol, you need to see a doctor about this,' he said, picking up the wet present. He then picked up the glass, which was still intact on the thick carpet. 'You nearly gave me a heart attack before.'

A mobile phone chimed somewhere to announce that a text message had been received, and Carol looked at her iPhone to see no text had arrived on her mobile. Larry looked over at his armchair and saw that he had left his mobile there, and he walked over pretty fast to it and picked it up. He scanned the text quickly then his eyes looked at Carol. 'From Jay,' he said, but he was not very convincing.

'*This* time of night?' Carol asked. She was suspicious.

'Yeah, he wants to know if I'm going to the pub with him on erm, Boxing Day,' Larry replied, and Carol could see him going into the messages on his phone and deleting the one he had just received. He then looked back at her and said, 'Are you coming to bed? These things seem to happen when you're overtired.'

'Larry, who texted you just then?' his wife asked, 'It wasn't Jay.'

He sighed and shook his head. 'Alright, it was a friend from work – a female friend – but I knew if I told you that, you'd start trying to make out I was seeing her.'

'Can I see what she texted?' Carol asked, and she got up off the sofa and walked towards Larry, but he bolted out of the living room and into the hallway, saying, 'No, you can't! If you don't trust me, we may as well call it a day!'

'So you *are* seeing her then!' Carol went up the stairs after him to get the truth.

Larry sat with his back to her on the bed, his face in his hands, and she sat on the chair in front of her dresser, looking at him in the mirror.

'Okay, I am going to tell you the truth, Carol,' Larry told her, turning to her with tears in his eyes, 'and you can ask Jay about this because he was there when it happened. In fact I *want* you to ask Jay because I know you just won't believe what I have to say without me needing to get it all backed up by someone else.'

'Go on,' she said, coldly.

Larry coughed, then said: 'We had a really pathetic Christmas party at work, in the afternoon, as I probably told you, and we went to a pub in town, and a woman in the firm named Taylor – '

'That name sounds young,' Carol interposed.

'She's nearly thirty,' expounded Larry.

'That's young compared to us,' sighed Carol.

'Anyway, this Taylor had the hots for me, and I don't know why, but she did, and she made it clear. Now, I had invited Jay to the pub – I texted him and he came down to the place so he is a witness. Taylor followed me into the toilets; she'd had a bit to drink, and she said, "Take me in there," and she meant the cubicle, and I said I was married and Jay came into the toilet, and he was obviously taken aback seeing a girl in the gents, and anyway, she asked me again to take her into the cubicle, and Jay heard her, and he also heard me say, "I'm married love, no way, behave yourself!" and then she walked out. Jay actually said I was loyal and told me he would have well taken her in there.'

Carol seemed perplexed. 'But Larry - she's got your number – '

Larry looked at the ceiling. 'I do not – repeat *not* know who gave her my number, but she keeps persecuting me.'

'Well I better go and have a word with her then,' said Carol, and her eyes seemed to flash with anger. 'Taylor's her name then? I'll get to the bottom of this.'

On Christmas Day, Carol went next door to Jay and quizzed him about Taylor and her attempted seduction of Larry in the toilet and Jay said he couldn't remember much because he was drunk and kept changing his alleged recollections. While Larry was having a shower later that morning, Carol searched high and low for his mobile, and finally found it outside in Larry's car. The ringer had been set to silent. She guessed Larry's passcode correctly and navigated her way to his messages. Taylor had sent nude pictures of herself to him and Larry had sent back texts telling her how beautiful she was. In one text he had told

Taylor to stop calling him on the mobile and he had sent her the number of another mobile phone.

It was the worst Christmas Day Carol had ever lived through, and by the New Year she had moved out and was living with her auntie. Larry begged her to come back and said he had been stupid and weak but claimed he had never slept with Taylor. He blamed drink and 'the male menopause' and promised he'd never be unfaithful again. Carol gave him a second chance and to date he has kept his word. Carol mentioned the weird ghost that had alerted her to Larry's infidelity to an old neighbour named Patricia, who was currently being looked after in a care home, and Patricia told her a very strange and disturbing story. In 1965, a woman named Maria had lived in the house where Carol now lived, and at the age of twenty-six, Maria's 5-year-old son died of meningitis. Maria's husband had been seriously injured in a car crash around the same time and could not even attend the funeral of his son. Maria took the loss of her son badly and on the night before the funeral, she kept the child's little coffin in her bedroom. Around 2:30am a noise in the bedroom awoke Maria, and she saw the very same silhouetted figure Carol would later see in 2014: it looked just like a jester except the horns of the jester's cap were huge. The shadowy entity picked the coffin of the dead boy off its stand, and Maria screamed, 'Leave him alone!' The ghost then placed the coffin back down heavily on the stand and vanished, but it returned four more times that night and tried to pick up the coffin containing Maria's son. In the morning, Maria was exhausted and when they laid the coffin in the earth that day, she collapsed at the graveside. When she told people about the thing that had tried to take her son's coffin, they assumed she had hallucinated the so-called ghost because of her sad loss and also because her husband was critical in hospital.

Carol lived in mortal fear of seeing the strange shadow being for months, and she eventually persuaded Larry to sell up and move to a flat, and they moved into their new home in August 2015. She still has the occasional nightmare about the jester but has thankfully not set eyes on it in her waking life since that eventful Christmas Eve. Just what the thing is remains a mystery, but I have a feeling it'll only be a matter of time before the new occupiers of the house in Knotty Ash encounter it.

# WHEN ROSE RETURNED

It was February 1971, and Britain had just gone decimal, and 50-year-old Sid Greymarsh just couldn't get to grips with the new money, but then he just couldn't get to grips with life in the Seventies anyway. He dressed old, wearing straight wide trousers with turn-ups and kept his hair short, and in these winter months he wore a flat grey cap. He despised long hair and flared trousers and lived alone with just an old radiogram for company. He was a filling station attendant but he was off on this Saturday and was slicking his hair back with a touch of Anchor butter on his fingers as he got ready to go to the Wellington pub to talk to old Paddy about bygone days. Sid left his home in Wavertree Gardens and upon reaching the alleyway leading from Paradise Gardens, he saw a ghost. She came hurrying out of that alleyway which gave access to cottages at the back of the Wavertree High Street. Sid clutched his chest as the shock coursed through his heart. Before that ghost had even turned around he could tell it was Rose – a beautiful woman who had been his first crush, back in 1939 when he was 18. But Rose had died in an air raid in 1940, Sid reminded himself, so this was a bona fide ghost. He slowed his gait, grabbed the stub of a cigar his hand had felt in his inside pocket, and lit it. He followed Rose to the corner of Grange Terrace, where she halted. She looked down the street, and then she turned to look at him and she seemed confused, and she was a vision of beauty to Sid as she stood there in a smart sapphire blue swing coat, under a similarly coloured hat with a scarlet bow tie, and she seemed taller in her black shiny heeled T-bar court shoes.

'Hello Rose,' Sid dared to say, noting how solid she looked for a ghost. He halted about nine feet from her.

The lady seemed surprised and said, 'Who are you?'

'It's me – Sid - Sid Greymarsh,' he replied, 'used to deliver your paper.'

'Sid's a young man – are you his father?' she said, eyeing him suspiciously.

Sid shook his head and asked, 'Why have you come back?'

A Number 79 bus roared past at that moment and drowned out Sid's metaphysical query, and she walked back up the street and as she passed Sid she said, 'I've been to my house on Stevenson Street and someone else is living there; it's all very odd. I don't know what's going on.'

'Rose, are you real?' Sid asked, going after her, 'You don't look like a ghost.'

She turned into the alleyway she'd first emerged from when Sid had spotted her and said, 'I left me mam's house along there in Paradise Gardens and went home to Stevenson Street but everything changed – all these strange cars and everyone looks silly, and no one knows me. I want to go home. I feel as if I'm losing my marbles.'

Just then, it dawned on Sid what might have happened. Through some strange quirk of nature, some bend in time, Rose had left the past and walked into 1971. He had to test his theory, so Sid asked her what the year was, and was told, 'What a daft question – 1939.'

'Ah, Rose, you're wrong, it's 1971,' said Sid excitedly, and he walked alongside of her now, and had no need to keep his distance because he was certain she was not a ghost but had just walked through the time barrier without even knowing it.

'How can it be 1971 if it's 1939?' Rose asked Sid with a charming raise of her eyebrow and a skew-whiff smile.

'Rose, such things are possible, honest,' said Sid, 'and we know things today about time and space that would astound you. We've even landed on the moon!'

'See, my mam's cottage should be there!' Rose pointed to a block of modern flats – and then suddenly, a cottage began to appear as if it was being glimpsed through a fog that was clearing in a breeze.

As Sid and Rose walked on down the alleyway, 1939 slowly returned. A man in a gabardine coat and a trilby came walking past and he said, 'Hiya Rose' as he passed by.

'Oh Jesus, the old days have come back,' said Sid, and his heart somersaulted with joy. 'Rose, I always wanted to tell you this but I was so shy when I was a teenager, but well, I love you. Rose you mean the world to me.'

Rose shot a puzzled look that turned to a smile and raised, perfect eyebrows as she walked along, back to her time.

Sid thought he was going back with her, and he had so many plans; a marriage proposal would be the first on the agenda.

Rose and the old cottages of Paradise Gardens started to fade away, and Sid tried to grab the arm of his love, but his hand went straight through her, and he heard her exclaim, 'Ooh!'

And there was silence all around him. The only witness to the strange spectacle was a tortoiseshell cat on a backyard wall.

'Rose!' Sid moaned, leaning against the wall with his head bowed. His cigar fell from his mouth onto the narrow road and he left it there. He walked about, looking at the walls and buildings and trees of 1971, hoping 1939 would return again so he could hop into it and stay with the only woman he'd really loved. He lingered there until a light rain started to fall, and then he left the alleyway and walked off, bound for the Wellington pub in tears.

# THE HELL RIDERS

Seven silhouettes of figures on motorbikes stood starkly in a row atop of the ancient landmark hill of Bidston that September evening back in the early 1970s. Many saw the audacious motorcyclists; dog walkers, an amorous couple courting on the hill, an observant policeman on his Vyner Road North beat, as well as a 'cocky watchman' sitting in his little tent overseeing roadworks on a twilit Eleanor Road. Against the fiery tangerine and vermilion skies of a spectacular autumn sunset, the seven ominous motorcyclists stood out as ink-black living shadows, and some with a keen eye noticed the horns protruding from their helmets. Then the seven riders made what looked like a suicidal daredevil descent of Bidston Hill on their machines, and many of the entranced observers noticed that the headlamps were crimson, and straight away the policeman set out to confront the bikers because the law is adamant that headlamps can only be white or yellow – and certainly not red. An old man walking his terrier on the slopes of Bidston Hill told the zealous officer of the law to keep well away from the maelstrom of motorcyclists roaring down the sandstone incline because they were devils. 'They'll leave us for dead,' said the nervous old man, snatching up his terrier before he crouched behind the trunk of a tree. 'The Hell Riders; that's what they call them; keep out their way, let them go past!'

'Hell riders? I'll give them hell,' The policeman remarked as he returned a smirking sarcastic look at the cowering elderly man and his whimpering dog, and he defiantly shone his torch at what he perceived to be seven idiotic youths who were flouting the law of land and road. The leader of the gang of motorcyclists accelerated to a phenomenal speed, and although his bike was thundering down a steep forty-five degree slope over hazardous rugged crags, his path was straight and did not swerve by a hair's breadth. In a flash the leader lashed out with a large hammer which smashed the copper's torch and the force of the impact sent the policeman into a spin. As the bikers and their thrumming machines flew through the air, landing on the poorly lit road below, the young constable rolled down the rocks, and he was left with sprains and bruises – and an incredible tale to tell them back at the station. Some of the older serving coppers at the station had heard of these Hell Riders – bikers who had supposedly returned from the dead as servants of some ancient god – or possibly even the Devil. The policeman who had come within inches of that lethal hammer recalled that the red headlamp of the leader's bike had a strange symbol in its glass; it had looked like an upside-down star; a pentacle in other words – an ancient talisman of magical evocation.

That very same night, a young motorcyclist lay dying in Wallasey's Victoria Central Hospital with brain matter oozing from his ears. He had deliberately driven into a tree at seventy miles per hour. Before he passed into the Great Silence, the young biker cried out, 'Satan, receive my spirit!' and he died at one in the morning with a slight grin on his face. Several staff members swore they later saw that dead biker outside the hospital on a motorcycle. Seven other black-clad bikers wearing weird horned helmets drove off with him. The parents of the dead man later revealed that their son had been obsessed with the occult and had a huge poster of Aleister Crowley over his bed.

In the summer of 1978, two 16-year-old girls – Maura and her cousin from Liverpool, Alice - decided to camp overnight on a field off Willaston Road because they wanted to go ghost hunting. They'd heard hair-raising stories of the Devil's 3am appearances at the crossroads formed by the Raby Mere Road and Willaston Road junction about half a mile east of the Wheatsheaf Inn and the curious girls wanted to see if the tales were true. Two young thugs in a stolen car spotted the girls camping around a fire that night as they listened to a portable radio, and tried to assault them. Maura put up a fight, clawing the faces of one of the juveniles but they dragged her cousin Alice to the car and drove off. Maura stood there in tears. The radio was playing the Blue Öyster Cult hit, *Don't Fear the Reaper* when the girl noticed a humming sound like a thousand bees. She turned to see a procession of red lights coming down Willaston Road with the full moon hanging high above them. As they drew nearer she saw it was nine motorcyclists, and not only did they have blood-red headlamps featuring a symbol she knew well – the inverted pentacle – the eyes of the bikers seemed luminous, and they wore horned helmets. Maura bravely stood in the middle of the road and waved at the uncanny riders and the leader halted his machine six feet away. The others also came to a halt. Maura went up to the leader and told him she'd been attacked by two men in a yellow car who had taken her friend. The leader said nothing, but gestured with the thumb of his gauntlet for Maura to get on the back of his bike. When she put her arms around him she found his body ice cold – and he grunted and slapped her hands away - making it clear he didn't want to be held. Maura had to lean back slightly and grab the back of the seat. That motorbike started to slowly move off and then it rocketed through the moonlit night at such a speed, Maura really thought she'd fall off and be killed. Hedges streaked past in silver blurs of reflected moonlight and within a minute, Maura saw the red tail lights of the yellow car of those youths drawing nearer on the road ahead. She felt nauseous as she wondered what they were subjecting her cousin to. The bikers overtook the car and surrounded the vehicle, forcing it into a ditch. The two males tried to escape but were captured by the encircling bikers. The weird horned motorcyclists roared with laughter as they lashed at the abductors with chains. Maura went to Alice, who was unarmed, and as the cousins hurried home over farmland, they heard the screams of the youths and Maura saw blood glistening on one of the chains the bikers were punishing the would-be rapists with. The girls later saw the bikers roar along Thornton Common Road – and Maura silently whispered, 'Thank you.' She developed a crush on that leader and his 'knights' but she never saw them again. About a week after this, just before

Alice went home to Liverpool, she and Maura went shopping in Birkenhead, and there in Woolworths was one of the men who had tried to snatch Alice. He had lost his eye in that attack and he now had a scar that ran from his forehead to his mouth – as if he had been slashed with a knife. The girls were terrified the young man would see them so they sneaked out of the store and ran off.

The Hell Riders have been seen all over the North West, and some years ago a retired police motorcyclist told me on a BBC radio programme about the occult that he had encountered them around 4am one October morning in 1979 as he rode his police motorbike through the Queensway Tunnel. They came from behind the policeman, rode their machines alongside him, then in a burst of speed they left the tunnel. The policeman pursued the uncanny bikers with their horned helmets onto The Strand, where the thirteen bikers took off at a phenomenal speed in excess of 300 mph – and then, they seemed to vanish as they all swung onto Parliament Street. The policeman radioed an alert to his colleagues and two officers who had been sitting in a police car that had been parked on Grafton Street at the time radioed back that no one had passed them. When I mentioned this incident on the radio we received many calls from residents in the Prescot and Rainhill area who said that a mysterious gang of motorcyclists with red headlamps had been seen roaring along Blundell's Lane on their machines in the wee small hours of the morning on many occasions, but whenever the police chase these bikers or attempt to intercept them, they literally vanish off the face of the earth. Long before the age of the motorcycle, when the roads were traversed by people on horseback, there were tales of Highwaymen selling their soul to the Devil and afterwards appearing on red-eyed black steeds – even after the highwaymen had been hanged, so the Hell Riders may be some recurring archetypal manifestation of something much older. Going back centuries, we have the Wild Hunt – also known as the Wild Troop – a large ghostly group of dead hunters or warriors on horseback who travel across the country in a straight line, bringing death to those who see them. If the Wild Hunt passed through a dwelling in the dead of night where people were asleep, their souls would sometimes be dragged out of their bodies by the spectral huntsmen. The whole legend is said to have strong connections with the supreme Norse god Odin.

# THE MOONLIGHT HUNT

On the Friday afternoon of September 16 2016, 27-year-old Huytonian Ralph Winnington was already close to oblivion as he and his nine friends careered from bar to bar in the city centre of Liverpool. The stag night hadn't even started yet and they had plied Ralph with a myriad of leg-numbing mind-erasing shots concocted from permutations of absinthe and tequila, Creme de Menthe and the highly dangerous 95% alcohol Spirytus Rektyfikowany. They laughed as Ralph complained in slurred speech that they should be staying on lager so the stag night could start in the evening, and the four girls called him an old fogey because he told them in disjointed sentences that girls should not be allowed on stag nights and should never be the "best man".

One of the offended girls on the stag – Magda – was a trainee tattooist and she promised Ralph that once he went out like a light, she would tattoo the name "Rita" (his first crush when he was fifteen) on his manhood. A horrified and highly intoxicated Ralph shrunk back in shock at the threat and said he'd sue her and everyone fell about laughing – and then from Ralph's point of view the world turned black and he was gone.

He awoke to the hoot of an owl in the middle of nowhere with no clothes on in what seemed like the countryside. He was sitting up against a thick oak and the amber September harvest moon was on the rise. He recalled Magda's threat and looked down – and saw she had put the name of his first crush where she said she would – on his penis. He panicked then seethed and got to his feet swearing, but he felt a bit dizzy and fell back against the tree. He thought they might have tied him to a lamppost on Dinas Lane with just his boxer shorts on but this was extremely cruel for a stag night prank. When he married Kristine in the morning, how on earth would he explain who Rita was and why it was tattooed on his manhood? Ralph stormed off, and the cold evening air seemed to sober him up. He passed through a wood where he heard voices chanting a nursery rhyme he vaguely recalled from his childhood:

*Hector Protector was dressed all in green,*
*Hector Protector was sent to the queen;*
*the queen did not like him and nor did the king,*
*so Hector Protector was sent back again!*

Ralph thought whoever they were, they would lend him some clothes and he could get back to Huyton, but he stopped in his tracks when he saw about a dozen people on horseback, all wearing those red coats and black hats and white trousers tucked into black boots – a fox hunting party – but they all had on weird animal masks; one of the mounted figures had the face of a cat, another had the visage of a sinister-looking fox and so on. The one with the face of what looked like a wolf saw Ralph and he pointed to him and shouted "Look! Tally ho!"

As Ralph turned to run, he heard one of the 'huntsmen' blow a horn. He looked back briefly as he ran through a field of wheat and saw some of the hunting party had whips and one of them wielded a medieval spiked ball on a chain. The thought that these deranged people might be his friends pulling off some elaborate prank briefly crossed Ralph's mind, but somehow he knew that this was not them, and he ran off screaming for help. He could not outrun horses of course, and they toyed with him, and he was whipped hard against his back, and only when he saw his own blood trickling down his arm did he think they might actually murder him – but why? With his adrenalin pumping through his bloodstream, Ralph raced through a gap in the circle of huntsmen and as he ran, he thought he saw a motorway in the distance. He felt he was somewhere north of the East Lancs. If he could make it to that highway someone would notice the weird hunting party in their red coats. As he bolted through the wheat, there was a mighty crack and the whip coiled around his neck in a moment of horror, choking him. They all dismounted and chanted the Hector Protector rhyme, and they held Ralph down. The one dressed like a cat produced a small golden sickle and said, 'I am Hector and now I shall remove your staff of life!'

Guessing correctly that the masked cultist was about to cut off a cherished piece of his anatomy, Ralph screamed "No! Help me somebody, please!'

The cat-faced maniac halted, looked close at Ralph's penis and said, 'Oh we can't have this one, it's spoiled.'

They all started kicking Ralph, and then they got back on their horses and left him black and blue in the field with only the moon as a witness. When he finally got home he thanked Magda for saving him from a bloody fate. She said she had only used a marker-pen to write the name "Rita" on his penis and had not tattooed him at all. If you are male, you should stay well away from a certain swathe of countryside north of the East Lancs at the time of the Harvest Moon, for those cultists on horseback are still seen from time to time...

# GLORIA'S REVENGE

I've had to change a few names in this strange story for legal reasons. On the evening of Friday 3 August 1973, 35-year-old John Lonsdale was supposed to be at the home of his seriously ill cousin Stephen in North Wales as his wife Gloria lay in a hospital bed in Clatterbridge, recovering from a major operation – but that night John was seen with a blonde girl at the Kingsland Restaurant on Borough Road, Birkenhead. The person who saw the duplicitous John Lonsdale was Peter Kelly. Peter had attended the Collegiate Grammar School on Shaw Street with Liverpool-born John many years ago when they were both in their teens. Peter had been at the restaurant with his wife, watching the highly popular comic Tom O'Connor when he had noticed John kissing the blonde at a table across the room. She looked as if she was barely out of her teens. Peter knew John's wife was in hospital and wanted to go and punch him but his wife told him not to get involved - but Peter's wife subsequently told a friend about the way Gloria Lonsdale's husband was carrying on and it eventually got back to Gloria. She didn't want to believe it but she had long suspected that John was an incurable philanderer. She'd detected various perfumes on his clothes over the years and too many of his stories and explanations just hadn't added up, but she'd been afraid of losing him and so she never left him. All of Gloria's friends said she was a fool putting up with his infidelity and told her she was beautiful and had a lovely personality and could have anyone, but Gloria said she couldn't help loving John. Gloria's health deteriorated after the operation and her doctor told John to be there for his wife as much as possible, as Gloria had told him how she'd looked at John as her main reason for wanting to live. In a perfectly simulated choked-up voice, John cruelly told his wife on her sickbed: 'The doctor has informed me that your condition is much worse than he had previously thought and that the end might come sooner than he had imagined,' and then he pretended to burst into tears.

Gloria told a nurse what her husband had said and when the doctor heard about the lies John had told he threatened to have him prosecuted. 'I know your game, Mr Lonsdale,' the doctor roared down the phone to John one day, 'using a type of negative suggestion to finish your wife off!'

'You're supposed to be a doctor, not a psychiatrist, so stop trying to psychoanalyse me!' John yelled back, and added: 'And may I just tell you that you are one of the most incompetent doctors on the Medical Register? You bury all your mistakes, don't you? You didn't even spot Gloria's cancer until it was too late!'

John slammed the phone down on the doctor.

Just after this, Gloria heard that John's young blonde mistress was now pregnant, and already he was seeing someone else. Gloria's sister Jenny arrived from Australia, and when Gloria told her about John's evil and appalling behaviour, Jenny had it out with him and he threw her out of the house and refused to let her in. Then Gloria suddenly died.

Hours after they took Gloria's body to the mortuary,

John Lonsdale invited his latest girlfriend – a 21-year-old redhead named Natasha - into his home and they slept in the bed he had shared with his late wife.

'Don't you feel bad doing this on the day your wife passed away?' Natasha asked as she lay besides John.

He smiled and coldly told her: 'No, I don't feel bad at all. You see I am what is known as a nihilist – I believe life is meaningless and I reject all religions and pathetic morals. Gloria's death is just icing on the Nietzschean cake as far as I'm concerned. We live, we die, and that's it – we're just recycled carbon. No afterlife and angels and harps – just nothingness.'

'That's horrible John,' said Natasha, snuggling into his chest, 'I don't think death is the end.'

'Well no one ever comes back from the grave, do they?' he asked, and Natasha let out a scream, startling him.

She said she'd seen a woman looking at her from the wardrobe mirror. Then they both heard a woman outside shouting '*John...John!*'

'That'll be Gloria's sister Jenny!' John told Natasha, who was already getting dressed. 'What are you doing?' he asked. Natasha put on her boots and said: 'I'm leaving, that's what I'm doing! Your wife's haunting me!'

John smiled and told his scared girlfriend: 'Natasha you silly girl, its Gloria's sister Jenny, just trying to spook us! Now get back in this bed!'

'That was a ghost in that mirror! Bye John!' Natasha left the room and switched the light on outside on the landing and looked about nervously. She heard female laughter echoing somewhere in the house, and this prompted Natasha to hurry down the stairs to the front door. John let her struggle with the bolt on the door, but once she had slid it back she was out of there like a flash and had to walk almost a mile to her home.

That night as John Lonsdale tried to sleep, the bed started to tilt left and right until he rolled off the mattress. Then the wardrobe toppled over and the top half of it smashed into the bed. He heard plates being smashed down in the kitchen. Now he knew it wasn't Jenny trying to scare him. He heard Gloria's demented laughter, and it scared him so much he went to stay in a friend's house in Noctorum. Then, on the day of Gloria's funeral, John waited outside the church in his car, and he followed the cortege to Bebington Cemetery, keeping some distance away from the last car so he wouldn't be seen. After the mourners had gone and the coffin had been left in the ground for the gravediggers to fill, John sneaked over to the open grave carrying a wreath of pink roses. Two gravediggers looked on as they had a smoke behind a bush, and they saw John toss a wreath down the hole onto the coffin and shout, 'I'm sorry Gloria! Now leave me alone!'

Something hurled that funeral wreath out of the grave and it ended up around the neck of John Lonsdale. He fell back in shock, and the gravediggers were a witness to the strange spectacle. John took the thorny wreath off his head and threw it on the ground, and then he backed away from the bleak mouth of the grave and ran to his car.

After that day, John's constant attempts to approach any girl he fancied were always thwarted by very strange goings-on; poltergeist activity and weird telephone calls in the dead of night to girls John had started to date – and these calls were always from a woman with a raspy voice who warned them to stay away from John Lonsdale. One wealthy young socialite from London named Katrina received such a call one morning at one. The voice said, 'You are going with John Lonsdale, and he is cursed, and you will be too if you continue to see him. He has children everywhere and he is a carrier of VD [venereal disease], and he uses women and then casts them aside. You have been warned...'

And then the line went dead. Katrina telephoned John to ask him if he really had fathered children with other women and John said he hadn't, and when Katrina asked if he had venereal disease, John went ballistic and told her to never call him again.

One morning in 1975 John Lonsdale was found dead in a Mossley Hill flat he'd just moved into. They found him with his eyes bulging in terror at something. The coroner established that Lonsdale had suffered a massive heart attack as he sat in his armchair. A postman who had passed the window of the flat the morning John had passed away said he had definitely seen a woman in a long white gown leaning over the deceased – but a detective told the postman that no one could have left the premises because the bolt was still on the front door and police had to smash a window to gain access to the flat and admit the ambulance men. It would seem then, that Gloria Lonsdale had taken revenge on her disgraceful and wicked husband from beyond the grave.

# QUEENIE

One sunny Saturday afternoon in August 1973, an exceedingly pretty Tuebrook lady of nineteen named Frances left her home in Buckingham Road. Her coppery pre-Raphaelite curls had been tamed with Teeda hair straightener, and she wore a black velvet choker, an Alice blue skirt-suit patterned with marguerite daisies, Bear Brand suntan tights, and a pair of platforms from Dolcis. As Frances hurried for the bus she left a trail of the fragrance "Charlie" hanging in the air. She was in love with the man behind the counter at Barratts of Lord Street, and she didn't even know his name. She'd first set eyes on him a few days ago when she went to buy her Nan a pair of Duraflex shoes at the store, and now she was headed back there – but, alas, when Frances went into the store, her secret crush was nowhere to be seen. The lovelorn teen lingered there for half an hour, then left. As she reached Church Street someone slapped Frances so hard across the back of her head, she was thrown to the floor. There was a commotion as people rushed to her help.

'Who hit you, love?' a woman asked, but Frances didn't know and a witness said he saw no one by the girl when she was struck. Then the mystery deepened later that afternoon when Frances rode the bus home. A lady, aged about fifty, who was seated behind Frances tapped the girl on the shoulder and said,

'Excuse me chick, but who's "Queenie"? Have you lost someone of that name? I'm psychy see, and there's a spirit of a woman on this bus following you named Queenie.'

'I don't know anyone named Queenie, sorry,' Frances told her, blushing, because it seemed as if everyone on the top deck was now looking at her.

'Well there's definitely a female presence named Queenie hovering by you now,' said the alleged mediumistic woman. 'Maybe she's a relative who died when you were a little girl and you can't remember her.'

'She's just said she doesn't know anyone of that name,' said a very sarcastic man sitting across the aisle from Frances. He looked the psychic woman up and down in a very condescending manner.

'No one's talking to you, love,' said the woman, visibly ruffled by his comment, 'So don't get your knickers in a twist; they *are* your wife's knickers you have on, aren't they?'

The man went red as passengers sniggered. He suddenly got up, but whether his stop was coming up or whether the woman had hit on some kink of his is unknown.

Twenty minutes later the bus approached Tuebrook and Frances got up off her seat, smiled at the seemingly eccentric woman behind her, and went to the stairwell of the bus. Her stop was coming up, and she just wanted to get home now after the weird events of the day. When Frances was going down the stairs from the top deck something pushed her, and she screamed, thinking she was about to fall and break her neck, but a huge burly man who had been going down the stairs ahead of her quickly turned and grabbed the girl in the nick of time.

'Something pushed me!' gasped Frances, and an elderly wide-eyed passenger who had also been coming down the stairs behind Frances said: 'It was a woman with a big beehive, and then she vanished!'

'What?' gasped Frances, unaware she was still in the arms of the smiling man who had caught her as she fell.

'A ghostie!' said the old passenger, squeezing past the girl and her saviour to reach the bottom deck.

'We can't go on meeting like this,' joked the man holding Frances, but she struggled from his arms and went after the old man who said he'd seen the ghost and asked him again what he had seen.

'I told you,' he said, and his frightened eyes looked back at the stairwell as if he was expecting the woman he was talking about to come down the steps, 'it was a ghost, and she was in a long tight black dress, and her face looked ghastly. Her eyes were just black like sockets.'

'Cor, I'd love to have some of that stuff you're all on,' quipped the bus driver, pulling up at the stop. The driver looked at Frances and said, 'I can see everything upstairs on this,' and he pointed to the mirror of a periscope in front of him. 'And I never saw any ghosts pushing anyone down any stairs.'

'*Something* pushed me!' Frances insisted, 'I felt their hands on me!'

'Lucky ghost,' said the driver, and he opened the doors.

'It also attacked me earlier on Church Street – ' Frances was saying but the passengers behind her,

377

queuing to get off the bus started to grumble.

'Come on, move it!' shouted an impatient woman.

'I'd put the willies up you as well if I was a ghost,' said a young man who brushed past Frances to get off the vehicle, and she swore at him, then got off as the driver laughed.

Frances told her mother about the ghost pushing her over in the street and on the bus but her mum said, 'Love, that's been no ghost – it's those bleedin' platforms you've got on. Mrs McGarry's girl went flying in front of me the other day in a pair like those; she stepped on the end of her flares – '

Frances rolled her eyes and raised her voice to differ with her mother's explanation. 'Mum! I didn't trip - *something* pushed me!'

'Frances, why would a ghost want to push you over girl?' the girl's mother asked, 'It doesn't make sense.'

'Look, just forget it mum,' said Frances and as she went to the hallway, she said, 'as long as I know it's a ghost, I don't care who believes me.'

She went up to her room for a sulk and thought about something her mum had said: *why would a ghost attack her?*

On Sunday evening at 10pm, Frances got into her bath. It was just the right temperature and she'd put Radox bath salts in the water. She relaxed back into the bath and reached for a magazine called *Words* which contained all of the lyrics of the top 25 songs in the pop charts and the potted biographies of singers and musicians. Frances wanted to be a songwriter and loved reading the lyrics of songs for inspiration. The girl was reading the magazine in the bath, carefully keeping it a few inches above the waterline – when she felt a hand press down on the top of her head and the next thing Frances knew she was being ducked. She tried to get up but invisible hands were pressing down on her head and right shoulder, and she could see the ceiling light undulating through the water as she thought she'd be drowned. She thrashed about with her arms and legs, and as she tried to get her breath she took in the salty Radox-infused water, and then, the instinct for survival kicked in and the girl somehow accessed a tremendous amount of energy to get out of the bath – but she found herself choking on the water which had entered her lungs. She coughed and tried to breathe but it was impossible and she thought she'd pass out for a second. Then she managed to take in some air, and she heard her mother rapping on the bathroom door.

'Frances! What's wrong? Frances?' her mother shouted hysterically.

'Something tried to drown me,' gasped the girl, and she looked back at the bath and saw her magazine under the water. She coughed up a small quantity of water, then grabbed a towel and wrapped it around her. Then she turned the catch on the bathroom door, and the girl's mother pushed the door open immediately, but the bottom of the door hit Frances' big toe and it felt as if the nail had been ripped off. Frances screamed. Her toe had just been grazed.

'What happened?' her mother asked with a very worried expression.

'Mum, that ghost has followed me home!' Frances said, and her huge eyes looked in terror at the bath. 'It tried to drown me!' She cried and then she pushed past her mother and ran into the bedroom in tears, partly because of the shock of something supernatural trying to kill her and also because of the agonizing pain in her toe. She'd had enough. Her mum came into the bedroom and said to her, 'I hope you're not taking drugs!'

Frances screamed at her: 'Why don't you believe me you stupid cow? Something just tried to kill me!'

'Aye aye!' said the girl's father, peeping around the door. 'Don't you dare talk to your mother like that!'

'Just go away – the two of you! Just go away!' Frances said as she sobbed, and she felt her big toe.

'If this goes on Frances, I'm taking you to see Dr Forshaw!' her mother said, and seemed shaken at being the subject of such an outburst from her usually quiet daughter.

'Fine!' yelled Frances, 'And take yourself to see him too!'

'Come on love, let her simmer down,' the girl's dad said to his wife and her parents left the bedroom. Frances heard her mother say, 'You should see the bathroom floor, it's flooded. I hope she's not on drugs.'

At 1.30am, Frances was lying on her back in bed, fast asleep, when something started to strangle her. In the dream she was being throttled by a blonde female with mad-looking blue eyes, and when she awoke in the darkness, she realised the ghost was making another attempt on her life. She tried to remove the powerful hands from her neck and they felt hard as stone and ice cold. Frances reached out for the alarm clock on her bedside cabinet and she tried to smash it into the attacker's face – but there was no face or head there. The only part of the ghost that had any solidity was those strangling hands. Frances threw her legs sideways out the bed and managed to wrench herself from the icy hands. She ran to the door, opened it, and went into the bedroom of her mother and father. Her mother was asleep but her father was sitting up reading a book, and he looked over the top of his glasses with his mouth open, startled as his daughter barged in.

'It tried to strangle me!' Frances said, and her father got up and said, 'What are those marks on your neck?'

Something flew through the open door behind Frances and hit her head, knocking her to the floor. The impact sent glass everywhere and rang like a bell as it landed on the floor. It was the alarm clock from Frances' room.

'Frances!' her father stooped down and picked his daughter up. There was blood on the back of her head and she'd been knocked out by the clock. He placed her on the bed, shook his wife awake, and without explaining what had happened he went onto the landing and saw no one was about. He went into the bedroom of his daughter and found nobody there either – so who had thrown that clock so viciously? He hurried back to the bedroom and saw that Frances had now regained consciousness and his wife was holding a pillow case to the wound on the back of her head.

Frances was taken to the hospital by her parents and a doctor said it was just a superficial wound, but he advised Frances not to sleep for at least six hours as a precaution - as she was suffering from mild concussion.

Now the parents believed their daughter – they realised something had come home with her, and they went to see a priest, but he insensitively suggested that a psychiatrist was needed. 'What a waste of time it was coming to you!' Frances' father yelled at the priest, and the holy man said, 'I'm sorry but these are modern times. There are no such things as ghosts and the devil and all that. We've got to be realistic.'

'I wouldn't be surprised if you don't believe in God!' said Frances' dad, and parents and daughter left the priest's house in disgust.

News of the persecuting ghost spread through the neighbourhood and beyond, and an excommunicated priest named David – defrocked for allegedly dabbling in the occult – turned up at the house and asked to help Frances. The parents of the girl were naturally reluctant to let him help, but realised they had no one else to turn to, so they decided to give him a try.

'When I heard the thing's name was Queenie, I realised it was a spirit I'd tackled before,' said David, unpacking his Gladstone bag in the hallway. He had a bottle of holy water, a Bible, incense and all sorts of sinister-looking paraphernalia.

He went upstairs to the bedroom with Frances, and she told him there was a cold spot near her wardrobe in the corner. She felt as if the ghost was there most of the time, and she was so grateful for David's help; he really took the matter seriously and put her at ease. 'The medium you spoke about on the bus is right; her name is – or was – Queenie. She's the spirit was of a woman who hates redheads because her boyfriend left her for one, and she took her own life. She was pregnant at the time too.'

'That's so sad,' said Frances, 'fancy deserting her when she was having his baby.'

'I agree' said David, holding his hands out at the cold

spot near the wardrobe, 'it was a horrible thing he did, but Queenie has got to move on; she's earthbound because she's holding a grudge against all redheads.'

'Shall I leave you to it then?' Frances asked, watching David put on a crucifix.

'Yes please, if you don't mind,' he said, and Frances left the room. She stood outside on the landing with her mother and father, and the three of them listen to the ex-priest as he solemnly intoned the Rite of Exorcism. They heard a female shouting, and then someone crying, and then they all heard what sounded like the cry of a baby. The bedroom door creaked open, and David peeped through a gap of a few inches and quietly said, 'Frances, you don't have to do this, but she'd like to see you.'

'What?' Frances asked, and seemed shocked at the request. 'Who wants to see me?'

'Queenie,' David said, with a faint smile on his face.

'What? The ghost?' asked the girl's stunned mother.

'Yes, the ghost,' said David, all matter-of-fact.

Frances looked at her mother and father, and then she turned to look at David. 'Why does she want to see me?'

'To apologise I think,' he answered.

'Don't love! She tried to kill you!' said the girl's mother, grabbing at her daughter's forearm.

'Okay,' Frances said to the exorcist, and she gently removed her mother's trembling hand from her arm as she said, 'I'll be alright mum.' She walked into the room and straight away she saw a woman who was a bit taller than her, and she was in a black knee-length dress. Her platinum blonde hair was done up in a perfect beehive and her face was as pale as chalk. Her eyes were large and Frances could see the pale blue in them from nine feet away. Frances froze and tried to accept the ghost but this was so outside of her everyday experience, she found herself becoming weak with fear.

'It's alright Frances, she won't harm you,' said David, and he took hold of the girl's right hand and slowly walked towards the solid-looking apparition.

'I'm sorry – for what I did,' said the ghostly woman, and her huge blue eyes became filled with tears.

'Come on, Frances,' David gently placed his left hand on the shoulder of the nervous redhead and she walked towards the ghost, and when the apparition reached out, Frances drew back a bit, startled. The ghost came forward and embraced Frances and close to the scared girl's ear she whispered, 'Please forgive me, I am so sorry for the things I did to you.'

'I forgive you Queenie,' said Frances, and she put her arms around the ghost and it was like hugging something very light, and cold.

The sounds of a baby crying somewhere echoed in the room, and Queenie said, 'My baby – she doesn't give me a minute.'

A scream startled Frances and the ghost. It came from behind Frances, from the doorway. It was the mother of Frances; she's opened the door out of curiosity and looked in on the unearthly proceedings.

'Jesus Christ! Come here, Frances!' cried the teenager's mother, 'Get away from her, Frances!'

Frances then realised she was holding nothing but empty space – Queenie had gone. She'd been scared off by the scream.

'Calm down, it's alright,' the exorcist said to the girl's

distraught mother, 'she wouldn't have done anything to Frances.'

'You need to bless this place now,' said Frances' mother, 'keep that killer away from us!'

'Queenie has gone for good now,' said David, 'I don't have to bless anything. She has broken the pattern of her repetitive behaviour. She'll be at peace now.'

And Queenie was not heard from again. Frances started seeing David and they became engaged. They married in 1975.

# GUARDIAN DEMON

In the winter of 2012, a 22-year-old Litherland girl named Gina went to Birkenhead for an interview for a secretarial job at an estate agent's office, and three days later she was told that she'd landed the job. Gina had a girlfriend in Birkenhead named Lisa who was about to go and work in Spain, and she let Gina take over the tenancy of her little flat to make it easier for her to get to and from work without travelling all the way from Litherland to Birkenhead every day. Gina's father had died before she was born and her mother now lived in Birkenhead with her partner, Bryan, so she looked forward to seeing a lot more of her mum than she had in the past. The only thing Gina didn't like about the new job was the early starts, but then her boss started asking her to do overtime, and so Gina had to go home through some poorly-lit streets on these winter evenings and when she took a short-cut through Hamilton Square she felt it had a creepy atmosphere hanging over it. Gina's boyfriend Elliot was currently studying Art History at Sussex University, and if he'd been back in Liverpool he would have taken her to and from work in his battered Ford Focus. Gina texted him before work, on her lunch-break, and in the evenings she chatted to Elliot for hours on her mobile.

He made flying visits at weekends, but he had two more years to go at Uni. About a month into Gina's new job the stalking started. It began on Gina's Facebook page with someone named "Penketh John" commenting: 'Saw you walking thru Hamilton Square in your red coat and you never even noticed me. Maybe next time x'.

Gina had indeed worn a red coat a few days back, and she tried to recall if anyone had passed her but all she could remember was a middle-aged businessman with an attaché case and an elderly man in a trilby. On the following morning at 7:50am she received an anonymous text message which ran: 'Hope I bump into u on Hamilton Sq l8tr?'

Should she tell Elliot about this potential stalker or was it just someone she knew messing about? Gina was unsure what to do. She called her mother, who lived at The Woodlands, half a mile from her flat, and told her about the messages. 'Keep your wits about you when you go to work, love,' was her mum's advice, 'or just get a cab to and from work for a week.'

That evening after work, Gina circumvented Hamilton Square and on the 15-minute journey home she kept looking over her shoulder. Every man who passed was under suspicion. When she got home she couldn't get the key in the door. It transpired that someone had squirted superglue into it. The neighbour, Mr Jenkins, had to kick the door in, and he replaced the lock. That evening another anonymous text message was received by Gina: 'Stuck on you. Love that song :)'.

Saturday came and Elliot made a surprise visit, but was baffled as to why his key didn't open the flat door.

Gina had to tell him what had happened. Elliot was furious and told his girlfriend she shouldn't have kept the stalking business secret – 'unless,' he added, 'you know who he is and you like him!'

'I can't believe you just said that,' said Gina slowly shaking her head, 'I haven't a bloody clue who he is! You're so paranoid – and untrusting.'

'I'll have to tell the Uni I've had a family bereavement and take some time off!' Elliot decided, 'And I'll get to the bottom of this!'

There was a supernova of a row and Elliot broke the Marilyn Manson Vinyl Clock he had bought for Gina down in Brighton. He apologised, stayed for a few days, during which the stalker was inactive, and then he returned to Sussex.

As soon as Elliot was home he called Gina and asked her to come and live with him down in Brighton, but Gina said she'd deal with the stalker issue first; she was not going to live in fear of anyone – and then she'd consider moving to Brighton. There was a pause, and then Elliot asked, 'Have you got someone who's going to sort this stalker out?' and before Gina could answer he added: 'You've got someone haven't you? You don't want to come down and stay with me because you're seeing someone.'

Gina swore and hung up. The phone chimed from a text message. It was not from Elliot – it was from the stalker. 'Passed your place 'tother day and heard you and your fellah arguing lol.'

Gina had had enough, and she started to cry – and then she felt that presence – a presence she sometimes felt whenever she thought her life was in danger. She called her mother and told her about the presence. Her worried mother said: 'Gina, turn to God; go to church; you don't need that thing's help.'

Gina's father had died just before she was born, and he had been a hard-core occultist; even Satanists had said he had gone too far, summoning up ancient evil beings known as the Yovar (which I've written about before in my books); they are said to be even more evil than the Devil. Gina's father had dedicated his unborn daughter to one of the Yovar – and had begged it to act as a type of guardian angel – or should I say guardian demon? The entity who looked after Gina when her life was in jeopardy was Ubil (pronounced Yoobill), and she had fainted when she had first seen him when she was five, for he had a misshapen octopus-like head of tentacles and glowing eyes. On that occasion he had removed her from a pond she had fallen into. Three times he had saved her life.

On Tuesday evening Gina walked home through a deserted Hamilton Square. The presence of that entity, Ubil, was now so strong, the girl felt a prickling static-electricity sensation on the nape of her neck. A stocky man in glasses approached, heading straight towards Gina. She stepped aside, thinking he hadn't seen her, but he stepped aside too and walked into her, and she realised it was the stalker. He wore an angler hat a parka, and he said, 'Hello Gina, we meet at last.'

Gina was just going to run when the stalker looked at something over her shoulder with an expression of utter horror. A giant figure, well over six feet in height, made from dark swirling mist, brushed past Gina and flew towards the stalker. Gina saw the thing's three arms seize the man and she saw the tentacles of its head writhe about. She ran off and heard the terrible screams of the stalker. And then the screams came to an abrupt end. She hid for a while, then returned to Hamilton Square and found the stalker lying on the floor with his glasses next to his head. He was foaming at the mouth and seemed to be having a seizure. Ubil had gone – back to God knows where. Gina called for an ambulance and then she ran home. She later heard from a nurse who is a friend of her mother that the stalker had been so traumatized by his encounter with the demon, he had to be kept in a psychiatric ward. He went steadily insane, but what his fate was after that, I do not know. Gina went to live with Elliot in Brighton to try and forget about the distressing incident, but she knows at some time in her life. That guardian demon will come to her aid again.

Printed in Great Britain
by Amazon